World Series '48

World Series '48

*The Cleveland Indians
and Boston Braves
in Six Games*

JOHN G. ROBERTSON *and*
CARL T. MADDEN

McFarland & Company, Inc., Publishers
Jefferson, North Carolina

ALSO BY JOHN G. ROBERTSON AND CARL T. MADDEN
The Mustache Gang Battles the Big Red Machine: The 1972 World Series (2022)
Amazin' Upset: The Mets, the Orioles and the 1969 World Series (2021)

ALSO BY JOHN G. ROBERTSON
Hockey's Wildest Season: The Changing of the Guard in the NHL, 1969–1970 (2021)
When the Heavyweight Title Mattered: Five Championship Fights That Captivated the World, 1910–1971 (2019)
Too Many Men on the Ice: The 1978–1979 Boston Bruins and the Most Famous Penalty in Hockey History (2018)
The Babe Chases 60: That Fabulous 1927 Season, Home Run by Home Run (1999; paperback 2014)
Baseball's Greatest Controversies: Rhubarbs, Hoaxes, Blown Calls, Ruthian Myths, Managers' Miscues and Front-Office Flops (1995; paperback 2014)

ALSO BY JOHN G. ROBERTSON AND ANDY SAUNDERS
The Games That Changed Baseball: Milestones in Major League History (2016)
A's Bad as It Gets: Connie Mack's Pathetic Athletics of 1916 (2014)

ALL FROM MCFARLAND

ISBN (print) 978-1-4766-8990-6
ISBN (ebook) 978-1-4766-4783-8

LIBRARY OF CONGRESS AND BRITISH LIBRARY
CATALOGUING DATA ARE AVAILABLE

Library of Congress Control Number 2022048647

© 2023 John G. Robertson and Carl T. Madden. All rights reserved

No part of this book may be reproduced or transmitted in any form or by any means, electronic or mechanical, including photocopying or recording, or by any information storage and retrieval system, without permission in writing from the publisher.

Front cover: Members of the 1948 Cleveland Indians (left to right);
Thurman Tucker, Larry Doby, Lou Boudreau, Joe Gordon, Allie Clark,
Eddie Robinson, Ken Keltner, Jim Hegan and Bob Feller (Cleveland Public Library)

Printed in the United States of America

*McFarland & Company, Inc., Publishers
Box 611, Jefferson, North Carolina 28640
www.mcfarlandpub.com*

To the players on both the 1948 Boston Braves
and Cleveland Indians who served their country
in uniform during the Second World War.
As Bob Feller once said,
"The war was the only game we had to win."

Gene Bearden (U.S. Navy)
Vern Bickford (U.S. Army)
Clint Conatser (U.S. Coast Guard)
Alvin Dark (U.S. Marines)
Larry Doby (U.S. Navy)
Bob Feller (U.S. Navy)
Joe Gordon (U.S. Army Air Force)
Jim Hegan (U.S. Coast Guard)
Ken Keltner (U.S. Navy)
Bob Kennedy (U.S. Marines)
Bob Lemon (U.S. Navy)
Mike McCormick (U.S. Army)
Marv Rickert (U.S. Coast Guard)
Eddie Robinson (U.S. Navy)
Al Rosen (U.S. Navy)
Johnny Sain (U.S. Navy)
Sibby Sisti (U.S. Coast Guard)
Warren Spahn (U.S. Army)
Joe Tipton (U.S. Navy)
Earl Torgeson (U.S. Army)

Acknowledgments

The authors would like to gratefully acknowledge the help given to us by the following organizations and individuals:

- The Boston Public Library, specifically Aaron Schmidt, for his help in securing many of the photographs contained in this book.
- Bob Cullum, the curator of the wonderfully impressive Leslie Jones Collection of photos from the aforementioned Boston Public Library, for generously allowing us access to many of its terrific baseball images.
- Bob Brady, the president of the Boston Braves Historical Association, for his kind help.
- The Library of Congress for its ongoing unrestricted free use of its vast repository of public domain photographs and other images.
- Grant Robertson for his all-purpose assistance.

Contents

Acknowledgments	vi
Introduction	1
1. Returning to Prominence: The Resurrection of the Boston Braves	5
2. The 1948 Cleveland Indians: Baseball's Biggest Drawing Card	20
3. Down to the Wire: The 1948 American League Pennant Race	35
4. Game #155: A One-Game Playoff Decides the American League Pennant	48
5. Esoterica: A Collection of Happenings from the 1948 Baseball Season	60
6. Anticipation: Braves vs. Indians	70
7. Game One Scuttlebutt: Question Marks	78
8. World Series Game One: Picked Off? No, Ticked Off!	81
9. Game Two Scuttlebutt: Pressure Now on Cleveland	102
10. World Series Game Two: Cleveland Gets Some Lemon-Aid	104
11. Game Three Scuttlebutt: Bearden's Boast, Puzzled Paige, and Bickford Under Pressure	121
12. World Series Game Three: Bearden Blanks the Braves	123
13. Game Four Scuttlebutt: Boudreau Cautious, Gromek Disrespected, Absent Offense	137
14. World Series Game Four: Doby's Homer Does It	139

15. Game Five Scuttlebutt: Boudreau Still Cautious, Rickert Gets No Share	151
16. World Series Game Five: Brave Resistance	154
17. Game Six Scuttlebutt: Feller's Second Failure, Veeck Eyeing Chisox, Railroad Woes	169
18. World Series Game Six: Indian Summer Concludes	171
19. Why Cleveland Won	186
20. Postscripts	189
21. The Decline and Relocation of the Boston Braves	194
22. Whatever Became Of…	203
23. Has Anyone Seen the 1948 World Series Pennant Recently?	231
24. 1948 World Series Composite Statistics	233
Chapter Notes	237
Bibliography	245
Index	247

Introduction

> "I have observed that baseball is not unlike a war, and when you come right down to it, we batters are the heavy artillery."[1]—Ty Cobb

There were certainly more important things going on in the world during October 1948 than baseball. In fact, if one reads the chilling newspaper headlines in the dailies from the first two weeks of that month, the world seemed to be again teetering on global war.

The Soviet Union, erstwhile allies of the United States just three years before in the laudable effort to vanquish both Nazi Germany and Imperial Japan, had very quickly become a belligerent Cold War foe. Isolated West Berlin had become the world's hot spot. Josef Stalin intended to subdue this prominent enclave of capitalism by shutting it off from the rest of Europe and depriving its 2.5 million people from the necessities of everyday living. The Western allies were frantically trying to prevent this catastrophe by dropping hundreds of tons of food, fuel and medical supplies into the besieged city each day using a ceaseless stream of cargo planes. It was a mammoth undertaking—and one wrong step could lead to armed conflict in a new and dangerous nuclear age.

Winston Churchill, the former leader of war-weary Great Britain and its Commonwealth of Nations that no longer possessed much international clout, was gloomily predicting a Third World War would erupt soon. The world map and geopolitics were changing. India had gained its independence in 1947, but Mahatma Gandhi was assassinated the following January and the populous nation would soon be split into three along religious and cultural lines. Communists had already taken over the postwar government in Czechoslovakia. The Truman Doctrine was trying to make sure this did not happen to other European states.

Americans heard and read about these ongoing crises daily, but they generally got on with their postwar lives to the fullest. Conspicuous consumption was fashionable once again. A resurgent economy was finally providing the public with goods they could not afford during the Great Depression and could not buy due to wartime shortages. Suburbia was rapidly growing as the men who returned from the battlefields of Europe and the Pacific were settling down to marriage and family lives. They sought more room than major cities could offer. Automobiles, paid vacations, cheap gasoline prices, improved highways, and plenty of places to visit were all changing how Americans spent their leisure time and money. Television was in its infancy in 1948; Ed Sullivan's *Toast of the Town* began its 23-year run on Sunday nights on CBS although TV sets were still a rarity in American households. However, it was patently obvious that the number of these magical boxes would grow exponentially, soon change the entertainment routines of millions of people, and pose a serious threat to radio, Hollywood, Broadway, and, yes, even to baseball's grass roots.

America's musical tastes had undergone some changes since the end of the war. Although big bands were still touring, the hit parade had mostly given way to individual artists. Songs from Bing Crosby, Doris Day, Dinah Shore, Perry Como and Peggy Lee were year-end chart-toppers. (Even radio superstar Arthur Godfrey got into the recording business with his comical "Too Fat Polka" that cracked the top 25 for 1948.) That same year, the long-playing 33⅓-speed disc was introduced, giving listeners up to 25 minutes of uninterrupted music—about six times the length of a typical 78-rpm platter.

In 1948 readers could peruse new books about serious topics such as *The Naked and the Dead*, *The Gathering Storm* and *Cry, the Beloved Country*, or lighter fare such as *Cheaper by the Dozen*. They could also put their word knowledge to competitive use as the board game Scrabble was first marketed.

Hollywood's studios were busily churning out memorable films in all genres such as *The Treasure of the Sierra Madre*, *I Remember Mama*, *Red River* and *Easter Parade*, although the Oscar for Best Picture went to a British entry: *Hamlet*, starring Laurence Olivier. That was a first. The typical adult admission price for a night (or afternoon) at the movies was an affordable 60 cents. Most filmgoers in 1948 had the good sense to avoid seeing William Bendix star in *The Babe Ruth Story*, a highly fanciful version of the life of baseball's biggest hero.

War-scarred London hosted the 1948 Summer Olympics in July and August while St. Moritz, Switzerland, was the locale for the Winter Games in January and February. (The Soviet Union believed such events to be bourgeois at the time and summarily snubbed them.) In America, 34-year-old Joe Louis was still the world heavyweight champion, but his title reign was nearing its end; Citation became the eighth thoroughbred

Introduction 3

to capture the Triple Crown; and college football had its passionate regional followers, but baseball was undoubtedly still king among American sports—as it had been for as long as anyone could remember.

Nothing else really came close to the grand old game on a national scale. In 1948 some 21 million spectators attended major league games, more than double the total of fans who turned out in 1940. Minor league baseball flourished, too. The 16 MLB teams had nearly 300 affiliated clubs of all levels of pro ball scattered across North America. The National Pastime continued to saturate the land, its players and games dominating discussions in offices, watering holes, barber shops, schoolyards, and anywhere else where people gathered. In a year that saw the formation of the World Health Organization, baseball seemed as vibrant as it ever had. Someone who did not follow baseball even peripherally in 1948 must have surely felt left out of something special.

The 1948 World Series brought together two formerly have-not teams. Both the Boston Braves and Cleveland Indians had been absent from MLB's postseason showcase for a generation. In Ohio, the Tribe's AL pennant was the nail-biting culmination of three years of rebuilding—and it was not decided until *the day after the final day* of the regular season. Truly, the 1948 AL pennant race was one of history's greatest. In Massachusetts, the Braves' relatively comfortable march to the NL pennant was something of a one-off; it would never be repeated again. No one could have foreseen that just four and a half years after more than 1.45 million fans had poured into Braves Field in 1948 that public interest in the team would wane to the point where the club would sadly and suddenly sever its ties with the city it had proudly represented for more than eight decades.

As the years went by, the 1948 Fall Classic turned out to be a bit of an aberration as it had no New York team vying for MLB's top honor. From 1949 through 1964, every World Series but one—the 1959 Los Angeles Dodgers–Chicago White Sox clash—featured at least one Gotham-based club. It did not matter much to the millions of Americans who listened to the radio broadcasts, or watched the games on that newfangled television gizmo, or read the batter-by-batter recaps that sometimes appeared on the front pages of their daily newspapers. The World Series was always worthy of special attention regardless of which two teams were participating.

One could argue that the 1948 World Series—the 45th such clash in the modern era of MLB—did not possess any special historical significance. It did represent its time, however. That year's Fall Classic reflected and reaffirmed baseball's seemingly unshakable grip on the American public. The World Series was hugely important on the sports calendar. People who cared little about the sport for its first six months of the season would routinely become acutely interested in October baseball when the champions of the two major leagues squared off. When Mel Allen stated during his Game Three radio broadcast that "the World Series is as much a part of the American scene as ham and eggs and apple pie. It's just one more symbol of our heritage," no one could seriously argue the point. With plenty of military veterans on both teams, Allen's words rang very true.

It is time to revisit that 1948 World Series to re-examine the pitching prowess of Feller, Lemon, Bearden, Spahn and Sain and the offensive exploits of Doby, Boudreau, Stanky, Dark, and Torgeson, plus two colorful supporting casts, and relive a time when baseball was the undisputed kingpin of American sports—a moment in history when the tribal clash between the Cleveland Indians and Boston Braves captured the public's fancy; a bygone era when the Fall Classic took center stage for one week in October—as it always did.

— 1 —

Returning to Prominence
The Resurrection of the Boston Braves

> First we'll use Spahn, then we'll use Sain,
> Then an off day, followed by rain.
> Back will come Spahn, followed by Sain
> And followed, we hope, by two days of rain.
> —Gerald V. Hern, *Boston Post*, September 14, 1948

The 1948 Boston Braves could proudly trace their rich baseball history to a time that predated the National League's foundation in 1876.

A Boston club called the Red Stockings was part of the first professional baseball league—the National Association—that operated with mixed results and remarkably survived five tumultuous seasons from 1871 to 1875. Today's baseball historians are divided over whether or not the circuit should be considered as the game's first major league. Be that as it may, Boston won the last four NA pennants handily. Their clear dominance was certainly a major factor in why the NA collapsed. Few other teams could compete with the strong nines from Beantown. Most gave up trying.

In 1876, a Boston outfit joined the newly formed National League of Professional Baseball Clubs. The team had no official nickname, although newspapers often referred to the Boston club as the Red Caps. On April 22, 1876, Boston won the first NL game ever played, defeating the hometown Philadelphia Athletics, 6–5. (Joe Borden—who was pitching under the pseudonym "Joe Josephs"—was the winning hurler that Saturday afternoon. Boston's Jim O'Rourke got the first hit in NL history. Twenty errors were committed in the game by the gloveless fielders.) During the 19th century, the Boston club—known as the Beaneaters starting in 1883—became a force, winning the NL pennant eight times with such star attractions as King Kelly, Tommy McCarthy and Hugh Duffy. Frank Selee was the club's manager for most of those titles. Only the Chicago White Stockings, who won six pennants, came close to rivaling the success of the Boston club over the NL's first 23 seasons. No other team won more than three.

In 1901, the American League established itself as a major circuit. The Boston AL entry lured most of the best of the Beaneaters away with substantial salary offers. The result was catastrophic for the remnants of the NL squad. The onetime baseball superpower was reduced to a laughingstock and remained that way for a decade. Boston's NL team managed just one winning season between 1901 and 1913. Fans also abandoned the city's NL entry in droves, opting for the cheaper admission prices charged by the AL club that began as the Pilgrims and eventually would call itself the Red Sox.

During that disheartening period, Boston's NL club was known as the Doves starting in 1907, then the Rustlers in 1911. The team adopted the noticeably tougher nickname "Braves" just before the 1912 season got underway. Interestingly, the moniker had no substantial connection to indigenous people. Club president John Montgomery Ward named it after team owner James E. Gaffney, a bit of a roguish figure who was often referred to in the press as one of "the braves" of New York City's dominant political figures within Tammany Hall. That group used an Indian head as its symbol; the baseball club just permanently borrowed it.

In 1914, under the stewardship of manager George Stallings, the

Hall of Famer King Kelly was one of the 19th century's most colorful ballplayers. He starred for Boston's NL club for parts of five seasons from 1887 to 1892 (Library of Congress).

1. Returning to Prominence

Braves got off to another miserable start, winning just four of their first 22 games. "The Braves, in fact, look none too strong," conceded Boston baseball scribe Francis Eaton in the May 14 issue of *The Sporting News*. Remarkably, the cellar-dwelling team, which was 15 games behind the league-leading New York Giants after losing both ends of a Fourth of July doubleheader to Brooklyn, rebounded spectacularly, winning 41 of their next 53 games. Their roster is barely recognizable to modern-day baseball fans. (Hall of Fame shortstop Rabbit Maranville perhaps is an exception). With a lineup largely consisting of obscure players such as Possum Whitted, Butch Schmidt, Hank Gowdy and Charlie Deal (and pitchers Dick Rudolph, Bill James and Lefty Tyler), the Braves eventually cruised home atop the NL with oodles of room to spare, winning the pennant by a comfortable 10½ games ahead of the Giants. Before MLB expanded and adopted divisional play in 1969, the 1914 Boston Braves were the only team in either major league to be in the basement on July 4 and rally to win a pennant. In fact, the Braves occupied last place in the tight NL standings as late as July 18.

As impressive as the Braves were in the second half of the 1914 regular

Hall of Fame shortstop Walter (Rabbit) Maranville starred for the Braves' NL pennant winners that swept the mighty Philadelphia A's in the 1914 World Series in a tremendous upset. It would be 34 years before another NL title came to Boston (Library of Congress).

season, few people gave them any hope of beating the vaunted Philadelphia Athletics—a club, replete with stars, that had dominated the AL since 1910—in that October's World Series. In mid-August, when the Braves were not yet atop the NL standings, several cocky A's players expressed a preference for playing the Braves in the World Series rather than New York because, according to an article in *The Sporting News*, beating the Giants in the Fall Classic had become monotonous to them. Philadelphia baseball writer William G. Weart agreed, noting that a new NL champion would give the scribes a lot more interesting matter to discuss rather than having to "rehash the old dope" connected to a Giants-A's World Series. Even Tim Murnane, a respected Boston correspondent for that same periodical, foresaw an easy triumph for the A's in the 1914 Fall Classic. He admitted, "I find very few [fans] who will admit to the Braves having an equal chance with the Mackmen." He thought the NL champs would accord themselves well if they could extend the World Series to six games. However, Murnane

Boston city officials gather with Braves players, mascot and management at Fenway Park prior to the first game of the famous 1914 World Series. Fenway was borrowed by the Braves because its seating capacity greatly exceed that of South End Grounds. Spacious Braves Field was opened in 1915. The ballplayer in the center is catcher Hank Gowdy. To the left of Gowdy is Boston mayor John F. Fitzgerald (the grandfather of John F. Kennedy). To Gowdy's right is Braves president James Gaffney. Others are unidentified (Library of Congress).

1. Returning to Prominence

did conclude his article by noting the old baseball truism: "You can never tell what might happen in a short series of games."[1]

Despite the dire predictions, the Braves exceeded the hopes of their most rabid supporters by taking Connie Mack's crew in a jaw-dropping four-game sweep. The A's scored just six runs over those contests. There has never been a more shocking World Series result in MLB history. Game Three was typical of the plucky 1914 Braves when they rallied from a two-run deficit in the *bottom of the tenth inning* to eventually prevail 5–4 in 12 innings. It was almost as if baseball fans refused to believe what they were seeing. Amazingly, the Athletics were 5:4 favorites to win Game Four after losing the first three games to Boston! Tim Murnane of the *Boston Globe* gushed a laudation that appeared on the front page of the October 14 edition. He proclaimed, "It was by all odds the cleanest cut victory ever attained on the ball field … with nine-tenths of the best critics claiming that the Boston team had very little to show to carry off the honors."

Fifty years after the fact, Herbert Simmons giddily concurred in the October 1964 issue of *Baseball Digest* when he wrote, "Someday, somewhere, a cow will kill a butcher, a mouse will marry an elephant, or Liz Burton [Taylor] will enter a nunnery. Until then, the most improbable happening of the twentieth century has to be the miracle of the 1914 Boston Braves."

After the Miracle Braves' surprising victory in the 1914 World Series, owner Gaffney decided that the club's South End Grounds—which had hurriedly been rebuilt after a catastrophic fire in 1894—was no longer deemed suitable for a championship MLB team and the swarms of fawning fans who would now want to see them in action. It could only accommodate 11,000 paying customers. Accordingly, Braves Field was rapidly built in just five months on ten acres of land only about a mile from Fenway Park. (The Braves used Fenway for many home games during 1914 until their new ballpark was ready.) "More than anything else, Braves Field represented the triumph of James E. Gaffney, his vision of baseball as it should be played, and his appreciation for the fans, or cranks, who flocked to see it," wrote Bob Russo in an article for SABR's Fall 2012 *Baseball Research Journal*.

Built in an amphitheater-like depression that had once been a golf course, Braves Field could accommodate about 45,000 spectators who could efficiently get to their destination by two Boston streetcar lines. The playing field was situated 17 feet below street level. It was first opened to the public on Wednesday, August 18, 1915. Close to 47,000 fans squeezed into the new venue and saw the home team defeat St. Louis 3–1 that afternoon, including the remarkable total of 15,000 children who were special guests of Boston mayor Curley. (It was a fantastic turnout. By comparison, the 1914 Braves drew fewer than 349,000 customers during the entire regular season—and still led the NL in attendance.) J.C. O'Leary of the *Boston Globe* exuded typical civic pride when he described brand new Braves Field as "the finest ballpark in the world. There is not another like it anywhere, and the probability is that it will stand preeminent for the next 25 years." The occasion also featured the overdue raising of the club's championship pennant from the previous year. The new ballpark did not bring another NL pennant to Boston in 1915, however, as the Braves finished second to Philadelphia that season.

If home runs were appealing to you, Braves Field was probably not. Never had a 20th-century MLB ballpark been constructed to keep the ball in the yard as it was at The Wigwam—the quaint nickname Braves Field came to be called frequently in Boston's newspapers. When the ballpark opened, the deepest point of its center-field wall was located 550 feet from home plate while the left-field fence was located more than 400 feet away. The August 26, 1915, edition of *The Sporting News* commented, "To drive a home run beyond these bounds is a feat to challenge the heaviest hitter." Those daunting distances were gradually reduced over the years with the addition of inner walls. The great Ty Cobb was a huge advocate of the dead-ball style of the game where runs had to be manufactured; he believed that over-the-fence homers demeaned the pure game. Cobb predictably loved Braves Field at first sight. "This is the only field in the country in which you can play an absolutely fair game of ball without interference of fences,"[2] he said admiringly. Indeed, no MLB player cleared the outer wall with a home run until Frank Snyder of the New York Giants did it in 1922.

Apart from its ornate ticket and business offices, Braves Field was not a visually appealing ballpark. In fact, it was rather dull in its construction and was often called charmless. A horseshoe-shaped covered grandstand ran from well beyond third base, around home plate, and then well beyond first base. The only permanent outfield seats were bleachers located in right field. Although it could accommodate 2,000 fans, this section of The Wigwam became known as the Jury Box because a reporter once spotted precisely 12 fans sitting there at one poorly attended game. One plus that many fans liked about Braves Field was the minimum of stair-climbing. Ramps were used to access various parts of the ballpark. City dwellers commonly rode special trolleys to Braves Field while out-of-towners typically traveled by automobile or train. The trolleys were derisively called "cattle cars" by the locals for their distinct plainness and overall lack of passenger comforts.

The Braves were competitive in both 1915 and 1916, but the club struggled both at the gate and on the field over the next 15 years. Only twice did the Braves post a winning record between 1917 and 1932. Interestingly, the attendance at Braves Field was better during the first few years of the Depression—when it reached half a million fans for three straight seasons—than it was in the 1920s when money was circulating more freely. In 1935, an aging Babe Ruth was signed by owner Emil Fuchs as a much-needed drawing card during the dark days of the Great Depression when the club was on the verge of insolvency. (Ruth knew a bad baseball team when he saw one; he chose to retire at the end of May, fleeing a woeful club that would eventually lose a record 115 games.) In August of that same season, a new ownership group renamed the team the Boston Bees in hopes of changing the club's declining fortunes. Accordingly, their home ballpark was blandly rebranded as National League Park and nicknamed the Bee Hive during that era. Those changes did not bring any on-field success.

Lou Perini and two other wealthy magnates associated with the contracting industry—Joe Maney and Guido Rugo—bought the club in 1940, with Perini owning a majority share and serving as the team's president.

Phil Masi is shown in a photograph taken when the Braves were the Boston Bees. He is best known as the baserunner who, quite probably, got a favorable safe call on Bob Feller's pickoff throw in Game One of the 1948 World Series (courtesy Boston Public Library, Leslie Jones Collection).

Dubbed the "Three Little Steam Shovels" by the Boston press for their take-charge approach to ownership issues, the trio quickly reclaimed the team's old, familiar and popular Braves nickname that has remained in use by the franchise to this day. Its ballpark was once again called Braves Field. In a June 28, 1947, interview for an article in *The Saturday Evening Post*, Perini recalled why he and his colleagues had bought the Braves. He quaintly recalled to sportswriter Harold Kaese, "We had been successful as businessmen. We knew little about baseball, but we figured that by using sound business methods, we could succeed in baseball as we had succeeded in building bridges, roads, and ammunition dumps."

Perini became a familiar face in Boston sports circles. He frequently interacted with fans. (With the open-air owners' box being adjacent to the grandstand, such close contact was unavoidable.) During and after games, if the paying customers wanted to debate anything about the team and its operations, Perini was happy to oblige them.

In the early 1940s the Braves slowly ascended the NL standings. By 1946 they were a fourth-place outfit. In 1947 Boston finished a strong third with 86 wins. With a young, exciting team under the capable management of 55-year-old Billy Southworth—who had already won three NL pennants in the 1940s while piloting the St. Louis Cardinals—the Braves entered the 1948 NL campaign with justifiably high hopes. Warren Spahn, age 27, and Johnny Sain who would turn 31, were the two best hurlers on the staff. Tommy Holmes was a thoroughly reliable batter; he connected for 190 hits and batted .325. (In 1945, Holmes had set a post–1900 NL record for consecutive games with a hit—37—that lasted until Pete Rose broke it in 1978.) Eddie Stanky, a gifted agitator who had a knack for playing on championship-caliber clubs, was a proven winner at second base in wherever city he played. That trend continued in Boston. In the June 5, 1946, edition of *The Sporting News*, editor J.G. Taylor Spink wrote of Stanky's unrivaled ability to draw walks, start rallies, and put a noticeable dent in the opposing pitcher's confidence:

> Pitchers "lose" Stanky more than they "lose" any other player in the game. They go to the mound with the burning desire to get the ball over to the pestiferous little purloiner of first base, who walked 148 times last year. They may get two strikes and no balls on him. But almost invariably they "lose" him. And, when they do, a saturating annoyance sets in. They are not the pitchers they were before Stanky upset them.

Stanky was destined to represent the Braves in the 1948 All-Star Game in St. Louis, but he seriously hurt himself in a collision with Dodgers third baseman Bruce Edwards during a game in Brooklyn on Thursday, July 8. The injury was diagnosed as a broken right ankle and a torn ligament. Stanky was out of the Braves' lineup for 60 days until September 19. He did not regain his former speed for the rest of the 1948 season—or the remainder of his playing career.

Alvin Dark was a promising rookie shortstop and a former football star from Louisiana State University who notched 175 hits in 1948 and batted .322. Moody Jeff Heath patrolled left field. Phil Masi and Bill Salkeld skillfully shared the Boston catching duties. Bespectacled Earl Torgeson was only an average hitter, but he committed just eight errors at first base all season. (Physically imposing, Torgeson was so highly regarded as a baseball prospect as a teen that civic leaders in his small hometown of Snohomish, Washington, reputedly prohibited the local high school football coach from recruiting the youth. They did not want Torgeson risking an injury on the gridiron.) Center fielder Mike McCormick was no slouch, either. He hit a productive .303.

Boston's Earl Torgeson was a highly touted high school athlete in Washington. Here the bespectacled first baseman sports a warmup jacket bearing the name of his small hometown (courtesy Boston Public Library, Leslie Jones Collection).

For the 1948 season the Braves installed two new features at The Wigwam which were years ahead of their time. One was an electric scoreboard—enormous for its time—measuring 68 feet in length. It not only kept track of the action on the field, it was an information center, providing periodic updates from other MLB games. It was, by far, the largest such contraption in the major leagues at the time. The other novelty for 1948 was the introduction of Sky View box seats, a very distant forerunner to today's luxury suites. For $200 a year, a Braves fan could reserve a seat located on the grandstand roof behind home plate—if he or she did not mind ascending very steep staircases to get there. Any unsold Sky View seats were put to use as an expansion of the ballpark's press box whenever necessary. Few Braves supporters bothered with the extravagance, though, preferring more traditional ballpark seating priced from 60 cents for a place in the bleachers to $2.40 for a box seat. The Braves also offered a 60-cent "boy's grandstand admission" for any youngster accompanied by an adult. Apparently, the club's management did not think girls attended baseball games.

The Braves entered the 1948 season with confidence garnered from a fine 1947 campaign and a solidly reinforced lineup featuring elite outfielder Jeff Heath, and the aforementioned twosome of scrappy veteran second baseman Eddie Stanky, and Alvin Dark (usually called Al by his teammates) who was expected to do wonderful things as a rookie shortstop. They augmented a lineup that contained National League MVP Bob Elliot at third base, steady hitting Tommy Holmes in right field, and promising Earl (Torgy) Torgeson at first base. Boston's pitching staff was anchored by its pair of formidable 20-game winners: Johnny Sain and Warren Spahn. Altogether, the Braves looked poised to capture the NL pennant in 1948. They were certainly the darlings of the preseason prognosticators. In a preseason poll of 238 members of the Baseball Writers Association of America by *The Sporting News*, the prevailing opinion was there would be a Braves–New York Yankees World Series in October. That same publication, in its April 21 edition, calculated the Braves to be 2:1 favorites in the NL to cop the 1948 flag.

Accordingly, a sense of optimism and excitement was palpable in Massachusetts as the 1948 MLB season was about to open. The First National Bank of Boston sponsored a newspaper advertisement that echoed the greedy hopes of the Hub's confident baseball fans. The poetic ad said,

> Here's to the Sox
> And here's to the Braves,
> An April wish that's hearty,
> Good luck along the pennant trail

1. Returning to Prominence

> To Southworth and McCarthy!
> And when September rolls around,
> Imagine this.... Oh Brother!
> One pennant flies at Fenway Park.
> Above Braves Field, the other!

While Boston's baseball fans hoped for what sportswriters dubbed a "Trolley Series" in October, six months earlier the Braves and Red Sox faced off in their annual City Series of preseason games. Their April 16 clash at Braves Field was a 19–6 rout easily won by the AL team, but it featured a bench-clearing brawl triggered when Red Sox baserunner Billy Hitchcock became entangled with Braves first baseman Earl Torgeson. Hitchcock tried to advance to second base on a wild throw, but paused briefly to sneakily grab one or both of Torgeson's legs to slow down his pursuit of the loose ball. Torgeson later told reporters it was not the first time that Hitchcock had used that illegal maneuver on him that spring. The Brave was not about to stand for it a second time. Punches flew. "Action became rapid," wrote Burt Whitman in the April 17 edition the *Boston Herald*. "It looked like a free-swinging of fists, both from the supine Hitchcock and from the now thoroughly aroused Torgy. Players of both teams rushed to the center of the battle. [Red Sox] manager Joe McCarthy was there as soon as some of the players. So was Ted [Williams]. So was umpire [Charlie] Berry. They pinned the two men, now on their feet, and both were sent to the showers." Both Torgeson and Hitchcock were Second World War army veterans. One journalist joked that Torgeson, who clearly got the best of the scuffle before the mob intervened, had committed an egregious military violation: an ex-private had punched out a former major.

Once the games that counted in the 1948 standings began, the Braves started poorly, winning just one of their first seven games. They had improved to 5–7 by the end of April, but that mark only put them in seventh place in the competitive eight-team NL. By the end of May the Braves were a .500 ballclub—and in fourth spot—despite enduring a discouraging four-game losing streak at the conclusion of the month.

In June the team found its stride and began playing to its potential. A six-game winning skein from June 6 to 11 propelled Boston into first place and baseball fans everywhere began to notice the quality of Billy Southworth's club. After June 13 the Braves were only once out of top spot in the NL standings—and that was just for a single day.

As summer drew to a close, Boston began relying more and more on their best two pitchers, Warren Spahn and Johnny Sain, to provide reliable hurling to remain the front-runners in the NL pennant chase. This prompted Boston sportswriter Gerald V. Hern to pen the quaint doggerel that appears at the top of this chapter. "Spahn and Sain and two days of rain" or "Spahn and Sain and pray for rain" has become the historically accepted "battle cry" for Braves fans in 1948—although researchers and statisticians have noted that the Braves performed just as well throughout the season even when neither of the twosome pitched. (In 1986, Boston's baseball fans again had similar rhymes as Roger Clemens and Bruce Hurst were clearly the strength of the Red Sox pitching staff: "Clemens and Hurst ... then expect the worst" and "Hurst and Clemens and the rest are lemons.")

The Sporting News recognized a 14th-inning double by Boston first baseman Earl Torgeson during a Labor Day doubleheader versus Brooklyn as the publication's Hit of the Year as it dramatically thwarted the hopes of the Braves' closest pursuers.

Things were not completely trouble-free inside the Braves' clubhouse during their highly successful 1948 season. The contentious issue of a promising 18-year-old lefthanded pitcher named Johnny Antonelli had several players upset. It did not have much to do with Antonelli himself—only his status as a Bonus Baby. Under MLB rules of the day, any young player who signed for a bonus of $4,000 or more had to be kept on the team's roster for two entire seasons. During that time, he could not be sent to the minors for seasoning. The rule was a well-intentioned, egalitarian one as it dissuaded the enormous signing bonuses that some of MLB's wealthier teams were using to sign the top amateurs and stockpile them throughout their farm systems. Antonelli certainly qualified: he got $50,000 for signing with the Braves. Thus, Antonelli spent all of 1948 with Boston but saw very little action: He only pitched a total of four innings in four games, mostly mopping up one-sided contests. Many longtime Braves resented his enormous $50,000 bonus and that Antonelli was occupying a roster spot that could have better been filled by a veteran who could truly help the team. The matter irked star pitcher Johnny Sain so much that he marched into owner Lou Perini's office late in the season and demanded his contract be sweetened to better match his undeniable value to the Braves. It was a gutsy move in 1948, but Boston Perini agreed—and also extended Sain's upgraded salary through 1949.

A doubleheader sweep over the St. Louis Cardinals on September 21 gave Boston a huge seven-and-a-half-game edge over their closest pursuers, the defending NL champion Brooklyn Dodgers. It was the greatest lead the Braves would hold during the 1948 pennant chase. The Dodgers mounted a late charge, but the Braves' nail-biting 3–2 win over the New York Giants on Sunday, September 26—a week before the schedule ended—clinched the NL flag for the Boston club for the first time since the triumph of the Miracle Braves back in 1914. Bob Elliott's three-run homer in the first inning provided all the necessary Boston offense in what was the Braves' final home game before the World Series. Associated Press scribe Joseph B. Kelley wrote that the Braves' 1948 pennant "ended 34 years of frustration and groveling in the dust of others."³

Carl Lundquist of United Press summed up the 1948 NL champs this way: "Manager Billy Southworth of the Braves believes that a so-so ballplayer who hustles is better than a great one who loafs. It must be so because he won a National League pennant with a team generally considered to be third-best in the circuit."⁴

It was a restrained celebration in the Braves' clubhouse. Manager Billy Southworth was the most animated of the bunch, giddily talking to reporters, only stopping to receive a vigorous handshake from John Quinn, the team's general manager, and to take a congratulatory telephone call from NL president Ford Frick. "These boys won it the hard way," Southworth insisted. "It was an uphill battle all the way. They're deserving of the pennant and deserving to meet any club in the American League in the World Series."⁵

While the Braves rejoiced in the confines of their clubhouse, giddy owner Lou Perini descended to field level and used the public-address system to thank the paying customers. "This is the happiest day of my life," he declared. "I can only wish that each of the players were out here to thank you for your fine support all this year."⁶

The Boston Fire Department put on an ostentatious display of support for the Braves: As soon as the pennant was officially clinched, numerous fire vehicles turned on their sirens. Police whistles added to the joyous clamor.

Whom the Braves would meet in the Fall Classic—tentatively scheduled to begin on Tuesday, October 5—was still very much up in the air. With a week to go in the schedule, the odds favored the front-running Cleveland Indians to take the AL pennant in what was turning into a deliciously tight three-team race to the wire.

In playing out the rest of their schedule, the Braves suffered an unfortunate setback that was probably avoidable. Ralph Roden of the Associated Press called it a "severe jolt" to Boston's World Series chances. Left fielder Jeff Heath broke the lower part of his leg while awkwardly trying to slide into home plate during the sixth inning in a meaningless game versus Brooklyn on September 29 at Ebbets Field. The Braves led 3–0 at the time, too. Johnny Cooney was coaching third base in lieu of manager Billy Southworth who was absent from the game with dental issues. Heath was on second base Cooney when teammate Bill Salkeld singled to right field. Cooney waved Heath onward to his fate at home plate as strong-armed outfielder Carl Furillo's throw sailed accurately toward catcher Roy Campanella. A widely circulated photo captured Heath grimacing in pain with his left foot at an unnatural angle from the rest of his leg. (The man who snapped the picture profited by it: He won a $500 prize in a photo-journalism contest.) To add insult to injury—literally—Heath never got to the plate and was easily tagged out by Campanella. Boston won the game, 4–3.

Jack Barry of the *Boston Globe* accurately commented, "Manager Billy Southworth's policy of hustling his champion Braves through their remaining games boomeranged at Ebbets Field today. Jeff Heath, [Boston's] number-one slugger, fractured his fibula and will not play in the World Series next week."[7]

The volatile 33-year-old Canadian was, of course, looking forward to playing in his first Fall Classic. Years later, Heath recalled the circumstances leading to his grisly mishap with no personal regrets about it: "I guess I didn't tuck my leg while sliding. [Brooklyn right fielder] Carl Furillo made the throw. He had a great arm and I was out by a mile. They [the baseball writers] said it was an unnecessary slide in a game that didn't mean anything. The hell it was, you always slide. Besides Johnny Sain was after his 23rd win and we wanted to shove Brooklyn into third place."[8]

A headline in the September 30 issue of the *Milwaukee Journal* declared, "Jeff Heath Suffering from a Broken Heart." Billy Southworth visited Heath in Brooklyn's Swedish Hospital and promised his teammates would win the World Series for him.

Heath had once been a Cleveland Indian. He had been traded to the Washington Senators after the 1945 season because of attitude issues. When the 1948 AL pennant was still very much in doubt, Heath told a reporter than his biggest disappointment in missing the World Series was that he had been looking forward to playing against the Indians. This statement rankled a few Red Sox players. "I hope he broke his leg up to his neck,"[9] growled one member of Joe McCarthy's squad.

Heath eventually received another bedside visitor, a complete stranger who had a remarkably shared experience. It was James (Red) Smith, a third baseman on the 1914 Boston Braves—who, like Heath, broke his ankle just before that year's Fall Classic was set to begin. "The only difference was that I broke mine on the last day of the season," the 58-year-old Smith pointed out. Smith was on his way to Boston to catch Game One. The cheerful Atlantan heard about Heath's untimely mishap and decided to pay him a social call and swap stories despite never having met him before. Smith tried to console Heath by pointing out that modern circumstances made him a lucky fellow. "They got him all fixed up so he can go back home for the World Series and sit on the sidelines and enjoy it," Smith noted. "I didn't even know how the games were coming out [in

1914] until a day later. After all, we didn't have any radios in our hospital rooms in those days."[10]

Outfielder Marv Rickert, whose season with the minor league Milwaukee Brewers had concluded, was summoned to the Braves to fill the roster spot vacated by Heath's injury. His addition to the club for World Series participation required the formal approval of MLB Commissioner Albert (Happy) Chandler, which was almost a certainty. Chandler was just the second man to hold the post as baseball's czar. A onetime U.S. senator and Kentucky governor, he was considered by many players as an ally in their battles against the club owners.

Earlier in the season, the Braves had lost another one of their players—Jim Russell—to a dangerous health ailment. Russell had been acquired by Boston, along with catcher Bill Salkeld, from the Pittsburgh Pirates in a November 1947 trade. Russell was doing well with his new club in 1948. On July 22, however, the speedy 29-year-old outfielder was hospitalized in Cincinnati with what Boston's newspapers originally labeled "a slight fever" or "an infected tooth." It turned out to be far more serious than that. Five days later Russell was released from the hospital after having both an infected tooth and a decaying jawbone removed. These problems were thought to have contributed to the fever that first sent Russell to seek medical care. Russell had been deemed well enough to rejoin the Braves by the end of July. He played in no further games, however, as his health issues grew more serious. On August, 13 Russell was sent home to Pennsylvania for a long-term recuperation by Braves team physician Dr. Roger T. Doyle. The eventual diagnosis was subacute bacterial endocarditis. A blood infection had damaged one of Russell's heart valves. After appearing in 89 of Boston's games in 1948 and batting .264, Russell was done for the season. Fortunately for Russell, the new wonder drug penicillin was now available to save his life. Previously, the malady would have almost certainly been fatal. Ray Sanders took Russell's place on the team's World Series roster.

During the 1948 season, the Boston Braves attracted a record 1,455,439 spectators to The Wigwam—the highest attendance total in their 73 years of NL membership. They would never come anywhere close to duplicating that mark again.

— 2 —

The 1948 Cleveland Indians
Baseball's Biggest Drawing Card

"The most beautiful thing in the world is a ballpark filled with people."[1]—Cleveland owner Bill Veeck

"My tastes, I have found, are so average that anything that appeals strongly to me is probably going to appeal to most of the customers."[2]—Bill Veeck

In 1920, in their twentieth season of operation, the Cleveland Indians won their very first AL pennant and the subsequent World Series. During that regular season, the Indians drew 912,382 spectators to tiny League Park—a terrific total in those days. In 1948, the year the next AL pennant flew in Ohio, the Tribe attracted a remarkable sum of 2,260,627 fans to cavernous Municipal Stadium—an average of better than 33,000 per game. It was a new MLB record for a single-season turnstile count that would last until the Los Angeles Dodgers broke it in 1962. (The 1948 figure remained the Cleveland club record until 1995—the first full season the Indians played at Jacobs Field.) Several factors were responsible for this fantastic fan support: a huge ballpark, a fine pennant-contending team, and a maverick owner whose sole aim in life seemed to be to attract people to come see his baseball team.

Cleveland had been one of the original eight teams in the American League's inaugural 1901 season. When it was founded, the team's official nickname was the Bluebirds. Nobody liked the moniker very much—especially the players who thought it was somewhat effeminate. The newspapers often shortened it to the Blues. An attempt by the players to rename the team the Broncos in 1902 went nowhere. Shortly thereafter, they were commonly called the Naps as a salute to Napoleon Lajoie, their terrific second baseman and captain, who was one of the sport's true superstars of

2. The 1948 Cleveland Indians

League Park was the undersized home of Cleveland's AL club from 1901 to 1947. First opened as a wooden structure in 1891, it had an original capacity of just 9,000. After its final renovation in 1910, it could hold about 22,500 fans. This photograph of its exterior was taken circa 1913 (Library of Congress).

the early 20th century. Winning seasons were a rarity in Cleveland—even with Lajoie and a young Shoeless Joe Jackson in their lineup. The club's best finish in their first 17 years of existence was a second-place showing in 1908. One wag in the local press started calling the team the Napkins. His reasoning: They fold up so easily.

When Lajoie left the team after the 1914 season, the Naps nickname no longer made sense. The name Indians was eventually selected. For years, the story was that the nickname was an homage to Louis Sockalexis, a troubled native American who had played sporadically for Cleveland's NL team from 1897 to 1899. Recent scholarship has cast some doubt on that narrative, however. Whatever the origin of the nickname was, it stuck. On January 17, 1915, a story in the *Cleveland Leader* noted, "In place of the Naps, we'll have the Indians, on the warpath all the time."

In 1918 the Indians were a pennant contender for the first time in a decade. They finished second and did the same in 1919. The following year was an iconic one in Cleveland's baseball history. The club's first pennant and World Series championship were both realized. Led by player-manager

Tris Speaker, the Tribe won 98 games to finish two games in front of the Chicago White Sox. The Indians then handily defeated the Brooklyn Robins five games to two in a best-of-nine World Series. Game Five, an 8–1 Cleveland victory at home, was an especially memorable contest. It featured three Fall Classic firsts: an unassisted triple play by second baseman Bill Wambsganss, a grand slam home run by Elmer Smith, and a homer struck by pitcher Jim Bagby. All three players wore Cleveland uniforms. Defeated Brooklyn manager Wilbert Robinson could only shake his head in disbelief at what had occurred that afternoon. He told a reporter, "I've been in baseball 40 years and I never saw [a game] like this."[3]

Superstar Napoleon Lajoie was so much identified with the early years of Cleveland's AL club that the team was commonly referred to as the "Naps" by fans and the press. When Lajoie left the team after the 1914 season, the club adopted the "Indians" moniker starting in 1915 (Library of Congress).

Sadly, the 1920 season is also remembered in Cleveland for a horrible incident in which the team's popular second baseman, Ray Chapman, was killed after being struck in the head by a pitch in a game at the Polo Grounds in New York on August 16. To date, it is the only on-field fatal injury ever suffered by an MLB player. In retrospect, it was quite remarkable that Chapman's bereaved Indian teammates were able to continue as strongly as they did for the final six weeks of the 1920 campaign to win the city's first AL flag.

The Indians dropped to second place in 1921 as the New York Yankees began ascending to their perch as the dominant AL club for the next four decades. Over the next 20 years the best two Cleveland finishes were as AL runners-up in both 1926 and 1940. As late as 1947, the Indians were

2. The 1948 Cleveland Indians

a fourth-place outfit that won just six more games than they lost. Few people would have predicted great things for the club in 1948. In the April 7, 1948, edition of *The Sporting News*, the Indians were reported as being 20:1 long shots to capture that season's AL pennant, putting them just fourth best in the eight-team loop. The New York Yankees, Boston Red Sox and Detroit Tigers were all given better odds by baseball's premier periodical to take the flag.

In 1946, the Cleveland Indians were bought by Bill Veeck, a 32-year-old Second World War veteran with reddish hair and some unusual notions. He had previously owned the minor league Milwaukee Brewers and made the club a roaring success at the turnstiles thanks to his own flamboyant personal touches. His father, Bill Sr., was a former sportswriter who once served as the president of the Chicago Cubs. In Veeck's memoirs, he recalled his dad showing him a sizable pile of gate receipts from one Chicago home game and noting it was impossible to tell who had spent the money and why those people had decided to attend the game. Cash was cash regardless of who had spent it or why. The lesson stuck with the younger Bill.

When Veeck Jr. became a baseball club owner himself, he made a point of trying to cater to everybody and make the ballpark a truly fun and friendly place to visit. Veeck believed in being totally accessible. (Accordingly, he removed the door from his office and had his home number listed in the Cleveland telephone directory.) No ploy to entice fans to buy tickets was too outlandish for Veeck to at least consider. Any allurement would do. Giveaways proved to be especially popular. By 1947 Veeck had made enormous Municipal Stadium the Indians' primary home field. Cleveland last played a home game at tiny League Park that season. (Within a couple of years, the abandoned site was converted into a playground.) It was simply too tiny for the big plans Veeck had for his AL baseball team.

Always aiming to be helpful, Veeck made a point of talking to Cleveland's fans to find out what they were thinking. At one game—while sitting in the bleachers, as he liked to do to get to know the paying customers—Veeck discovered for himself that Municipal Stadium's sound system was insufficient; fans in the distant seats could barely hear it. Veeck had it improved. Another time he overheard female patrons complaining that there were no mirrors in the ladies' washrooms. Veeck quickly rectified that oversight. Simple things—such as pregame entertainment at the ballpark and making it possible for fans to buy tickets over the telephone—were Veeck's ideas. Municipal Stadium even offered a free babysitting service for patrons who brought their young children, aged two to six, to a game.

In Bob Feller's 1990 autobiography (*Now Pitching, Bob Feller*), the star hurler recalled one popular peripheral attraction Veeck acquired for the amusement of the Cleveland fans:

> [Veeck] hired one of baseball's premier attractions, comedian Jackie Price, to entertain the growing crowds before games. As the pregame fans sat there buying Veeck's hot dogs, cold drinks and peanuts, Jackie kept them entertained with his showbiz routine—hanging upside down from the batting cage by his spikes and spraying line drives to every part of the outfield, holding three balls in this throwing hand at home plate and firing a strike to each base all in one throw, and catching fly balls from behind the wheel of a jeep while motoring across the outfield grass.

Veeck was also one of the first MLB owners to completely embrace radio and have all his team's games broadcast, home and away. Many owners thought radio was counterproductive to their business; they assumed fans would surely stay home and listen to the games free of charge instead of buying tickets. Veeck took an opposite stance. He recognized radio as a valuable avenue to cultivate new fans and perhaps entice them to see the Indians in action. They might just bring their friends and families with them too. That first season under Veeck's control, Cleveland compiled a disappointing 68–86 record and finished 36 games out of first place.

In 1947, Veeck came up with a novel twist to the concept of home-field advantage at Municipal Stadium: He had a secondary portable outfield fence at the ready for any home game. It could be moved backwards or forwards—or removed entirely—based on who the visitors happened to be. Thus, power-laden teams had to cope with longer home-run distances than some weaker-hitting teams. It was an ingenious ploy while it lasted. (There is some dispute among baseball scholars whether it was actually ever done.) Be that as it may, in response, MLB instituted a sensible new rule for 1948 that forced a team to establish the distance of its outfield fence on Opening Day and stick with it through the entire season. One long-term advantage the inner fence gave Veeck was the opportunity to allow thousands of fans to buy discounted standing-room admissions for important games in the area between the temporary fence and the stadium's wall. This boon was put to use often at Municipal Stadium in 1948 as the Indians became a huge AL drawing card.

Veeck also made history in 1947 by bringing a 23-year-old lefthanded hitter named Larry Doby to the Indians. Some three months after Jackie Robinson smashed the informal color line that had been in the major leagues since the mid-1880s by playing first base for the NL's Brooklyn Dodgers, Doby became the first black man to compete in the AL. Doby, a second baseman at the time, was recommended to Veeck because he was youthful and an outstanding ballplayer. Just as important, Doby was impeccably behaved off the field.

2. The 1948 Cleveland Indians

Unlike Branch Rickey—who refused to pay the Kansas City Monarchs anything for Jackie Robinson's contract—Veeck felt morally obligated to acquire Doby's services from the Newark Eagles of the Negro National League in a legal and ethical manner. Effa Manley, the business manager of the Eagles, eventually received $15,000 in exchange for Doby's contract when Doby stayed on the Indians' roster for 30 days. She is said to have told Veeck that if Doby were a white free agent with similar talents he would be getting a $100,000 signing bonus. The mainstream press knew nothing whatsoever about Veeck's plans.

Without any fanfare, Doby, accompanied by an agent of Veeck's, was quietly taken by train from Newark to Chicago to play in Cleveland's July 5 game at Comiskey Park versus the White Sox. Flanked by private security hired by Veeck, Doby was escorted into the Indians' clubhouse that Saturday where he was greeted less than enthusiastically by his new teammates. According to Doby's memoirs, four Indian players absolutely refused to shake his hand. Two of them even turned their backs to him. After several awkward minutes passed, the ice was broken when second baseman Joe Gordon offered to loosen up with Doby before the game by playing catch. Gordon and Doby soon became good friends. Doby was struck out by Chicago righthander Earl Harrist in his only at-bat that day when he appeared as a pinch hitter in the seventh inning. (A photo of Doby going down on strikes appeared in the July 16, 1947, edition of *The Sporting News*.) The White Sox won the game, 6–5. Afterward, Doby had to stay in a different hotel than the other Indians as Chicago's Del Prado Hotel did not accept black guests.

When asked why he had signed Doby and rushed him to the majors, Veeck told Oscar K. Ruhl of *The Sporting News*, "[Jackie] Robinson has proved to be a real big leaguer, so I wanted to get the best available Negro boy while the getting was good. Why wait?"[4] In that same article, Branch Rickey predicted in a very short time that a ballplayer's race would no longer be newsworthy. Indeed, by the end of July 1947, the St. Louis Browns had signed two black players (Hank Thompson and Willard Brown) without much accompanying fanfare. In a 1977 interview, Veeck said Doby was a fine ballplayer who could have been better if he had broken into MLB a decade later when ethnicity was less of an issue than it was in the 1940s. Veeck figured the virulent racism Doby encountered in rival AL cities greatly affected his play because it was something he had never experienced before.

The Indians already had a strong infield in 1947, so player-manager Lou Boudreau initially could not decide where to play Doby who had been a second baseman in Newark. Doby appeared in 29 games for Cleveland that season and, mostly as a pinch hitter, batted an unimpressive .156. By the 1948 season, Boudreau eventually shifted Doby from second base to the Indians' outfield—usually center field—where he became a mainstay and a .300 hitter. The Indians recorded an improved 80–74 mark in 1947, but they were still 17 games out of first place when the season ended.

The irrepressible Veeck was in a class by himself regarding special promotions. "Veeck had plenty of ideas," recalled first baseman Eddie Robinson, the last surviving member of the 1948 Indians, in a 2020 podcast. "Many of them were lots of fun!" Making the ballpark experience fun for the fans was the whole idea, according to baseball's version of P.T. Barnum. Creative giveaways, contests, and all types of oddball amusements were Veeck's forte. Pregame entertainment featuring clowns, acrobats, contortionists, and who knows what else were common at Cleveland's home games. Robinson himself was occasionally part of the peripheral goings-on. He, Jim Hegan, Joe Gordon and trainer Lefty Weisman formed a barbershop quartet as a hobby. They often entertained restless patrons during rain delays.

In 1948, Veeck had so many different "nights" at Municipal Stadium that one Indians fan, a 26-year-old war veteran named Joe Earley, wrote to the *Cleveland Press* to complain that he did not fit any of Veeck's demographic groups and argued that he ought to get his own night of special recognition. The letter was only semi-serious, but Veeck sagely saw it as yet another opportunity for a memorable publicity stunt. Proving that the squeaky wheel does indeed get the grease, Veeck quickly contacted the letter-writer and organized Good Old Joe Earley Night for Tuesday, September 28. At first, Earley and his wife were presented with numerous gag gifts—including an array of livestock because it was also Farm Night at Municipal Stadium. Then Earley, who held a modest job as a night watchman at an auto plant, was overcome with joy when he was given (among other goodies) a 1949 Ford convertible, a dishwasher, a TV set, a washing machine, and a special gold pass that granted him lifetime admission to every AL ballpark. That same night another hundred Indian fans were chosen at random by Veeck to receive a variety of prizes from light-hearted gifts to extremely valuable ones. Veeck was certainly eccentric and full of himself, but the ticket-buyers loved him for his unique ideas and seemingly boundless generosity.

In truth, Veeck probably did not need so many promotions to draw plentiful and enthusiastic fans to Cleveland's home games in 1948. His club was a good one. "We went into the 1948 season with a pretty damn good ball lineup—and the whole team just gelled," Eddie Robinson recalled. Veeck augmented his club with an impressive, all-star assemblage of coaches that included Bill McKechnie, Muddy Ruel and Tris Speaker. (The latter was there specifically to tutor the Indians outfielders on the

2. The 1948 Cleveland Indians

finer points of defense.) Rogers Hornsby was hired as an occasional batting instructor, although Robinson said the formidable ex-batting champion seldom did much teaching. The Indians were embroiled in a terrific four-team AL pennant race with the Philadelphia Athletics, Boston Red Sox and New York Yankees for most of the year which meant heady business at the box office. The Indians were special though; they drew fans from unlikely sources. One visiting baseball writer was astonished to learn that at one Cleveland home game there were several chartered buses filled with baseball fans from Detroit on a day when the Tigers were also playing a game at home.

On August 5, Cleveland broke their single-season attendance record of 1.53 million fans that had been set just the previous year—and had almost two full months left on the schedule to add to it. On August 11, Ed McAuley reported in *The Sporting News*, "The Indians are driving toward the two-million mark at home—and toward what their followers are certain is the American League pennant." That same baseball newspaper pointed out that the Indians were outdrawing the Yankees despite having only about one-sixth of New York's population.

The Indians' greatest asset in 1948 was Lou Boudreau. He had been with the club for almost a decade. Boudreau was elevated to Cleveland from the minor leagues toward the end of the 1938 season. He would be with the club until 1950. Boudreau was a graduate of the University of Illinois, and his higher education rankled some of his teammates who, like many ballplayers of that era, did not care much for college boys. Very soon he was one of the AL's best shortstops. His natural leadership qualities also made him destined to become an MLB manager. Starting in 1942, he was both simultaneously the shortstop for the Indians and the club's manager. When Veeck acquired the team, he and Boudreau often did not see eye to eye. After the 1947 season, rumors abounded throughout Ohio that Veeck was about to sell or trade Boudreau to the St. Louis Browns. By and large, Clevelanders were outraged at the idea. One newspaper poll showed that its readers opposed the move by a 10:1 ratio. Always taking public opinion into account, Veeck did not go through with the move—proving true the saying about the best trades are often the ones that are not made. That adage is said to have begun with Veeck—when, in later years, he discussed keeping Lou Boudreau. One memorable Boudreau highlight in 1948 occurred in the first game of a home doubleheader versus New York on August 8. Though injured, late in the game Boudreau inserted himself into the Cleveland lineup as a pinch-hitter and rapped a game-winning hit off Yankees' star reliever Joe Page.

The face of the Cleveland franchise in 1948, however, was probably still the aforementioned Bob Feller who had attained MLB stardom while only a teenager more than a decade earlier. The righthanded fireballer had made his MLB debut with the Indians in 1936 when he was just 17. One biographer has suggested that Bob "was perhaps the first [boy] to be raised by his father to be a major league star."[5] William Feller, an Iowa farmer, would roll a ball to Bob and use a pillow to catch and gently return the boy's tosses before his youngster could even walk. By the time he was nine years old, Bob could reputedly throw a baseball in excess of 270 feet. Seeing his son's obvious potential, William set up arc lights in his barn so he and Bob could play catch indoors during the harsh Iowa winters long into the night. William later went several steps further: He built a full-scale baseball diamond on the farm where local teams could play—and his son, of course, could be properly showcased. Sometimes, when young Bob Feller was pitching, 1,000 people would be present to watch the prodigy in action.

After Bob struck out 18 batters in a national amateur tournament game in Dayton, Ohio, in September 1935, scouts descended upon the Feller household. Bob eventually signed with the Cleveland Indians. (His father had to sign the contract too because young Bob was still a minor.) To make the transaction legal, Bob received a very modest bonus of $1 from scout Cy Slapnicka—and a ball autographed by the Indians. Late in the 1936 season, in the first MLB game he ever started, the precocious Robert Feller struck out 15 St. Louis Browns—just one short of Rube Waddell's longstanding AL record for whiffs in a single game. That result got Feller's picture on the front page of the September 10, 1936, edition of *The Sporting News*. Although "the baseball newspaper of the world" got the year of his birth wrong (listing it as 1919 instead of 1918), it accurately proclaimed, "[Feller] is described as one of the greatest pitching prospects to come up in years." When the 1936 AL season ended, Feller returned to Van Meter, Iowa, to complete his high-school education. (Such was the public interest in the precocious baseball phenom that NBC broadcast his graduation ceremony!) A smiling Feller, age 18, appeared on the cover of *Time* magazine on April 19, 1937. Because of his youthfulness, some newspapers commonly referred to him as "master" Feller—a polite term for a minor that the pitcher despised seeing in print. He perceived it as demeaning.

From that point onward, Bob Feller was an MLB star. By the age of 22, Feller was a veteran of six MLB campaigns. He had accrued 107 victories for a team that was not quite championship caliber, although the Indians came enticingly close to capturing the AL pennant in 1940. Feller had also acquired a pair of alliterative nicknames: Rapid Robert and Bullet Bob. The Van Meter Heater would come later. Three times Feller had led the AL in wins. Four times he topped his league in strikeouts. He had thrown a no-hitter on Opening Day 1940 versus the Chicago White Sox. (Through the 2021 season, no other MLB pitcher has yet matched that feat.)

About a month past his 23rd birthday, on December 7, 1941, Feller was driving to Chicago to negotiate his contract for the upcoming 1942 season when he heard about the Japanese attack on Pearl Harbor that Sunday morning. Feller quickly forgot about baseball and instead headed to a recruitment center where he enlisted in the U.S. Navy. (Feller could have been exempted from any military service—even if he had been drafted—as his father was terminally ill with brain cancer and he was now the sole provider for his family.) Instead of being out of harm's way, Feller actively sought out and was given dangerous duty. While serving on the USS *Alabama*, Feller eventually earned eight battle stars as the head of a gunnery crew. He later said an elongated combat stint in the Battle of the Philippine Sea in 1944 "was the most exciting 13 hours of my life. After that, the dangers of Yankee Stadium seemed trivial."[6] The combination of schoolboy baseball star and patriotic navy man, along with his impeccable middle-American virtues and piety, made Bob Feller something very close to a folk hero. In *Our Team*, Luke Epplin's book about the 1948 Indians, the author accurately wrote,

> Feller had resonated among wide swaths of white America. He possessed the uncanny ability to embody whatever the public craved at a particular moment: homespun values during the Depression, selfless patriotism during the Second World War, and entrepreneurial drive during the postwar consumer boom....
>
> In his years since returning from the war ... Feller had dedicated himself as much to striking out batters on the field as to cashing in on his name and persona off it, setting the template for the athlete as businessman.

Most importantly to the Indians, Feller combined those personal qualities with being a thoroughly dominant hurler. Both Ted Williams and Joe DiMaggio labeled the Iowa farm boy as the greatest pitcher either of them had ever seen. As if the war's interruption of his baseball career was meaningless, Feller again led the AL in wins in both 1946 and 1947. In 1946, Feller thought he had established a new AL record for most strikeouts in a season with 348, surpassing Rube Waddell's 1904 mark. However, further research and recalculations later revealed that Waddell had actually whiffed 349 batters that season. Waddell held the record until Nolan Ryan struck out 383 men in 1973.

In July 1948, Feller found himself in the unusual position of having many fans turn against him. The point of contention was the 15th annual MLB All-Star Game which was going to be held in Sportsman's Park in St. Louis on Tuesday, July 13. Feller had been selected to the AL team in 1947 (as he had been in 1939, 1940, 1941, and 1946), but that year he had withdrawn due to a sore back. In 1948 he was selected again, but once more he declined the invitation because he had pitched a complete game against the St. Louis Browns on July 11 and, to Feller's credit, he believed his mediocre record to that point in 1948 did not merit his selection to the team. Furthermore, teammate Bob Lemon—who was having an excellent season on the mound—had also been selected for the game. Bill Veeck did not want both of them pitching in St. Louis as it would disrupt Cleveland's rotation. Veeck suggested that Feller don a bandage on his pitching hand and announce he had injured himself in some type of household mishap. Feller declined to do that—but it did not stop Veeck from publicly declaring Feller was hurt and therefore would not be participating in the All-Star Game. Feller only found out about this untruth via the media and angrily demanded Veeck issue a retraction. The Indians' owner sheepishly complied, but the damage was done.

Feller's decision to skip the All-Star Game rankled a great many fans and baseball writers alike. The fact that Feller was almost certainly the highest paid pitcher in MLB history did not help matters. Ironically, controversy had also enveloped Feller nine years before at the 1939 All-Star Game at Yankee Stadium—this time for being too prominent. In that game, AL manager Joe McCarthy brought Feller in with the bases loaded in the top of the sixth inning. Feller coaxed Pittsburgh's Arky Vaughan to hit into an inning-ending double play. McCarthy then left Feller on the mound for the seventh, eighth and ninth innings. McCarthy was roundly criticized by NL fans for violating an unwritten All-Star Game "rule" that dictated no pitcher should hurl more than three innings. In facing 12 NL batters, Feller had pitched three and two-thirds innings.

Veeck tried to defend Feller's decision not to make the trip to St. Louis, stating that Feller's first duty as a ballplayer was to his team and the fans of the Indians as it appeared that Cleveland was going to be battling in a tight AL pennant race until the end of the season. (In the July 21 edition of *The Sporting News*, Veeck went a step further and insisted it was he who had advised Feller to skip the All-Star Game to rest his arm.) Feller's absenteeism did not sit well with many neutral fans or other MLB players, managers or owners. New York Yankees manager Bucky Harris, who would be piloting the AL team in the All-Star Game, denounced Feller and suggested he should be barred from all future events as a punishment. Feller got little support from his MLB brethren who viewed his snub as an attack upon the sport—and its main source of income for their pension fund. Dixie Walker stated, "I can't see how any player selected for the All-Star Game by either the fans or the managers can fail to look upon this selection as an honor."[7] When the All-Star Game was played, Feller was relaxing at home, but three other injured AL players (Joe DiMaggio, Ted

Williams and Hal Newhouser) were present—and in uniform—for their league's 5–2 victory. Feller was roundly booed the next time he pitched at Yankee Stadium and elsewhere, but he remained a popular figure among Clevelanders over his long career with the Indians. The feeling was mutual. Feller once noted, "A ballplayer doesn't spend ten years on the same team without developing an affection for the uniform, the city, the park, and certain teammates."[8]

Just before all the kerfuffle about Feller and the All-Star Game broke loose, on July 7, 1948, Bill Veeck brought in Leroy (Satchel) Paige for a tryout supervised by Lou Boudreau. Paige, whose true age was anyone's guess, was undoubtedly the best and most famous pitcher in the Negro Leagues—and had been for two decades. Cleveland's manager liked what he saw. On that same day—Paige's alleged 42nd birthday—he signed his first MLB contract, for a hefty $40,000 for the three months remaining in the 1948 season. Paige, one of baseball's true characters, thus became the first black pitcher in the American League. Two days later, Paige became the oldest man ever to debut in the major leagues at any position. Paige would go on to post a 6–1 record in 1948 and quickly become another huge attraction at Municipal Stadium whenever he was scheduled to pitch. He would also be Larry Doby's roommate on road trips where racially segregated hotels were still an issue in some cities. According to *The Sporting News*, some critics of Veeck accused the Cleveland owner of "exploiting a colored pitcher." America's foremost baseball publication itself was one of them. Publisher J.G. Taylor Spink negatively wrote in an editorial in the July 14 issue, "Page said he was 39 years of age. There are reports that he is somewhere in the neighborhood of 50. It would have done Cleveland and the American League no good in the court of public opinion if, at 50, Paige were as Caucasian as, let us say, Bob Feller. To sign a hurler at Paige's age is to demean the standards of baseball in the big circuits."

When Paige threw an impressive 1–0 shoutout against the Chicago White Sox on August 20, Bill Veeck sent a cheeky telegram to Spink that read, "Paige Pitching. No runs three hits. Definitely in line for Rookie of the Year." Spink found Veeck's message quite amusing and happily printed it verbatim in his newspaper's next edition on the front page. Nevertheless, one wag commented that Paige was too old to be a rookie *and* too old to be a veteran.

An interesting story in that same July 14 edition of *The Sporting News* claimed that people who came to MLB ballparks for the sole purpose of booing certain players or teams was on the rise in 1948. One unidentified noteworthy member of the Indians told a reporter from the *Cleveland Plain Dealer* that the negative attitude of many of the customers at Municipal Stadium in 1948 was at least partly responsible for the team only playing around .500 baseball at home to that point in the season while winning about three-quarters of their games in rival AL ballparks. "During our last home stand," said the disgruntled veteran, "our players were saying 'I wish to hell we were playing on the road.'" Although the player admitted that fans booing the home team was not unique to Cleveland, he believed it was worse on the shores of Lake Erie than anywhere else in the AL. He conceded that Philadelphia fans were probably a close second.

The article took a scholarly approach by noting, "Students of the abnormal booing, which has been evident in the major league parks in the last few years, attribute it to everything from a new social consciousness to overindulgence in alcohol." Bill Veeck thought it was an occupational hazard the players had to accept as professional athletes. "As for the few who seem to find pleasure in booing," he opined, "they have paid their way into the ballpark and it is their privilege." Veeck dismissed the theory that booing by the home fans had any substantial ill effects on his team. "You can't tell me that a few boo-birds account for the lack of base hits which has caused us to lose so many games at home. The presence of 70,000 fans in the park should inspire the players to give their best."[9]

Perhaps the booing was the result of high expectations from the locals. The Indians got off to a terrific 6–0 start to begin the 1948 AL season and talk of an AL pennant was in the air as early as late April. Then they dropped four straight games to fall into third place. By June 5, Cleveland was back atop the AL standings and stayed there until a losing streak hit the team in late July. On July 31, the Tribe had fallen into third place behind both the Boston Red Sox and the surprising Philadelphia Athletics with the New York Yankees close on their heels. The remainder of the 1948 AL season promised to be a dogfight.

It was not all fun and merriment for the 1948 Indians. On Thursday, July 15, Bob Lemon—who had blossomed into a formidable pitcher—suffered a mild concussion. A throw by Philadelphia Athletics second baseman Pete Suder struck him in the head as he scored on a double by teammate Dale Mitchell. Lemon initially shook it off and went back out to pitch the next inning. After Lemon gave up two hits and a walk, Lou Boudreau removed him from the game. Despite not being fully recovered, Lemon pitched in relief three days later in a 12-inning game in Washington. He got a hit in his only at-bat.

The club suffered an unexpected and nearly deadly setback as the AL pennant race tightened late in the season. On Monday, September 13, pitcher Don Black suffered a cerebral hemorrhage while batting during a home game against the St. Louis Browns. Black had pitched two shutout innings and had struck out three men. In his first time at bat, Black had just fouled off a pitch when he collapsed to the ground while holding onto his neck. Black was able to talk coherently to plate umpire Bill Summers and walk to the dugout under his own power, but he had lost consciousness by the time an ambulance arrived at Municipal Stadium. Black was transported to Cleveland's St. Vincent Charity Hospital; he was conscious for a time, but he soon lapsed into a coma. Although his doctor publicly stated that Black was likely to make a full recovery, the physician noted Black was "through with baseball for this year and possibly for good."[10] Privately, Veeck was informed that Black only had a 50/50 chance of surviving. After a few days in critical condition, however, Black had begun to recover. His condition was reported to have improved greatly. However, even though he signed a contract for the 1949 season, Black never played baseball again.

Black had been something of a personal reclamation project for Bill Veeck, so this unexpected setback bothered the Indians owner deeply. Discarded by the Philadelphia A's because of unreliability, Black was directed to Alcoholics Anonymous by Veeck after the 1946 season when he admitted to having a drinking problem. By the start of the 1947 season, Black was sober. On July 10, 1947, Black threw a no-hitter in a home game against his former team, Philadelphia. (Black also got two hits in the game and drove in a run with a superbly executed squeeze bunt.) It would be the apex of his baseball career. Ed McAuley glowingly wrote in *The Sporting News*, "Not many of us can identify with absolute certainty the happiest moment of our lives. Don Black can—and did. If the world had ended ten seconds after Don had tossed that historic ball to Eddie Robinson for the game's final putout, Don would have said, 'Okay, I'm ready.'"[11]

Ten days after Black was felled by the brain hemorrhage, on September 23, Veeck organized a rare serious event at the ballpark for a change: Don Black Night. It was an important game in the AL pennant race as the Boston Red Sox were the visitors. Black's teammates paid their way into the ballpark that evening, walking through the turnstiles in their Indian uniforms as a show of solidarity. Donations were collected at various stations throughout Municipal Stadium to help collect funds to offset Black's steadily mounting medical bills. In a game watched by 76,772 fans, $40,370 was raised.

Veeck himself had to contend with ongoing health issues. He had injured his right leg during the Second World War while serving with the Marines. A recoiling piece of field artillery had crushed it. He eventually had his foot amputated in late 1946. (Reputedly, after the operation, the first thing Veeck did was telephone a favorite Cleveland baseball writer to inquire about his club's selections in an amateur draft.) *The Sporting News* reported that a further part of that same leg was also removed in July 1947.

Veeck admitted that he tried to do too much too soon on the artificial leg and he would go at a slower pace this time. (Few people who knew the energetic Veeck well believed him.) A third surgery that occurred during the 1948 season removed most of the damaged limb.

The August 28 issue of *The Sporting News* painted a thoroughly rosy picture of the Tribe's chances to cop the 1948 AL flag. "The pitching looks all right and the hitting looks even better," wrote optimistic Cleveland correspondent Ed McAuley. "The club leads the league in batting average. Why shouldn't the Indians be in first place?"

Three other AL teams would certainly have something to say about it in the final five weeks of the 1948 regular season.

— 3 —

Down to the Wire

The 1948 American League Pennant Race

"Fans all have their memories of pennant races, good memories, sick memories."[1]—Author George Vecsey

"The 1948 Indians were locked in one of the tightest pennant races in history. On August 3, the top four teams—Cleveland, New York, Boston, and Philadelphia—were separated by only .006 [percentage points] in the standings."[2]—SABR biographer Warren Corbett

At the end of play on August 31, 1948, four of the eight American League teams were still in contention for the pennant with slightly more than a month to go in the 154-game schedule: Boston, New York, Cleveland, and Philadelphia. Fifth-place Detroit, 15 games out of first place, was still theoretically in the race, but a Tiger championship would require a highly improbable combination of both baseball and mathematical miracles. They would need to leapfrog all four of the teams ahead of them and overcome a huge deficit in games. Realistically, the Tigers were a nonfactor in the race. The league's also-rans—St. Louis, Washington, and Chicago—were either already officially out of the running for the pennant or very close to it. Here are the AL standings for the top four clubs heading into the circuit's games on Wednesday, September 1.

Team	W	L	GB
Boston	76	48	---
New York	75	49	1.0
Cleveland	75	50	1.5
Philadelphia	73	54	4.5

Given their shaky start to the 1948 campaign, the Boston Red Sox had to be thrilled to be leading the pack when August turned to September. They started the season 0–3 by dropping a series to the Athletics in Philadelphia. After playing the St. Louis Browns on June 4, their 42nd game of the 1948 AL schedule, the Red Sox were in seventh place with an 18–24 record despite being on a four-game winning streak. Although they were considered a strong threat to win the AL pennant in 1948 in preseason scuttlebutt, the Red Sox were hardly looking the part. But things were about to rapidly improve for them. By the end of June and for most of July, Boston was in fourth place. On July 25 they crept into the AL lead for the first time. They stayed there for a week.

The New York Yankees did not get out of the gate well, either. The defending World Series victors from 1947 began the defense of their championship laurels by winning just one of their first four ballgames. By the end of April, the Yankees were in third place and spent most of the summer either in second or third spot. It was very un–Yankee-like, but New York did not climb to the top the AL standings until August 3. They were in first place for just one day. By August 19, the perennial front-runners were back sitting in fourth place and truly had a battle on their hands to secure what they likely thought was their rightful berth in the World Series.

To most baseball observers, the Cleveland Indians looked like the best team in the AL for most of the 1948 season. Strongly backed by excellent starting pitching and consistently solid hitting, the stars seemed aligned for a rare Indian summer of championship baseball for the team on the shores of Lake Erie. The Tribe resided in the first division of the AL all season, usually in first or second spot. Cleveland occupied first place in the AL standings continuously from June 5 to July 22. The Indians' largest lead, however, was just three and a half games over their closest pursuer, which they last attained on June 22. One elongated bad streak could change Cleveland's elevated spot in the standings dramatically.

The Philadelphia Athletics were likely the sentimental favorites among neutral fans—if there is such a thing in baseball. It had been 17 long seasons since the A's had last won the AL pennant, and time was running out on their aging owner-manager Connie Mack. He would be 86 years old in December. Since the last championship flag was hoisted at Shibe Park in 1931, Mack's Athletics could usually be found near or at the bottom of the league standings. In 1947, the A's finished two games above .500 and came in a lofty fifth. A quick start in 1948 gave their dwindling number of fans a smidgen of hope for one last hurrah under old Connie's leadership.

Mack was the subject of a lengthy feature article, penned by esteemed journalist Bob Considine, in the July 29 issue of *Life* magazine. Throughout

3. Down to the Wire

Connie Mack, shown here (wearing hat) circa 1913 during the Philadelphia Athletics first heyday, was a beloved national figure by 1948. His club lingered near the top of the AL standings for much of the season, kindling hopes of one last AL pennant for the octogenarian manager. Alas, the A's faltered badly in September and finished fourth (Library of Congress).

the piece, the author practically gushed praise about baseball's undisputed greatest living ambassador:

> Mr. Mack has possibly had more personal friends than any American now alive, for he has several crops of them and is still enormously popular. A devout Catholic who never misses a Sunday mass or a holyday of obligation, [he] seems to attract waves of sports-minded priests at each stop along the big-league circuit.

> The old gentleman has no thought of retiring, not even if by some dazzling and dramatic accident he wins the pennant to crown gloriously his sixty-fourth year in professional baseball.

Philadelphia had a regular lineup that was a capable outfit, but it did not possess names that would be overly familiar to many 21st-century baseball followers. It included Ferris Fain, Hank Majeski, Elmer Valo, Eddie Joost, and Sam Chapman. Outfielder Barney McCosky, a 6'1" Pennsylvanian who batted left but threw with his right hand, was the team's best hitter throughout 1948, registering a .326 average—the fifth-best mark in the AL. The core players on the A's were an old bunch who lacked speed; only Fain and Valo were under 30. (Connie Mack especially rued one loss to Cleveland in which his slow-footed club grounded into five double plays.) The Athletics had four pitchers on their staff who won at least 14 games: Joe Coleman, Dick Fowler, Carl Scheib and Lou Brissie. Only Fowler, a Canadian war veteran, won as many as 15 games, however. With this group of largely unheralded players, the A's were positioned at or close to the AL lead for much of the summer. Surprisingly, Mack's team occupied first place all by themselves as late as August 11.

The Athletics were still within striking distance of the top of the AL table as they entered September, but with three talented clubs ahead of them, they could not afford to falter for long. But falter they did, enduring a catastrophic eight-game losing skid from August 29 to September 6. Even worse, the games were against Cleveland, Boston and New York—the three teams the A's were pursuing in the pennant chase. Realistically, their chances of finishing first were now hopelessly wrecked at that point.

After splitting a Labor Day doubleheader in New York to snap their awful winless skein, Connie Mack's squad was nine and a half games out of first place and languishing in fourth spot. Disappointing Mack's well-wishers, the A's would not climb any higher in the standings. A doubleheader loss to the Indians in Cleveland on September 19 officially eliminated Philadelphia from any possibility of winning the AL pennant. To conclude the campaign, Mack's team disappointingly collapsed, winning just one of their final 10 contests. They finished 1948 with an 84–70 record, 12½ games out of first place. Mack believed two shortcomings combined to doom his A's. "I'd like to make a number of trades," he told writer Art Morrow of *The Sporting News* as the season neared its end and Mack began planning for 1949. "We need speed and greater power. But where are we going to get [such players]?"[3]

When one examines the record of the 1948 Philadelphia Athletics that season, it truly shows they deserved to finish precisely where they did in the AL standings. Mack's team fared quite well against the league's three weakest clubs (Chicago, St. Louis and Washington) but they routinely struggled when they played Boston, New York, Cleveland—and even Detroit. Frank Gibbons of the *Cleveland Press* quipped that the Indians—if they won the AL pennant—ought to voluntarily give the Athletics' players World Series shares for having aided them so much down the stretch. (The Indians won 16 of 22 games versus Mack's crew in 1948.) Oddly, the A's were a considerably better road team (compiling a fine 48–29 record) compared to being a sub-.500 club (36–41) at Shibe Park.

Nineteen forty-eight was an unusual year for the vaunted and tradition-laden New York Yankees. The AL's most glamorous club spent exactly two days in first place over the entire season—and on both occasions they were tied with another team for the circuit's lead. Those two days were August 3 and September 24. Apart from that pair of brief apexes, the defending World Series titlists from 1947 fluctuated all season long from second to fourth place in the standings.

The elegant Joe DiMaggio was still the face of the Yankee franchise, but, nearing age 34, he was hobbling a bit with a bad right heel. Although injured, DiMaggio still played in 152 games as the team's center fielder. He batted .320 and hit 39 home runs and 11 triples despite the discomfort. (DiMaggio would require surgery to remove bone spurs in 1949 and miss much of that season.) Although he did not hold a regular position, a 23-year-old utility player named Lawrence Peter (Yogi) Berra was so good wherever he played that he garnered a handful of MVP votes to finish in 29th place. Eventually Berra would find his niche as the team's catcher and become one of the all-time greats at that position. Phil Rizzuto was not much of a threat at bat, but he was still an excellent shortstop at age 30. Lesser lights such as George McQuinn, Snuffy Sternweiss and Billy Johnson rounded out the infield. No Yankee pitcher won 20 games in 1948. Vic Raschi came the closest with his 19 victories. Eddie Lopat won 17 games for New York; Allie Reynolds won 16. The team's 94 wins in 1948 were spread among 11 different Yankee pitchers. Clarence (Cuddles) Marshall—the possessor of one of MLB's most memorable nicknames—was not one of them. The righthander, who bore a striking resemblance to movie star Tyrone Power, just pitched one inning in a mop-up relief stint for New York that season.

The Yankees entered September riding a three-game winning streak. They extended it to nine games during the first week of the ninth month. Remarkably, they could not seem to make any upward movement in the AL standings. New York remained firmly in second place over that period, anywhere from half a game to one and a half games in arrears of the Boston Red Sox. A run of three consecutive Yankee losses followed—including two to the Red Sox at Fenway Park. That setback temporarily dropped the New Yorkers to three and a half games behind the frontrunners from Boston. The streaky Yankees then went on a positive tear, winning six of their next seven games to get within a single game of the AL lead on September 17. Perhaps the invincible mystique of the almighty New York Yankees would prevail after all. Outfielder Tommy Henrich certainly thought so. In a somewhat arrogant manner, he told *The Sporting News*, "The Yankee tradition of winning is going to be a big factor in our success from now on. We know we won last year and that Yankee teams were coming out on top before some of us were born. On the other hand, Boston has only snagged one flag since 1918 and Cleveland has a record of bogging down."[4]

According to numerous accounts, the future of Bucky Harris' career as manager of the Yankees depended entirely on whether or not his club won the AL pennant. Rumors abounded that anything less than a World Series berth for New York would prompt Harris' swift dismissal.

Despite Henrich's optimistic predictions about Boston and Cleveland falling apart, the checkered histories of both the Indians and Red Sox seemed to be a nonfactor as the 1948 AL schedule approached its climactic end. Neither club seemed burdened by its reputation for failure. The Red Sox had at least ended their pennant drought in 1946 after a 28-year absence of championships. In 1948, Cleveland was trying to end their own negative run of 28 seasons without an AL flag to celebrate.

Boston began September by rolling off 10 wins in 11 games, including taking two of three contests from New York at Fenway Park. But by the middle of the month, a run of mediocrity began for the Red Sox where they won just six of 13 contests. A 6–2 loss to New York at Yankee Stadium on September 26 knocked the Red Sox out of first place in the AL standings for the first time since August 25. The surging Cleveland Indians supplanted Boston as the circuit's frontrunning squad on that date.

When September began, the talented Cleveland Indians were sitting in third place in the AL standings. They promptly won nine of 12 games to put pressure on both New York and Boston. After suffering two straight losses, Cleveland won seven consecutive contests. When they beat the Red Sox 5–2 at Municipal Stadium before 76,772 excited fans on Wednesday, September 22, the Indians attained a tie atop the standings with Boston. Each club had 91–55 records and eight games left on their respective 154-game schedules. Here is what the top of the congested standings looked like in the morning newspapers after the AL games of September 23 had been completed:

3. Down to the Wire

**American League Standings
(on September 24)**

Team	W	L	GBL
Cleveland	91	55	---
Boston	91	55	---
New York	90	56	1

The balance of the AL schedule seemed to favor the Indians. Six of Cleveland's remaining games were against the disappointing Detroit Tigers; the other two pitted them against the lowly Chicago White Sox. Five of Boston's last eight games were against the still hopeful New York Yankees. The other three were versus Washington. The Yankees finished their schedule with those five huge games versus the Red Sox and three contests against the badly fading Philadelphia Athletics. With most fans expecting the Red Sox and Yankees to essentially eliminate each other in their head-to-head games, it appeared to be Cleveland's pennant to win. All they had to do was vanquish two teams that, at least on paper, should not put up too much of a struggle against the hungry and powerful AL Tribe.

On September 24, the Indians surprisingly lost to Detroit at Briggs Stadium by a 4–3 score, ending a seven-game Cleveland winning streak. Bob Lemon, mired in a bit of a pitching slump, took the loss for the Indians. All three Cleveland runs came on solo homers off winning pitcher Freddie Hutchinson. Meanwhile, the Yankees upended the Red Sox, 9–6, in a slugfest at Yankee Stadium. Those results produced an eye-catching three-way tie atop the AL with everyone in contention having seven games left to play. New York manager Bucky Harris diplomatically told the press he figured Boston had the best chance of winning the pennant. "The Red Sox have five games at home," he explained. "Three of those are with lackluster Washington." Then Harris added with a smile, "But they still have two to play with us."[5]

Some sports editors began referring to the battle for top spot as the greatest pennant race in AL history—or at least close to the three-team struggle that had occurred exactly four decades before in 1908. Many scribes were genuinely surprised to learn that if the regular season was to conclude in an awkward three-way deadlock, there was no specific rule in the AL's constitution that offered any guidance on how to break such a tie. Only the situation of how to settle a two-way deadlock was addressed. In that case, a dramatic, winner-take-all, one-game playoff would settle matters.

Saturday, September 25 saw the AL standings revert to what they had been two days earlier—only there were just six games left to play for each club still in contention. Cleveland pounded Detroit, 9–3, while Boston drubbed New York, 7–2. The Indians and Red Sox were back in a two-way tie for the league lead, with New York a game behind both frontrunners. Nevertheless, Yankee manager Bucky Harris remained an optimist about New York's pennant chances. "The top three teams in the American League are 33:33:33," he stated in ratio form. "Don't count the Yanks out of it." Harris then made an extraordinary claim: "Everyone says that Cleveland has the edge because of a fine pitching staff. Cleveland's pitching staff is no better than Detroit's. Detroit may have the best staff in the league. Detroit's pitchers are loose and carefree. I wish mine were."[6]

On Sunday, Cleveland beat the Tigers again, 4–1, but New York topped Boston, 6–2. In the Cleveland win, the Indians fireballer Bob Feller beat Detroit's Hal Newhouser for the eighth straight time that the two fine hurlers had squared off against one another. Now Cleveland was alone atop the AL with both New York and Boston trailing the Indians by a game. Lou Boudreau cockily figured the pennant was now a sure thing for his first-place club. "I sincerely believe we're in now," the Cleveland player-manager told reporters after the important win was safely in the books. "[This game] meant the pennant for us."[7]

It was certainly fun to watch the daily rearrangement of the AL standings if you had no particular rooting interest, but for the players on the Yankees, Red Sox and Indians, the pressure was already immense and it was growing by the day. Some of that tenseness was relieved for 24 hours as there were no games at all on the AL schedule on Monday, September 27.

The diamond battles resumed the following day. On Tuesday, Cleveland thoroughly throttled the discouraged, last-place Chicago White Sox at Municipal Stadium, 11–0. A six-run sixth inning for the home team basically decided matters. The Indians were both amused and delighted to learn that their two pursuers had faltered that same day. Boston lost at home to Washington, 4–2, while the Yankees dropped a 5–2 decision at Shibe Park in Philadelphia. Thus, with their win over the hapless White Sox, Cleveland extended its AL advantage in the standings to two full games over both Boston and New York with just four games to play for all three of the battling clubs.

On Wednesday, September 29, Cleveland, Boston and New York all posted important victories in games they were supposed to win, but time was running out on the Yankees and Red Sox. With only three games left on each club's itinerary, the Indians seemed to be a lock for the AL pennant. After Boston's 5–1 win over Washington, first-year Red Sox manager Joe McCarthy singled out catcher George (Birdie) Tebbetts for special praise, believing the 35-year-old backstop had not been adequately recognized by baseball writers for his fine work. "I don't know anyone else who has out-caught him," McCarthy insisted. "Tebbetts really has been a big help to our pitchers [and] I don't think he's ever hit as good [sic] in his life."[8] New York almost threw away a 4–2 win over the A's when Joe DiMaggio stunningly dropped a routine fly ball in the ninth inning, but Philadelphia could not capitalize on the Yankee Clipper's rare defensive blunder.

Cleveland had no game scheduled on Thursday, September 30—but the Red Sox and Yankees both won theirs. (One scribe wrote, "The Cleveland Indians sat by smugly today and watched the Red Sox and Yankees try to squirm out of the noose."[9]) Boston bested Washington, 7–3, at Fenway Park. New York almost squandered a 6–0 lead versus Philadelphia, but hung on to win the game, 9–7, in an ugly affair that featured the two teams combining for 23 hits and making four errors. The Yankees and Red Sox each now trailed Cleveland by one and a half games as the drama of October baseball began.

On Friday, October 1, it was the Indians who played while the Red Sox and Yankees had a day off to prepare for their crucial two-game series to be played at Fenway Park on Saturday and Sunday. With the spotlight all to themselves—and a chance to guarantee themselves no worse than a tie for the pennant—Cleveland lost to Detroit at home, 5–3, before a puzzlingly small turnout of fewer than 16,000 fans. Considering the manner by which the home team lost, perhaps it was good for the Indians that there were so few witnesses to how the game concluded. Slumping Bob Lemon suffered another loss—and it was an excruciating one.

Cleveland led the tight contest, 3–2, heading to the top of the ninth inning. However, Detroit rallied with three runs to earn a surprise victory over the Tribe. Tigers manager, Steve O'Neill, who had managed the Indians for three seasons in the mid–1930s, made plenty of tactical substitutions in his club's final turn to bat as if it were his out-of-contention team that was vying for the AL championship.

In that fateful ninth frame, Detroit third baseman Eddie Mayo reached first base on an infield hit down the third-base line that Lemon could not field in time. Lemon compounded his problem by flinging a hopeful but wild toss in the general direction of first base that allowed Mayo to chug into second base on the overthrow rule. Lemon regained his poise and struck out the next Tiger batter, pinch hitter Johnny Bero, but he then issued two straight walks to load the bases. Lou Boudreau yanked Lemon from the mound and replaced him with Russ Christopher to try to preserve the Indians' slim one-run lead. He failed. Instead, Christopher could not find the plate either and walked in a run. Stunningly, the game was tied 3–3—thanks to Detroit using three pinch hitters. The damage was inflicted by a piddling infield hit, an error by Lemon, and three bases on balls.

Neil Berry batted next for Detroit. His ground ball to third baseman Ken Keltner should have been an inning-ending 5–2–3 double play. Lead runner Johnny Groth was quickly forced out at home plate, but catcher Mike Hegan's relay throw to first base was dropped by Wally Judnich who normally played right field. Instead of the side being retired with the game tied, the bases were loaded with Tigers with two men out. Jimmy Outlaw, a 35-year-old utility player with a .250 batting average, punished the Indians for Judnich's untimely error with a dramatic two-run single to give the visiting Tigers their margin of victory. (It was the only ball that left the infield in the top of the ninth.) All three Detroit runs in the top of the ninth inning were charged to Bob Lemon. The rattled Indians failed to score in the home half of the inning. Relaxing somewhere in Boston on their day off, both the Yankees and Red Sox were applauding the surprising turn of events at Municipal Stadium and the plucky Tigers' refusal to lie down. Cleveland's lead over Boston and New York had shrunk to just one game, thus markedly improving both those teams' chances of catching the Tribe as the schedule wound down.

To their credit, the Indians managed to forget about Friday's ninth-inning fiasco. Against a rookie Tiger pitcher named Lou Kretlow who had won just two games in 1948, Cleveland regrouped and thumped Detroit, 8–0, on Saturday, October 2 to finally clinch no worse than a tie for the league championship. Backed by 11 hits, Gene Bearden, a tricky lefthanded knuckleball specialist, earned the complete-game shutout for the home team without facing much difficulty.

Meanwhile, at a jammed Fenway Park—where New York had not won two straight games in their previous nine contests in Boston in 1948—the losing team in Saturday's contest would be mathematically eliminated from the AL pennant race. The Red Sox pleased their vocal supporters by jumping out to a 5–0 lead after four innings. (Two of the home team's runs came on a first-inning blast by Ted Williams with Johnny Pesky standing on first base via a walk.) Boston cruised home with a comfortable 5–1 victory. Jack Kramer, a 30-year-old righthander, pitched a complete game for the happy winners before 32,118 partisan rooters. Over the course of the important game, four New York pitchers generously combined to allow 11 walks to the Red Sox.

The ugly loss conclusively meant that the Yankees would not be defending their 1947 World Series title in 1948. It also sealed the fate of manager Bucky Harris, with 59-year-old Casey Stengel rumored to be the likely new man to pilot professional baseball's most storied franchise in 1949. Winning 94 games but finishing two games out of first place was

3. Down to the Wire

not an unacceptable outcome. (Harris had recently received a large dose of adverse publicity in his own hometown newspaper in Pittston, Pennsylvania. In the pages of the *Pittston Gazette*, Harris was accused of rudely "brushing off" a championship youth team from that city who had traveled to New York City to attend a late-season game at Yankee Stadium. On the other hand, three Yankee players—Yogi Berra, Vic Raschi and Spec Shea—were lauded by the newspaper as wonderful hosts and ambassadors. They felt badly for the teenagers and, to make amends, treated them to dinner.) Stengel was formally introduced as the Yankees new manager on October 12, one day after the World Series ended.

With New York now completely out of the AL championship picture

Bucky Harris led the New York Yankees to the AL pennant and World Series title in 1947. When the Yankees finished a disappointing third in 1948, Harris was quickly fired and replaced by Casey Stengel (courtesy Boston Public Library, Leslie Jones Collection).

for 1948, all the Yankees could do on Sunday, October 3 in Boston was attempt to spoil the pennant aspirations of the home team. Even if the Red Sox won their game, they still required underdog Detroit to beat Cleveland for a two-way tie to exist atop the standings. At Fenway Park, the Yankees—who had nothing tangible to play for—raced out to a 2–0 lead after two innings, but Boston scored five times in the bottom of the third inning and added four more runs in the bottom of the sixth to turn a slim 5–4 lead into a much safer 9–4 advantage and generally take the remaining fight out of the New Yorkers. The final score was 10–5 for the hometown Red Sox. It had been a long battle by 1948 standards: two hours and 40 minutes, but the important game being contested near the shores of Lake Erie was a slow-paced affair, too. The fans in Boston and the Red Sox players were being kept abreast of the encouraging news that kept trickling in from Cleveland's cavernous Municipal Stadium.

Veteran pitcher Bob Feller—the most recognizable of all the Indian players—was on the mound for Cleveland. Although he was trying to win his 20th game of 1948, Feller was more focused on clinching the Tribe's first AL pennant since 1920—and his first taste of World Series competition. Feller had won his last seven decisions, but he did not come close on this day. Feller was removed from the game with one out in the third inning after giving up four Detroit runs. In his brief outing, Feller was noticeably subpar. He faced 14 Tigers and allowed five Detroit hits and three bases on balls. Feller departed the ballpark with his 15th loss of the season. Cleveland would eventually use six pitchers in the game but still ended up on the wrong side of a 7–1 trouncing. Detroit's batters piled up 15 hits in the rout as more than 74,000 fans who had anticipated a pennant celebration instead trudged home unhappy and worried. According to Jim Doyle of the *Cleveland Plain Dealer*, "The only bells heard in Cleveland late yesterday were the church bells calling the devout to prayer."[10]

Cleveland did not score until the bottom of the ninth inning, when the game was well out of reach, as Hal Newhouser tossed a complete game to conclude Detroit's 1948 campaign on a high note, finally inflicting a defeat on Feller in a head-to-head confrontation after being the losing pitcher in their previous eight matchups. The Tigers had accepted the "spoiler" role well during the season's final weekend in Cleveland. Displaying the best of professionalism, they played for pride alone and beat the Indians in their home ballpark two out of three times.

When Cleveland's Ken Keltner softly flied out to Detroit left fielder Dick Wakefield to end Sunday's game, the Red Sox and Indians found themselves in an unusual predicament: they were knotted in a rare first-place tie after completing their full schedules. The deadlock would have to be broken to determine the AL's representative in the 1948 World Series with a single winner-take-all game.

Forty-two years later Bob Feller wrote in his autobiography, "What could never happen did. The Indians and the Red Sox played 154 games each and finished dead even. It was a hair-raising, nail-biting time for everybody in the game, including the fans, but it was even more so for us because we were the ones making history."[11]

— 4 —

Game #155

A One-Game Playoff Decides the American League Pennant

> "Joe McCarthy—in what remains one of the most controversial decisions a Red Sox manager has ever made, a decision that is still debated among old-timers and baseball afficionados—eschewed Parnell, Kinder, and the rest of his of starting rotation in favor of [Denny] Galehouse...."[1]—Ted Williams biographer Ben Bradlee, Jr.

Monday, October 4, 1948, presented a first in American League history: Never before in its 48 seasons of play had an AL regular season ended with two teams tied atop the standings. But that was the reality of 1948. Boston and Cleveland both finished their schedules with 96–58 records after 154 games. Not that it really mattered, but the two teams had also evenly split their 22 games with each notching 11 victories versus the other.

Remarkably, such a scenario had only occurred once in 73 seasons of National League history—and that was just two years earlier when the St. Louis Cardinals and Brooklyn Dodgers finished in a dead heat in 1946. (Coincidentally, the Dodgers and Cards also posted 96–58 records through 154 games.) The NL broke that tie in the standings by ordering a best-of-three playoff—which the Cards won in a tidy two-game sweep by scores of 4–2 in St. Louis and 8–4 in Brooklyn. The Cardinals then beat the favored Boston Red Sox in the 1946 World Series in seven games.

The AL was not bound to follow the NL's lead on how to conduct a tiebreaker—and it did not. Instead, its rules stated that a simple, one-game, winner-take-all playoff was sufficient to settle matters between the deadlocked Indians and Red Sox in 1948. At the very least, it certainly set the table for high drama. To determine the home team, a series of coin

4. Game #155

On opposing teams during the one-game playoff to decide the 1948 AL pennant, Bob Feller (left) and Ted Williams pose together at Fenway Park a few years earlier. Williams said Feller was the greatest pitcher he ever faced (courtesy Boston Public Library, Leslie Jones Collection).

tosses—with reps from New York, Cleveland and Boston present—had taken place a week earlier in Chicago, just in case such a game was necessary. The toss concerning a Red Sox–Indians playoff game had been won by Boston giving them the home-field advantage on October 4. The Red Sox had compiled a fine 55–22 mark in 77 games at Fenway Park in 1948, so the prospect of playing the crucial pennant-decider at home was thought to be a boon for Boston. Bookmakers certainly agreed, listing the Red Sox as 6:5 favorites to take the tiebreaker. There really was not much to choose from between the combatants. Apart from being the home team, perhaps the Red Sox were also slightly favored because they had caught the Indians at the wire while the Tribe had faltered badly on the final Sunday of the schedule.

If the Cleveland players quietly feared defeat, their management outwardly exuded an air of confidence. It was reported that seven dozen new baseball bats were shipped to the Indians from the Louisville Slugger factory. They were sent to Braves Field in anticipation of Cleveland winning the AL pennant and playing at Boston's NL ballpark in the first game of the World Series on Wednesday, October 6.

Boston had concluded their schedule at home on Sunday, as had Cleveland. That meant the Indians had to quickly arrange travel plans to Massachusetts for the tiebreaker on Monday. The Indians did not arrive in Boston with excessive time to spare. Their overnight train was delayed due to numerous stops along the way. Upon detraining, the visitors from Cleveland headed directly to Fenway Park to prepare for Game #155.

While most baseball fans' eyes were upon Fenway Park, the New York Yankees announced, to no one's great surprise, that manager Bucky Harris' contract would not be renewed for 1949. A terse statement issued by the club said Harris and the Yankees had parted ways by mutual agreement. Harris had won 191 regular-season games in his two years with New York, but that impressive sum was apparently insufficient. The vacancy created by Harris' dismissal had not yet been filled, but the new man at the helm in 1949—whoever he might be—would be the fourth different Yankee manager since 1946.

No one knew for certain whom Red Sox manager Joe McCarthy would select to be his club's starting pitcher for the most critical game of 1948. The obvious choice seemed to be Mel Parnell, a second-year lefthander who had last pitched on Thursday in Boston's 7–3 win over the Washington Senators. (In that game, the 26-year-old Parnell had started, pitched six and two-thirds innings, and got his 15th win of the season.) Ellis Kinder, who was even better rested that Parnell, was also a reasonable option. Jack Kramer and Joe Dobson were available for the home team, too. When the Red Sox arrived at Fenway, they were shocked to discover that McCarthy had abruptly chosen Denny Galehouse for the important task.

Parnell was startled for two reasons. First, he had found a baseball placed under his cap in the Red Sox clubhouse—a longstanding sign that he had been chosen to start the game by manager McCarthy. Second, Galehouse had spent much of the previous day periodically warming up in the bullpen for the better part of six innings during Boston's crucial win over New York, so he was likely fatigued. Parnell recalled McCarthy approaching him, almost apologetically, to say he had decided to go with the journeyman righthander because the wind was blowing out over Fenway Park's Green Monster. "The wind was blowing out, but hell, I pitched a lot of games at Fenway with the wind blowing out,"[2] Parnell recalled years later. McCarthy sent the team's clubhouse boy onto the field to fetch Galehouse, who had been vigorously shagging flies in the outfield for exercise. When Galehouse learned from McCarthy that he would be the Boston starter in Game #155, he reputedly turned ashen.

In 1989 Galehouse, then 77 years old, gave what was believed to be his first interview solely about Game #155. He disputed several longstanding

4. Game #155

notions about his start that afternoon. First, Galehouse said he had an inkling immediately after Sunday's game that he might be asked to pitch the tiebreaker on Monday. According to Galehouse, he and the other Boston pitchers were polled about their eagerness to start the most important game of the year for the Red Sox—and only he gave a 100 percent positive response, saying that he would pitch if McCarthy asked him to do so. Galehouse also said he found a ball in his glove in his locker when he arrived at Fenway Park on Monday.

Galehouse, to his credit, had big-game experience. He had won the opening game of the 1944 World Series as a member of the St. Louis Browns. Galehouse had posted an overall 8-7 record thus far in the season and he was known to have good control, but his 3.89 ERA heading into the October 4 game was not especially eye-catching. Galehouse had pitched against Cleveland three times in 1948, winning once, losing once, and posting a no-decision in his other start versus the Tribe. In one game versus the Indians, on July 30, Galehouse pitched quite well for eight and two-thirds innings in relief. Still, Galehouse was, at best, only his team's fifth starter. When Lou Boudreau and his teammates saw Galehouse warming up, the Cleveland player-manager could scarcely believe his eyes. For a while Lou Boudreau thought McCarthy was orchestrating some sort of sneaky ruse. He figured the Red Sox had their real starting pitcher warming up in secret somewhere within the hidden confines of Fenway Park.

The Indians' choice of starting pitcher raised a few eyebrows too. Gene Bearden, a 28-year-old lefthanded knuckleball specialist from Arkansas, was given the nod by Lou Boudreau. Years later Boudreau recalled, "Bearden was my best pitcher [in 1948]—better than Bob Feller, better than Bob Lemon, better than Steve Gromek. He'd come through in the tough games for us all season, and I had absolute confidence in him."[3]

Certainly, nobody at that point of the season seriously questioned how good Bearden was. (His record in 1948 going into the decisive October 4 game was a sparkling 19-7 with a 2.53 ERA.) The fact that Bearden was a lefty—and the Red Sox could flood their lineup with righthanded hitters to take advantage of the short wall in left field—was cause for alarm among Cleveland's studious baseball fans. Furthermore, Bearden was technically a rookie. He had never faced such an important game in his young MLB career. (Few pitchers had!) Perhaps the most compelling concern for Indian supporters was that Bearden had pitched on Saturday. Thus, he was coming into the most important ballgame in Cleveland history since 1920 on just a single day's rest. After the game, Boudreau said he had no qualms about starting Bearden. "I wasn't concerned. He's that type," Boudreau noted. "You can't keep him off the mound. After pitching on Saturday, he was in the bullpen yesterday."[4] In his autobiography, Bob Feller called Boudreau's decision to start Bearden "a stroke of genius and a shock to all of us."[5]

Although it made no difference on the diamond, Bearden was also a wonderful human-interest story. A navy veteran, he had suffered serious injuries during the Second World War while serving aboard the light cruiser USS *Helena* in the Pacific Theater. During the Battle of Kula Gulf on July 6, 1943, he was working in the *Helena*'s engine room when the vessel was struck by three enemy torpedoes. While trying to abandon the sinking ship, Bearden fell from a ladder on the *Helena*'s deck. He sustained a fractured skull and a crushed kneecap. Bearden spent the better part of two years in military hospitals, undergoing surgeries in which aluminum plates were inserted in both his head and damaged knee. Bearden seldom discussed his naval service or his harrowing, life-threatening ordeal except to praise the surgeons and hospital staff who saved his life and nursed him back to health. His storybook comeback from near death to being a star MLB pitcher in 1948 was absolutely inspirational.

Lou Boudreau made one bizarre and risky entry in his starting nine: He put reserve outfielder Allie Clark at first base—a position he had never played before, at least professionally. Clark learned about his odd assignment by finding a first baseman's mitt in his locker at Fenway Park. Clark recalled being utterly puzzled. He asked Boudreau what it meant. Boudreau explained that he wanted Clark's right-handed bat in the lineup to take advantage of the ballpark's enticing left-field wall. Cleveland's regular first baseman, Eddie Robinson, was a lefthanded hitter. Clark would be in the second spot of the Indian batting order. It was a throw of the dice.

An enormous crowd of 33,957 emotionally charged fans crammed into chilly Fenway Park to watch the critical game that would decide the AL pennant winners for 1948. Many fans had camped out overnight to buy bleacher seats. When the box office opened at 9 a.m., there were at least 15,000 fans in the meandering queue. To prevent scalpers from gobbling up the precious ducats, sales were restricted to one ticket per person. Speculators were getting the fantastic sum of $50 apiece for grandstand tickets. The *Boston Globe* reported that 20 of 22 city councilors opted to attend the ballgame at Fenway Park rather than their weekly meeting—which had to be canceled for the first time in ten years due to the lack of a quorum.

Among the spectators were MLB Commissioner Happy Chandler and the entire roster of the Boston Braves. They would host Game One of the World Series two days hence. Manager Billy Southworth ran a brief morning practice at Braves Field before the NL champions departed *en masse* to Boston's AL ballpark less than a mile away to view the unfolding drama—and to exploit the rare opportunity to scout both the Indians and Red Sox

4. Game #155

simultaneously. One of them would be the visiting club when the Fall Classic began on Wednesday afternoon at 1 p.m.

One would expect that the Braves would have been rooting for the Red Sox for the sake of having a unique all-Boston World Series. That was not the case, however. The substantial financial rewards of a Cleveland victory were not lost on the NL champs. "So far as baseball rivalry is concerned, I would like to play the Red Sox," explained Braves rookie shortstop Alvin Dark, "but for business reasons I naturally want to see Cleveland win the pennant."[6] Dark was referring to the enormous crowds who would surely attend the Fall Classic games at Cleveland's cavernous Municipal Stadium if the Indians won the AL championship. The seating capacity there was more than twice that of Fenway Park. The higher the turnstile count, the bigger the World Series shares the players would receive.

Although no one could know for certain, the number of reporters present to cover the AL tiebreaker may have been the greatest ever to report on a non–World Series game. The scribes had to battle their way into the park as local police had their hands full trying to intercept gatecrashers along with more than a few miffed Red Sox season-ticket holders who angrily learned at the last moment that their 1948 passes did not grant them admission to the all-important Game #155.

Journalist Hugh Fullerton reported that Red Sox owner Tom Yawkey was offered $50,000 for the radio rights to broadcast the AL tiebreaker. Instead, he refused payment, claiming that having Game #155 on the radio was something akin to a public service. Bill Veeck, always scrambling to earn every possible nickel of revenue for his Cleveland club by any means possible, was apparently horrified when he heard what Yawkey had done.

Things began poorly for the nervous Denny Galehouse in the very first inning. Although he retired the first two batters, the third Indian he faced, Lou Boudreau, Cleveland's player-manager, slammed a solo home run into the screen above the Green Monster to put the visitors ahead 1–0. The Red Sox got the run back in the bottom half of the inning when Johnny Pesky hit a double and Vern Stephens drove him in with a single, tying the game at 1–1.

The score remained that way until the top of the fourth inning. The Indians began that key frame with a bang: Two straight singles and a three-run homer by Ken Keltner—again into the screen atop the Monster—put the visitors into a healthy 4–1 lead. That was the last pitch Denny Galehouse threw in 1948. Ellis Kinder was summoned from the home team's bullpen for some long relief work. Kinder did not get off to a particularly stellar start. A double by Larry Doby followed by a sacrifice bunt and an infield out increased Cleveland's advantage to 5–1.

When the Indians roared out to a four-run lead in the top of the fourth inning, Boudreau replaced Allie Clark with regular first baseman Eddie Robinson. For Clark, being lifted from the game brought on an overwhelming feeling of relief. "I was the happiest guy in the ballpark,"[7] Clark remembered years later. Boudreau's gamble had resulted in a no gain/no loss outcome: Clark had failed to get a hit in his two at-bats, but more importantly for the Indians he did not make any errors in handling five chances defensively. *New York Herald Tribune* baseball writer Rud Rennie sensed Clark's apprehension at the unfamiliar position. He wrote, "Clark played the position as one might expect it to be played by a man who had never played it before. He did not drop any ball, but he always looked as if he might."[8]

Cleveland's lead rose to a daunting 6–1 when the red-hot Boudreau drilled another home run into the left-field screen in the top of the fifth inning. (It was just the second time in 1948 that Boudreau had homered twice in a game.) The AL pennant was a virtual certainty for Cleveland at this point.

Meanwhile, Gene Bearden was meticulously moving toward his twentieth victory and fifteenth complete game of the season. (For statistical purposes, Game #155 was considered an extension of the 1948 AL regular campaign, so its numbers would be included in the seasonal records of both the Indians and Red Sox and in the individual stats of both teams' players.) Bearden allowed two unearned runs in the home half of the sixth inning when a Ted Williams fly ball was misplayed by second baseman Joe Gordon. Bobby Doerr followed shortly thereafter with a home run to slice the visitors' lead to only 6–3. Those runs, both unearned, were the last the Red Sox would score in 1948. Bearden only allowed one more harmless Boston hit over the final three frames—an eighth-inning single by Ted Williams—while the Tribe added an insurance tally in the eighth inning and another in the top of the ninth to assume a commanding 8–3 lead. Ellis Kinder was still on the mound for Boston when the game was salted away by the Indians.

The Red Sox got a man on base via a walk in the bottom of the ninth inning, but they otherwise capitulated rather quietly. Boston's catcher, Birdie Tebbetts—who would later manage Cleveland for four seasons in the 1960s—grounded out to Indians third baseman Ken Keltner to end matters. The game had taken 144 minutes to play. Moments after the final out was made at first base, the Indians surrounded Bearden. Several teammates happily hoisted him off the ground and carried him into the Cleveland clubhouse in joyful triumph. J.G. Taylor Spink of *The Sporting News* put a monetary value on the result of the game. "Bearden's artful left arm," he wrote, "with its sharp-dipping knuckleball, clever slider and baffling fastball, picked more than $5,000 right out of the pockets of each member of the Red Sox."⁹

Journalist Franklin Lewis described the scene at Fenway Park—and beyond—when the Tribe knocked off the Red Sox: "Lou Boudreau rushed toward Joe Gordon and wrapped both arms around [him]. The Indians stormed from the dugout, picked up Gene Bearden, and carried him off the field. In Cleveland, thousands poured out of offices and stores and celebrated in the streets. Business was suspended."¹⁰

Cleveland certainly deserved to win the October 4 tiebreaker at Fenway Park. The Indians outhit the Red Sox 13 to five. Everyone in the visitors' lineup contributed to the victory. Seven different Indians got hits while six different Cleveland players scored runs. On the other hand, the bottom four spots in the Boston batting order managed just a single hit off the thoroughly dominant Bearden. Cleveland scribe Ed McAuley wrote in *The Sporting News*,

> From vanquished foe, delirious friend, and impartial sideliner came the same comment as the Indians whooped their way of the field with their 8–3 decision and their first title since 1920: "The best team won."
>
> The Indians were the best team because they were sounder defensively than any of the other contenders; they hit more consistently if not more noisily as some of their rivals; and most of all, in the moment when they needed it, they had the pitching.¹¹

Years later it was revealed by Lou Boudreau that Bearden had been stealthily sipping on brandy between innings. The bottle had been hidden in a satchel carried by team trainer Harold Weisman. Weisman nervously walked around the visitors' dugout during the game with the bag and sat beside Bearden whenever the pitcher indicated he needed to be refreshed with a snort.

Many of the Indians' wives were present at Fenway Park to watch their husbands capture the Indians' first AL pennant in 28 seasons. With a Cleveland victory becoming more and more likely as the contest wound down to its conclusion, they sensibly muted their cheering as nearby Red Sox fans grew progressively angrier at what was occurring to the home team in 1948's most important ballgame. This led to one amusing incident: When the final out of the ninth inning was recorded by the Indians, Sandy Harder, the wife of Cleveland pitching coach Mel Harder, began weeping with joy. Mistaking her sobs for tears of sadness, a compassionate Red Sox fan approached Mrs. Harder and kindly offered these words of condolence: "Don't worry, lady. We'll get them next year."¹²

There would be no Trolley Series in 1948. As of October 2022, the Red Sox and Braves have never met in a World Series.

In the clubhouse of the defeated Red Sox, Boston second baseman Bobby Doerr was generous and sportsmanlike in his comments about the winning pitcher. "Give credit where credit is due," conceded Doerr. "Bearden was great. He had all kinds of stuff. That he could come back with so much stuff after only one day of rest was remarkable."[13] An Associated Press correspondent was also praiseful of the winning hurler. He wrote, "Bearden did it with a little bit of this and a little bit of that—but mostly his knuckleball. He threw the dipsy-doodler four out of every five pitches. The knuckler got him home—parlayed with the raw courage that brought him back to baseball from Pacific war action with aluminum plates in his head and left knee."[14]

Lou Boudreau thoroughly agreed. "The knuckler did it," he told a crowd of reporters after the game. "They just couldn't hit it. I know one of their coaches was tipping the hitters every time [Bearden] threw it—and they still couldn't connect."[15]

Arthur Daley of the *New York Times* wrote, "Fenway Park is supposed to be poison on left-handed pitchers, particularly when the wind blows the wrong way. But Bearden fed the poison in large doses to the Red Sox and killed their pennant hopes."[16]

From an offensive standpoint, the most impactful player in Game #155 was Lou Boudreau himself. He was 4-for-4 at the plate and scored three runs. Two of his hits were homers. "You've just got to hand it to this guy Boudreau," wrote Canadian journalist Laurie Brain of the *Galt Daily Reporter*. "He's been pacing the Indians from start to finish. His tremendous hitting, sensational fielding, and outstanding field generalship stamps him as one of the greatest player-managers of all time." Brain felt compelled to remind his readers: "And this is the guy that Cleveland last winter was going to sell down the river to St. Louis."[17]

The Indians were having a boisterous celebration with plenty of liquid refreshments in the visitors' clubhouse at Fenway Park when a moment of somber seriousness was interjected by Boudreau. He silenced everyone momentarily. "I want everyone to raise his glass," Boudreau asked, "to a great pitcher who is not with us tonight … to a fellow we really won this pennant for … to Don Black."[18] Black was still resting in a Cleveland hospital, in serious condition, since being afflicted by a brain hemorrhage on September 13. His future, baseball and otherwise, was a very uncertain one.

Excluding the players and team officials, probably the happiest and most thankful man in Cleveland after the Indians' playoff victory was a small business owner named Ronald Mazur. Before the season had concluded, Mazur had ordered the considerable amount of 50,000 pennants for his novelty shop. The flags proclaimed the Tribe as AL champions for

4. Game #155

1948. With the real pennant safely in the hands of Cleveland's baseball team, the miniature souvenir versions were now quite desirable items. However, had Cleveland lost the playoff game to Boston on October 4, their value to anyone would have been very questionable. In all likelihood, they would have been unsellable.

After the game, Ellis Kinder lamented the lost and relished opportunity to play in a unique all-Boston World Series against the NL champion Braves. He sadly told reporters, "If it hadn't been for my arm trouble, we'd have won this [AL championship] easy [sic]. Well, I'll show them next year. I'll win 20 games or more for this club and we'll win the pennant."[19] When he was asked about McCarthy's questionable choice of starting Denny Galehouse in Game #155, Kinder bluntly gave his honest opinion. He said, "With everything riding on the game, it didn't make a lot of sense."[20] Often overlooked by Red Sox aficionados is that Kinder allowed as many runs in in Game #155 as Galehouse did (four), although just three of Kinder's were earned runs.

Reaction in the street of Cleveland was, predictably, unrestrained joy and merriment. According to an Associated Press story that ran in many of the continent's newspapers the following day, general bedlam broke loose among the city's long-suffering, pennant-starved inhabitants:

> This lakefront city, after biting its fingernails down to the second knuckle the last few weeks as the Indians dilly-dallied in their attempt to win the American League pennant, was a debris-littered mess today.
>
> A celebration set off by the 8–3 victory over the Boston Red Sox yesterday in the American League's first sudden-death playoff, lasted into the wee, small hours.
>
> To a casual visitor, not knowing the pent-up emotions of the oft-frustrated Cleveland fans who have been denied a pennant since 1920, the celebration—a swashbuckling, noisy affair—must have resembled the Armistice Day blowout.
>
> The hotels were first to take action as the final score winged in. They immediately cleared their lobbies of furniture, and it was a good thing they did, for a few minutes later a flock of bands, generally led by a big guy beating a drum, roared in.[21]

Some 90 tons of confetti and streamers had to be collected from Cleveland's streets. People generally behaved themselves, but there were 45 arrests for drunkenness. One freak injury was reported when rowdies toppled a lamppost which struck a hapless female bystander.

A Braves-Indians Fall Classic was going to be noteworthy for its novelty, if nothing else. "Well, at least we're going to have a change in the 1948 World Series," wrote Laurie Brain, who knew his baseball history well. "Between them, this year's American League and National League pennant winners have waited 62 years for a crack at the postseason pot of gold."[22]

In an editorial the next day, the *Youngstown Vindicator* acknowledged the victory but questioned people's priorities. It said, "So the Cleveland Indians have their first pennant in 28 years, and what Cleveland thinks about it is shown as the *Plain Dealer* devotes three-fourths of page one to the deciding game while giving the war threat a scant half-dozen inches."[23]

An Associated Press story from the following day noted, "Today the Indians and Braves settle down to plans for a series that must come as an anticlimax to the Indians. It won't come as any anticlimax to their pocketbooks."[24]

Baseball fans had Tuesday off to ponder and predict what might happen when the two major leagues' worthy champions of 1948 squared off in the World Series. The opener, weather permitting, was scheduled for Braves Field on Wednesday afternoon.

AL Tiebreaker Game
Monday, October 4, 1948, at Fenway Park

CLE A 1 0 0 4 1 0 0 1 1 - 8 13 1
BOS A 1 0 0 0 0 2 0 0 0 - 3 5 1

BATTING

Cleveland Indians	AB	R	H	RBI	BB	SO	PO	A
Mitchell lf	5	0	1	0	0	0	1	0
Clark 1b	2	0	0	0	0	0	5	0
Robinson 1b	2	1	1	0	0	0	9	0
Boudreau ss	4	3	4	2	1	0	3	5
Gordon 2b	4	1	1	0	1	0	2	3
Keltner 3b	5	1	3	3	0	0	1	6
Doby cf	5	1	2	0	0	1	0	0
Bob Kennedy rf	2	0	0	0	0	0	0	0
Hegan c	3	1	0	1	1	2	6	1
Bearden p	3	0	1	0	1	0	0	2
Totals	35	8	13	6	4	3	27	17

FIELDING: DP—3. Hegan-Boudreau, Gordon-Boudreau-Robinson, Bearden-Gordon-Robinson. **E**—Gordon (23).

BATTING: 2B—Doby 2 (23, off Kinder 2); Keltner (24, off Kinder). **HR**—Boudreau 2 (18, 1st inning off Galehouse 0 on 2 out, 5th inning off Kinder 0 on 2 out); Keltner (31, 4th inning off Galehouse 2 on 0 out). **SH**—Bob Kennedy 2 (4, off Kinder 2); Robinson (9, off Kinder). **GDP**—Mitchell (10, off Galehouse); Keltner (24, off Kinder). **IBB**—Boudreau (7, by Kinder); Hegan (17, by Kinder); Gordon (6, by Kinder). **Team LOB:** 7.

4. Game #155

BATTING

Boston Red Sox	AB	R	H	RBI	BB	SO	PO	A
DiMaggio cf	4	0	0	0	0	0	3	0
Pesky 3b	4	1	1	0	0	1	3	4
Williams lf	4	1	1	0	0	0	3	0
Stephens ss	4	0	1	1	0	1	2	4
Doerr 2b	4	1	1	2	0	1	5	2
Spence rf	1	0	0	0	2	1	1	0
Hitchcock ph	0	0	0	0	1	0	0	0
Wright pr	0	0	0	0	0	0	0	0
Goodman 1b	3	0	0	0	1	2	7	1
Tebbetts c	4	0	1	0	0	0	3	1
Galehouse p	0	0	0	0	1	0	0	1
Kinder p	2	0	0	0	0	0	0	1
Totals	30	3	5	3	5	6	27	14

FIELDING: DP—2. Stephens-Doerr-Goodman, Stephens-Doerr-Goodman. **E**—Williams (5).

BATTING: 2B—Pesky (26, off Bearden). **HR**—Doerr (27, 6th inning off Bearden 1 on 2 out). **GDP**—Goodman (18, off Bearden); Tebbetts (21, off Bearden). **Team LOB:** 5.

BASERUNNING: CS—Spence (2, 2nd base by Bearden/Hegan).

PITCHING

Cleveland Indians	IP	H	R	ER	BB	SO	HR	BFP
Bearden W (20-7)	9	5	3	1	5	6	1	35

Boston Red Sox	IP	H	R	ER	BB	SO	HR	BFP
Galehouse L (8-8)	3	5	4	4	1	1	2	14
Kinder	6	8	4	3	3	2	1	28
Totals	9	13	8	7	4	3	3	42

Galehouse faced 3 batters in the 4th inning.

WP—Kinder (2). **IBB**—Kinder 3 (6, Boudreau, Hegan, Gordon). **Umpires**—HP-Bill McGowan, 1B-Bill Summers, 2B-Eddie Rommel, 3B-Charlie Berry. **Time of Game**—2:24. **Attendance**—33,957.

— 5 —

Esoterica

A Collection of Happenings from the 1948 Baseball Season

"Trivia is a fact without a home."—Don Rittner

Every sport has its moments of highlights and lowlights each season, whether it be record-setting feats of brilliance or sometimes forgettable instances of futility and infamy. Baseball is certainly no exception. Here are just a handful of the memorable and offbeat happenings from the 1948 campaign throughout the vast world of professional baseball.

Even in 1948, the Boston Red Sox and New York Yankees tended to play long games. On March 29, in St. Petersburg, Florida, the two AL rivals set a record for what was believed to be the longest spring training game in MLB history—and they did not even finish the contest! The game was called after 17 exhausting innings that took four hours and two minutes to play and involved 34 players. The final score was 2–2.

Proving the Dodgers-Yankees rivalry was continuing well after the two clubs had played seven games in the 1947 World Series, the New York Yankees set a second spring training record on April 18. That day they hosted the Brooklyn Dodgers at Yankee Stadium before a crowd of 62,369 fans—believed to be the largest turnout for a preseason exhibition game in MLB history. Brooklyn took the meaningless game, 5–3.

On Opening Day, Monday, April 19, a monument to baseball legend George Herman (Babe) Ruth was unveiled at Yankee Stadium. Ruth, who had turned 53 in February, was in failing health. The inscription on the plaque reverently read, "A great ball player. A great man. A great American."

That same day, the Boston Red Sox became the first MLB team to hit three consecutive homers on Opening Day when Stan Spence, Vern Stephens, and Bobby Doerr went deep in the second inning. The trio of long balls proved to be inadequate for Boston, however. The Philadelphia Athletics prevailed 5–4 over Boston in 11 innings in the first game of a doubleheader at Fenway Park.

Also on April 19, New York Yankee starting pitcher Allie Reynolds, thinking the hometown Washington Senators were trying to trick him, refused to leave second base after he hit his first—and only—MLB homer. Reynolds never saw the ball clear the outfield fence at Griffith Stadium, which caused him to be doubtful of his rare achievement. In front of an amused President Harry Truman, New York, manager Bucky Harris finally convinced the skeptical Reynolds to circle the bases to complete his home run so the Opening Day contest could continue. New York won the game handily, 12–4.

Manager Leo (The Lip) Durocher of the Brooklyn Dodgers returned from a one-year suspension for consorting with unsavory characters. On April 21, Durocher employed 24 players in establishing a new MLB record for Opening Day in a 9–5 loss to the New York Giants at the Polo Grounds. By contrast, his counterpart, Mel Ott, used only 12 players. Ironically, Durocher would replace Ott as the Giants' pilot before the end of the season.

Cleveland Indians right fielder Larry Doby tied an unflattering MLB record on Tuesday, April 20 by striking out five times in a game. It did not affect the outcome, though. Doby's team still managed to defeat the Detroit Tigers at Briggs Stadium, 7–4.

On Thursday, April 29, Ted Wilks lost his first game in 77 consecutive appearances—a run of games that dated back to September 8, 1945. The righthanded reliever of the St. Louis Cardinals was 12–0 during the streak, including four appearances as a starting pitcher. Wilks' rare loss occurred in relief in a 14-inning defeat to the Cincinnati Reds at Crosley Field.

On Thursday, May 20, Joe DiMaggio put on a batting clinic as he hit for the cycle for the second time in his career. In front of a sparse gathering of only 5,001 fans at Chicago's Comiskey Park, DiMaggio sparked the Yankees' 22-hit assault with a pair of home runs and six RBIs as New York won in a rout, 13–2, over the lowly and overmatched White Sox.

On that same Thursday, the Cleveland Indians tied an AL record when they coaxed 18 walks out of the Boston Red Sox pitching staff in a 13–4 victory before their home fans at Municipal Stadium. Red Sox starter Mickey Harris walked seven Indians before being pulled by manager Joe McCarthy in the second inning. His replacement was 19-year-old rookie southpaw Mickey McDermott. He followed suit and gave up 11 more passes in the six-plus innings he tossed. Three of those walks came with the bases loaded. Every one of the Cleveland starters drew two bases on balls except for catcher Jim Hegan (one) and right fielder Pat Seerey (three). The 18 passes in one game tied a 32-year-old MLB record set by the pitiful 1916 Philadelphia Athletics—arguably the worst MLB team of the 20th century.

With a crowd of 49,641 fans emotionally singing "Auld Lang Syne" to their greatest star, the New York Yankees celebrated the silver anniversary of Yankee Stadium by holding Babe Ruth Day on Sunday, June 13. With members of the 1923 Yankees—the first installment of the club to play in the famous Bronx ballyard—looking on, the gravely ill former superstar had his uniform #3 retired and sent to the Hall of Fame in Cooperstown. The visiting club that day was the Cleveland Indians. Ruth dressed in their clubhouse and laboriously made his way to the field through the visitors' dugout. First baseman Eddie Robinson noticed that Ruth had a very unsteady gait, so when Ruth was about to walk to the batter's box, Robinson handed him a random bat from the Indians' rack to use as a cane. (It was one belonging to Bob Feller—who did not know until 1982 that it was his bat that Ruth had used; Robinson had quietly kept it as a souvenir for more than three decades.) A famous photo, taken by Nat Fein of the *New York Herald Tribune*, shot from the rear, shows Ruth standing in front of home plate, looking thoughtfully toward the outfield, and leaning against the bat for support. The poignant photograph won Fein a Pulitzer Prize. For many years the bat was displayed at the Bob Feller Hometown Museum in Van Meter, Iowa, until it closed in 2015.

The last of the stubborn AL holdouts opposing night baseball, the Detroit Tigers, finally hosted their first contest under the lights on Tuesday, June 15. The novelty drew a huge crowd. Before a throng of 54,480 onlookers at Briggs Stadium, the Tigers upended the Philadelphia Athletics by a score of 4–1. This left the Chicago Cubs as the only MLB team that had not hosted a nighttime game—and it would remain that way for another four decades.

On Monday, June 21, St. Louis Browns pitchers issued the godawful one-game total of 16 walks to opposing Philadelphia A's batters. Dizzy Dean, the former great St. Louis hurler, commenting from his radio broadcasting perch, was disgusted by a sequence in which one pitcher threw nine consecutive balls. Dean informed his listeners in his folksy Arkansas way, "If I had pitched nine straight balls when I broke into this game, I'd have [written] ma and pa and told them to put in another acre of cotton because I'd be coming home."[1] Dean blamed the decline in control pitching on the sport's new affluence. "Baseball has become so doggone ritzy that every team carries a batting-practice pitcher whose only duty is to toss [balls] for 30 minutes a day,"[2] he said in *The Sporting News*. Dean strongly believed a team's regular pitchers ought to throw batting practice every day to hone their control skills.

On Thursday, June 24, in a game in the Class D Eastern Shore League,

Gene Corbett, the manager of the Salisbury Cardinals, was ejected. On his way to the showers, Corbett gave the team's batboy a special instruction— which 13-year-old Paul Murrell dutifully followed. Murrell boldly told the plate umpire to get in the game and keep his eyes open! Murrell was also ejected.

Bob Lemon of the Cleveland Indians pitched a no-hitter on Wednesday, June 30 as he defeated the Detroit Tigers, 2–0 in just 93 minutes at Municipal Stadium. Lemon walked three batters while striking out four Tigers for his eleventh win of the season. Lemon thus became the first AL player in the circuit's history to throw a no-hitter in a night game.

In a July 4 game between the Boston Red Sox and the Philadelphia Athletics, the Red Sox entered the bottom of the seventh inning in a 5–5 tie—which they managed to break in record fashion, scoring 14 runs on their way to a 19–5 victory. Ted Williams came to the plate three times during the home half of the frame and failed to get a hit. (He walked twice and grounded into the final out.) A's pitcher Bubba Harris was tagged for 12 of the runs as the Red Sox finished the game with 20 total hits. Proving that they enjoyed playing Philadelphia on the Fourth of July holiday, Boston's 14 runs in a single inning tied the MLB record exactly nine years after the Red Sox scored a team-record 35 runs against the A's in a 1939 doubleheader sweep (18–12 and 17–7).

Throughout the 1948 season, Richard Muckerman, the owner of the lowly St. Louis Browns, criticized the baseball fans of his city for not adequately supporting his team. Muckerman had also frequently sold or traded his most promising players to other AL clubs. This prompted Dan Parker of the *New York Mirror* to scathingly pen in his baseball column, "In view of Muckerman's policy of peddling his best players to other clubs, I'd say the crowd of 2,787 which attended a recent [Browns] game versus the A's, was 2,786 more than Muckerman had reason to expect—assuming he himself was in the ballpark that night."[3] Parker's questioning of Muckerman's own attendance at Sportsman's Park was a fair comment. A photograph in the July 7 issue of *The Sporting News* taken during a Red Sox–Browns doubleheader on June 27 showed the owner's box to be conspicuously vacant. The St. Louis Browns had the worst attendance of the 16 MLB clubs by far: just 335,564 customers bought tickets in 1948. The Philadelphia Phillies had the next worst seasonal attendance total—but they drew more than twice the number of fans that the Browns did.

In an attempt to keep its ballparks family friendly, the American League decided to crack down on audible foul language and general misbehavior that could drive ticket-buyers away. Accordingly, fines and suspensions were being imposed on AL players, managers and even umpires whose actions and language brought the sport into disrepute. "I'm not trying to make the American League an adjunct to a Sunday School movement," insisted AL president William Harridge. "It comes down to this: Some very fine people attend ballgames. These folks represent a tremendous asset to the game. Women, children, entire families attend our contests. It took many years for us to arrive at our current situation. We cannot risk driving these families away from our parks, just because an umpire gets huffy or a player says things he later apologizes for and does not recollect having said."[4]

Along those lines, umpire Bill McGowan—a veteran of 24 AL seasons—was suspended without pay for ten days and fined $500 for an aggressive series of actions against the Washington Senators during two games in July. In the first game, on July 15, the 52-year-old McGowan threw his indicator at Ray Scarborough after the Senators pitcher complained about his plate umpiring. Washington manager Joe Kuhel and the coaching staff, not surprisingly, took issue with McGowan's cantankerous behavior. Four days later, while working at first base in a three-man system, the highly respected McGowan assailed Senators outfielder Bud Stewart with an onslaught of verbal abuse after Stewart had argued with plate umpire Joe Paparella. Later in that same game, McGowan threw a baseball at Stewart, who had his back turned toward the umpire at the time. By all accounts, these actions were highly atypical of McGowan's reputation. In assessing the unusual disciplinary penalty against one of its esteemed arbiters on July 30, William Harridge publicly stated that McGowan's behavior was "unbecoming of an umpire."[5] During baseball's off-seasons, McGowan ran the most famous umpiring school in the country.

On Sunday, July 18, Pat Seerey of the Chicago White Sox joined a very elite coterie, one whose members were Bobby Lowe, Ed Delahanty, Lou Gehrig and Chuck Klein: Seerey became just the fifth player in MLB history to belt four home runs in a single game. His club needed every run. His spectacular batting feat propelled the visiting White Sox to a 12–11 victory in 11 innings over the Philadelphia Athletics at Shibe Park. Seerey, who never lived up to his potential, hit just 86 homers in his MLB career. Seerey himself admitted he was a coach's nightmare. "I'm sort of a rockhead," he once said. "When somebody tells me something and I'm not sure it's right, I get stubborn and won't do it."[6]

Reverting to the norm, Pat Seerey made it into the record books again less than a week after hitting four homers in a game—this time in a negative way—as he became the first player in MLB history to strike out seven times in a doubleheader. It occurred on Saturday, July 24, against the New York Yankees. The White Sox and Yankees split the twin bill.

On Sunday, August 1, righthander Phil Marchildon of the Philadelphia Athletics may have thrown the wildest pitch in MLB history in a game versus the Tigers in Detroit. It occurred in the bottom of the fourth inning with Vic Wertz at bat for the home team. The toss sailed so far and wide of the plate that it struck a fan from Toledo, Ohio, named Sam Wexler who was occupying a seat in the tenth row of the grandstand about one-third of the way between home plate and third base! Wexler, who was leaning over to light a cigar, was struck on top of the head by Marchildon's pitch. Wexler was taken to a first-aid room as a precaution, but he was quickly deemed to be unhurt. Wertz drew a walk, but Marchildon was the winning pitcher in Philadelphia's 4–2 triumph.

In the second game of a doubleheader on Thursday, August 12, the Cleveland Indians rapped out 29 hits in a 26–3 route over the pitiful St. Louis Browns. Nine of the hits went for extra bases as the Indians established an MLB record with 14 different players hitting safely in the contest.

The very next day, the Philadelphia Phillies set an MLB record by scoring nine runs before making an out versus the New York Giants at Shibe Park on August 13. The Phillies would go on to score ten times in that inning on their way to a reasonably close 12–7 victory.

Four months after having his monument unveiled at Yankee Stadium, on August 16, at 8:01 p.m., one of the greatest players to set foot on a baseball diamond, the Sultan of Swat, the Bambino, the Babe, George Herman Ruth passed away after a lengthy battle with cancer. Ruth had been diagnosed with nasopharyngeal carcinoma two years earlier. Largely because of his enormous fame, Ruth became one of the first cancer patients to receive both drugs and radiation treatment at the same time. Thousands of New Yorkers stood vigil outside the hospital during his final days. Ruth, probably the most famous athlete in American history, passed away in his sleep. He was only 53½ years old. His body was placed in an open casket at Yankee Stadium. When the public was allowed to view Ruth for the last time, more than 100,000 people passed by it at an average rate of more than 100 mourners per minute.

Lefthander Sam Zoldak of the Cleveland Indians tossed a nine-hit shutout on Wednesday, August 18, extending the Tribe's impressive streak of scoreless innings to 30 innings. The Indians would eventually extend this skein to an impressive 47 innings encompassing four shutouts. One of those whitewashes was tossed by the recently signed Satchel Paige.

A news release from Charley Hurth, the president of the minor league Southern Association, was certainly an eye-catcher: "Umpire Angelo Guglielmo has been indefinitely suspended for his uncalled for and unjustified attack on a Chattanooga radio announcer." That announcer was Tom Nobles who called Chattanooga Lookouts games on WDEF. The incident occurred when Guglielmo and two of his colleagues decided to pay Nobles a visit while on their way to their next umpiring assignment. Nobles was broadcasting a Chattanooga-Nashville game on August 18 when he calmly told his listeners that someone representing himself as umpire Guglielmo had entered the broadcast booth to register a complaint. Guglielmo accused Nobles of calling him "meathead" during a recent game. Nobles denied doing so; he said he was only reporting what the spectators had been calling Bill Malesky, one of Guglielmo's partners. After the broadcast, Nobles headed to his hotel where he was accosted by Guglielmo in the lobby. The agitated umpire challenged the announcer to a fight. Both stepped outside to do battle. The local police arrested both men on disorderly conduct charges but not before Nobles got the worst of the scrap, suffering cracked ribs. They each posted $50 bonds and were released. Guglielmo failed to appear in court the next day, forfeiting his money. The charge against Nobles was dropped. Guglielmo was in his first year as a Southern Association umpire, having been promoted from the Kitty League on the recommendation of Commissioner Happy Chandler.

On August 18, in a Pacific Coast League game at San Francisco's Seals Stadium, the ballpark's supposedly "unbreakable" plexiglass backstop broke. It shattered after it was struck by a foul ball from the bat of Seals catcher Will Leonard in a game versus the Hollywood Stars. No spectators were injured by the flying shards.

Looking for any possible edge to move up in the tight AL pennant race, the New York Yankees "borrowed" the Philadelphia A's most renowned and effective fan/heckler, Pete (Leather Lung) Adelis, for an upcoming home series versus the Cleveland Indians. Adelis, an enormous man whose stentorian voice carried loud and clear throughout every inch of Shibe Park, was flattered by the Yankees' unusual offer. Still, he wanted to remain loyal to his hometown Athletics. He said he would only make the trip to New York City—with all his expenses paid by the Yankees— if the Athletics consented to it. They did, as they were still in the running for the AL flag and they wished to see Cleveland lose to New York too. Adelis abided by one stipulation put forth by the Athletics: He had to be back in Philadelphia when the Chicago White Sox played a Sunday doubleheader versus the A's on August 29 at Shibe Park. The twin bill would feature the return of the disappointing Pat Seerey to his former home ballpark. Adelis agreed with alacrity. "With Seerey coming back to Philadelphia—I wouldn't miss it!"[7] he happily exclaimed.

On Sunday, August 29, Jackie Robinson hit for the cycle as the Brooklyn Dodgers defeated the St. Louis Cardinals, 12–7, in the first game of a doubleheader played at Sportsman's Park. It was the sixth time a Dodger had attained that feat. Only four have done it since then.

Eight days later, the Dodgers were in Boston for a doubleheader on

Monday, September 6. During the second game, Bill Salkeld and Mike McCormick of the Braves batted out of order the first two times through the lineup unbeknownst to the Dodgers! McCormick was listed in the sixth position and Salkeld the seventh on the Boston lineup card that had been handed to plate umpire Artie Gore before the game, but they flip-flopped the order when they batted. The pair produced two runs before the visitors realized there was a problem. In the first inning, Salkeld singled Jeff Heath home after the latter's two-RBI triple off the center field wall. Then, in the third inning, Salkeld doubled to right field and scored on Sibby Sisti's single to left. After Salkeld made an out in the fifth inning, McCormick singled to left to advance a runner. Brooklyn coach Ray Blades then noticed the mistake and spoke to umpire Gore about the irregularity in the batting order. McCormick was correctly called out for batting out of turn. Despite the amateurish paperwork gaffe, the hometown Braves still swept the twin bill by scores of 2–1 and 4–0.

Also on September 6, the Chicago Cubs and Cincinnati Reds played a Labor Day doubleheader at Crosley Field. Cincinnati was up 1–0 in the first game when Chicago's second basemen Emil Verban came to the plate. With two outs and the count 0–1, Verban tied the game with a solo home run. It would be the only time in his career that Verban would have the opportunity to circle the bases in his seven-year MLB career spread amongst four teams. What makes this home run special was that Verban had gone 2,592 at-bats without ever hitting one before. Verban was a .272 lifetime batting average but only compiled a .325 slugging percentage. That futility streak established an MLB record number of at-bats for a player to hit his first career home run that still stands today. What made Verban's home run even more remarkable was that it came off Johnny Vander Meer—the only pitcher in MLB history to throw back-to-back no hitters.

On Thursday, September 9, Rex Barney of the Brooklyn Dodgers tossed a 2–0 no-hitter over the New York Giants at the Polo Grounds. Barney walked only two batters while striking out four Giants for his 13th win of the season. Barney had to endure a one-hour rain delay and intermittent showers through the seventh, eighth and ninth innings to accomplish his feat.

The Philadelphia Phillies lost 13–2 to the Boston Braves on Saturday, September 11, ensuring another dismal losing season for the 16th consecutive year. This would be a record of futility unmatched by another team until the Pittsburgh Pirates endured 20 consecutive losing seasons between 1993 and 2012.

On Thursday, September 16, Joe DiMaggio became the eighth player in MLB history to accrue 300 career home runs. The round-tripper accounted for the New York Yankees' only run in a 2–1 loss to the Detroit Tigers in the first game of a twin bill at Briggs Stadium.

Stan (The Man) Musial of the St. Louis Cardinals, hit his 38th home run of the 1948 season on Wednesday, September 22 against the Boston Braves. While not a particularly spectacular hit, it still helped to make MLB history. Musial would go on to rack up five hits in the game, joining Ty Cobb and Wee Willie Keeler as the only other players to ever have at least four games in an MLB season with five or more hits. Those five hits came off five different Boston hurlers. In all the years since, only Tony Gwynn (in 1993) and Ichiro Suzuki (in 2004) have achieved this feat.

As he always seemed to be in the news, it was only fitting that the Yankee Clipper, Joe DiMaggio, on October 4, became the first major leaguer to grace the cover of *Time* magazine for a second time. The first such honor for New York's magnificent center fielder occurred more than a decade earlier, during DiMaggio's terrific 1936 rookie season.

Wes Ferrell, one of the best hitting MLB pitchers in recent memory, showed that his batting skills had not declined significantly at the advanced age of 40. Playing in the low minors for the Marion Marauders of the Class D Western Carolina League—where he also served as the team's manager—Ferrell handily captured that circuit's batting title in 1948 with a superb .432 average. The former hurler for the Senators and Red Sox accrued 162 hits in 375 at-bats for the Marauders. For good measure, Ferrell clouted 24 home runs and 14 triples mostly playing as an outfielder. It was the league's first year of operations.

On Wednesday, December 15, the Brooklyn Dodgers traded the extremely talented but even more accident-prone Pete Reiser to the Boston Braves for Frolian (Nanny) Fernandez and Mike McCormick. Reiser had become one of the top NL outfielders of his time, but he had badly damaged his reputation—and routinely battered his body—after being carried off the field on a stretcher no fewer than 11 times throughout his injury-plagued MLB career. Recklessly crashing headlong into unpadded, concrete outfield walls in various NL ballparks was seemingly the Reiser trademark. Reiser biographer Mark Stewart sympathetically wrote, "Alas, in the heat of the moment, Pete Reiser just never could pull up and play it off the wall. Every fly ball was his to catch, and catch them all he would— or kill himself trying."[8]

Television was becoming a major concern for professional baseball as the 1948 season entered the history books. Many of the sport's moguls saw the burgeoning and exciting new medium as a dangerous scourge to their livelihoods. "Radio aroused the curiosity of the fan; television satisfies it," insisted Frank Shaughnessy, president of the International League. As evidence, Shaughnessy pointed to the sharp decline in attendance for the Newark Bears, the New York Yankees' top farm club, whose fans apparently now overwhelmingly preferred to watch MLB games on television from New York over paying to see minor league games. He continued, "Television encourages the fan to stay home. What's going to happen when sets run into the millions?"[9] MLB owners were concerned too. Horace Stoneham of the New York Giants blamed television for the noticeable dip in attendance at his club's night games. He said his Giants used to regularly attract 45,000 customers to the Polo Grounds for evening contests. In 1948, that figure had dropped to about 35,000 fans per game because many people were choosing to stay home to watch other forms of amusement on the tube. Wayne Coy, the chairman of the Federal Communications Commission, was utterly unsympathetic, believing it was a survival-of-the-fittest situation. As television coverage continued to expand to fully national enterprises, Coy predicted, "[The medium's growth] would have a great impact on present entertainment methods which will be pressed to compete for public favor."[10]

— 6 —

Anticipation

Braves vs. Indians

"When Billy Southworth's bravest of the Boston Braves take the field tomorrow against Lou Boudreau's tribe, they'll be boasting a record of never having been beaten in a World Series. There are a good many fans who don't expect that record to hold after tomorrow."[1]—Laurie Brain, *Galt Daily Reporter*

"What women want: To be loved, to be listened to, to be desired, to be respected, to be needed, to be trusted, and sometimes, just to be held. What men want: Tickets to the World Series."[2]—Humorist Dave Barry

As soon as the two combatants for the 1948 World Series had been determined, Leo H. Petersen, the sports editor of United Press, accurately wrote,

> One of the strangest World Series ever conceived—the Cleveland Indians against the Boston Braves—was at last a reality and the baseball world was enthralled over the possible outcome.
> It was a strange alignment because the Indians, the team almost unanimously conceded to be the winner, almost didn't get into it at all. And the Braves, the poor and supposedly mediocre club rated little better than a preseason second-division outfit, won their race by a comfortable margin.[3]

The Associated Press polled 44 baseball writers assigned to the Fall Classic to find out what each expected the final outcome of the World Series to be. Thirty of the 44 predicted a Cleveland victory. Only one of the thirty scribes thought it would last seven games. Likewise, only one journalist figured the Indians to be victorious in a four-game sweep. Not surprisingly, he was a Cleveland writer: Franklin (Whitey) Lewis of the *Cleveland Press*. All the others pro–Indian voters predicted a five- or six-game tussle for the AL

6. Anticipation

version of the Tribe to put away the NL champions. Of the 14 journalist who boldly foresaw a Boston victory, not one figured on a four-game sweep or even a five-game triumph. Two of them picked the Braves to take the World Series in six games. The remaining dozen thought it would take Boston the maximum seven games to prevail over Cleveland.

Boston third baseman Bob Elliott, who was called "Mr. Team" by his fellow Braves—decided to needle the Indians when both clubs were jointly working out for the benefit of reporters and photographers at Braves Field on Tuesday, October 5. "Don't you guys get too cocky," he warned all the members of the AL champs within earshot. "Those home runs you hit at Fenway Park yesterday are just outs here."[4]

The NL champions cared little what the baseball pundits thought of their chances. They appeared to be unimpressed with the AL pennant winners, according to one scribe who observed the workout. "The Braves were cocky and confident," he wrote. "So were the Indians, despite the report of there being a rebellion among some of the players over what they reportedly felt was the preferred treatment which [Lou] Boudreau was according [Bob] Feller." The reporter felt compelled to add, "If there had been any dissention in the Cleveland ranks, it clearly had been dissipated. There wasn't a growl among them when Boudreau disclosed that Feller would be his opening game nominee."[5]

A postcard of Braves Field features the newly installed floodlights at the ballpark. Night games were first played there in 1946 (Library of Congress).

As it was an even-numbered year, the 1948 World Series would begin in the NL park based on a simple annual rotation system. The 1947 Fall Classic had opened at Yankee Stadium. The 1949 World Series would start at an AL ballpark too. Typical of the era when the two major leagues were completely separate entities, few of the Indians had ever seen or set foot in Braves Field before. Journalist Gayle Talbot noted that Cleveland's righthanded sluggers "surveyed with open delight" the short distance straight down the ballpark's left-field line that its inner walls provided. It measured 337 feet. The right-field line was even more enticing at a mere 317 feet. Bob Feller took a look at the barrier and jested that a batter could spit over it.

Baseball writer Whitney Martin's attention was drawn to the high pitcher's mound at Braves Field. "It looks like the foothill of the Alps," he penned. "That is, it towers up abnormally over the flat infield. Feller standing out on it today looked like a colossus. When he turns loose his fast one from that elevation, it will be like a guy sniping at a traveler from behind a rock up in the mountains."[6]

The city of Cleveland embraced the chance to host World Series games for the first time in 28 Octobers. The occasion was certainly going to benefit the local hospitality industries—especially the hotels. It was reported that no rooms could be found at any of the city's downtown hotels for the weekend when Game Three, Four and Five would be played on the shores of Lake Erie. Accordingly, an October 5 Associated Press story issued this warning to traveling baseball buffs: "If you are counting on [finding] a hotel room in Cleveland during the World Series, [you had] better forget about it. Hotel managers said today there is nothing available. In fact, the Boston Braves themselves were fearful they would not be able to secure accommodations until one hotel got a hospital convention to postpone its meeting for a week."[7]

As a goodwill gesture, the booked-solid inns were going the extra mile to try to assist hopeful fans who could not secure lodgings in the usual manner. Seven Cleveland hotels were busily organizing "hospitality desks" in their lobbies to connect visitors with private citizens who had indicated they would kindly accept out-of-town guests in their homes while the World Series was being contested.

With outfielder Jeff Heath injured and relegated to the sidelines for Boston, the Braves formally petitioned Commissioner Happy Chandler for permission to use minor leaguer Marv Rickert in the World Series. Chandler approved—so long as the Indians had no objections. (As was customary and sportsmanlike in such situations, the Indians agreed to let Rickert join the Braves' roster for the Fall Classic.) Oddly, Rickert possessed one advantage his more illustrious teammates did not have; He was the only

6. Anticipation

member of the Braves who had ever faced Bob Feller before. However, those occasions were in games that carried no weight in the standings. Nevertheless, Rickert had fared quite well versus Rapid Robert and his fearsome fastballs. When he was with the Chicago Cubs, Rickert batted against Feller in a handful of spring training games—and impressively got six hits in nine at-bats. Rickert had been planning a fishing vacation along the Columbia River once his season in Milwaukee ended. Nevertheless, the opportunity to compete in October baseball thrilled him. As a souvenir, Rickert liked to carry around the surprise telegram that was delivered to his home in Tacoma, Washington. Summoning him to the Braves, it was sent by Billy Southworth. The wire read, "HEATH BROKE ANKLE, JOIN US IN NEW YORK."

The underdog Braves were experiencing good times at the box office, too, as Boston fans clamored for reserved seats for the first two games of the Fall Classic which would be held at Braves Field. (Games Six and Seven would be contested there too, if necessary.) "Tickets of any sort were at a great premium today," wrote Gayle Talbot the day before the World Series opened. "The Braves' medium-sized park is certain to be packed to its absolute limit with some 40,000 fans when [Johnny] Sain [throws his] first pitch at 1 p.m."[8] That hour would be the starting time for every game of the 1948 World Series. Leo H. Petersen of United Press added, "Tickets were harder to get than a new automobile, and scalpers, working undercover, were asking and receiving as high as $50 for a $6 reserved grandstand seat."[9]

Reserved-seat tickets for the games at Braves Field were indeed difficult to obtain. As soon as the team showed it had the potential to be a championship outfit in April, the club's offices began fielding inquiries about World Series tickets. They were all politely but firmly rebuffed by Raynhild Stenberg, the team's implacable secretary, in accordance with a debatable policy enacted by the club: Ticket requests from New Englanders would take precedence over those from outsiders—and no applications whatsoever would be considered until the NL pennant was clinched by the Braves. According to a story that appeared in *The Sporting News*, Stenberg said, in one case, she was on the telephone with a man from somewhere in the northern reaches of Canada for more than 20 minutes who desperately wanted to purchase ducats for the first two Series games. All she could do was repeatedly thank him for his long-distance interest in the Boston Braves—and nothing more.

One season-ticket holder who had two cherished grandstand seats for both Game One and Game Two sacrificed them for a good cause. The *Boston Globe* reported that James A. McDonough of Stoneham, Massachusetts, donated his tickets as a lottery prize to benefit a local family that had recently lost three of its six children in a horrific house fire. The raffle raised $3,800 to help pay the medical expenses of the survivors.

Fifty-five-year-old Boston manager Billy Southworth reminded writers that he had a connection to the AL champions that had been largely forgotten. A native of Harvard, Nebraska, Southworth had made his MLB debut with the Indians, appearing in one game for the then–Cleveland Naps in 1913 and 60 more contests for the same team as an outfielder in 1915. Southworth would eventually play 13 seasons in the majors, but those two abridged campaigns for Cleveland were the only ones he ever spent on an AL team's roster.

More substantially, Southworth verified that Eddie Stanky would be Boston's starting second baseman for the World Series. There was some speculation that Sibby Sisti might be handed the task given that Stanky was still hobbling slightly from his July ankle injury, but Southwood affirmed to the press that Stanky was his choice.

The Series created another reunion as Cleveland coach Bill

On Opening Day 1949 Boston Braves owner Lou Perini (at right, holding two corners of the pennant) raised the NL pennant won by his club the previous year. They failed to defend it; Brooklyn won the flag that year (courtesy Boston Public Library, Leslie Jones Collection).

6. Anticipation 75

McKechnie had a prominent link to Boston. Now 68, he had managed the Braves for eight seasons from 1930 to 1937. The Braves finished no better than fourth place in the NL during McKechnie's years of leadership. One of those seasons was the dreadful 1935 campaign in which the hapless Braves lost 115 times. McKechnie was a widely respected baseball man, but local reporters recalled that the ex-Braves pilot was renowned for his appallingly poor sense of direction. He often became hopelessly lost in large buildings. According to one anecdote, McKechnie once intended to fly from Boston to Pittsburgh in advance of his team's arrival by train. When the plane touched down, McKechnie hailed an airport cab driver to take him to a prominent Pittsburgh hotel. The experienced cabbie said he had never heard of it nor any of the streets McKechnie mentioned. The driver surmised that McKechnie had to be in the wrong city and asked the Boston manager where he thought he was. Indeed, McKechnie had somehow boarded a flight to Detroit instead of Pittsburgh.

Cleveland manager Lou Boudreau evoked a laugh from a group of newspaper photographers. He was asked to assemble "three or four heavy hitters" from his squad to pose for a group photo. After a moment of silence, Boudreau responded, "We don't have 'em!"[10] Boudreau was being modest, of course. The general feeling among baseball scribes was that the Indians, on balance, were a better slugging outfit than the NL champion Braves.

Boston's Game One starter, Johnny Sain, usually said little to reporters, but "the big, dour man" (as he was described in an Associated Press article) did offer this tidbit of pitching philosophy before the opener: "If you were pitching to a machine, you could work until you brought every kind of pitch to perfection. But batters aren't machines. You fool a man with a certain pitch one day, and the next [day] he belts it out of the park."[11] Sain, like Bob Feller, had lost 15 games in 1948. Unlike Feller, Sain had won 24 contests.

Jack Hand of the Associated Press duly warned the Indians against the dangers of overconfidence, despite the fact that some bookmakers were listing the AL champs as heavy wagering favorites to win the 1948 World Series. He wrote, "All season long, the Braves heard they didn't have a chance. When they were eight games ahead in July, they were expected to blow it. When the chips were down, they [succeeded]. They don't figure to be the kind to fold in rough going—not even against Feller, Bearden or Lemon."[12]

Retired NL batting champion Rogers Hornsby foresaw a Cleveland World Series triumph. "The Indians will win in five games," he wrote in his column for the *Chicago Daily News* that was being syndicated nationally. "Had the Red Sox or Yankees won the American League pennant, I would have picked the Braves to take the title in six or seven games, but the Indians have more power and more good pitching. They should have won the pennant by 10 games."[13] Hornsby also deemed Lou Boudreau to be the greatest overall MLB ballplayer of the present time.

One prominent Boston pitcher announced he was going to mock an old baseball superstition that claimed that patting the head of a curly-headed lad would bring good luck. Warren Spahn said he was planning to do just the opposite. Spahn cheerfully told a reporter he would be rubbing the head of a bald-headed boy—his five-day-old son, Gregory. "Just a wee pat on the head might do the trick,"[14] the Braves hurler chuckled.

It was reported that the cost for radio and television rights for the Fall Classic had reached lofty new heights in 1948. Each was valued at $175,000. In 1947, the radio rights for the World Series were sold for $150,000 and the television rights went for a measly $65,000. For the tenth consecutive October, the Mutual Broadcasting System had secured the radio contract for the event. Its signal would be carried coast-to-coast across the

All things associated with the Braves became fashionable in Boston in 1948. Here manager Billy Southworth signs boxes full of souvenir baseballs (courtesy Boston Public Library, Leslie Jones Collection).

6. Anticipation

United States on its network of more than 500 stations, overseas on Armed Forces Radio Service, and on airwaves north of the border via the Canadian Broadcasting Corporation. The Gillette Safety Razor Co.—as part of their popular *Cavalcade of Sports* programming—would be the one and only American sponsor for the dominant radio medium.

Anticipation was at its apex. With the Indians and Braves raring to go, the fans in Boston eager to watch, and millions more across North America ready to tune into the radio description of the action, the 1948 World Series would begin on Wednesday, October 6—as long as the iffy Massachusetts weather cooperated.

— 7 —

Game One Scuttlebutt
Question Marks

A major subplot leading into the opening game of the 1948 Fall Classic was Bob Feller's first ever appearance in it. One sportswriter, Carl Lundquist, penned, "Feller, strikeout king of the majors, has achieved everything he dreamed of in his baseball career except pitching in a World Series, and he can be depended upon to make the most of that chance."[1] Nevertheless, rumors persisted among reporters that Feller was hampered with a sore pitching arm going into his Game One start for Cleveland. Feller denied there was any truth to the scuttlebutt at all. "My arm feels fine; there's nothing wrong with it," he insisted to scoop-seeking reporters who pressed him on the issue. "I'm ready to go."[2]

Another journalist, the fawning Leo H. Petersen, declared, "Rapid Bobby has a chance to prove he is one of the greatest hurlers the game has ever known. Since he came up to the Indians in 1936, most baseball men have claimed he is the best thing to walk on a pitching rubber in the game's modern era."[3]

That same scribe penned that the biggest concern the Cleveland club faced going into Game One was an untimely head cold caught by player-manager Lou Boudreau. It prevented him from working out with his team on Tuesday, but Boudreau minimized the cold's impact on his overall health or his ability to play shortstop in the opening game. Nobody questioned Boudreau's ability to ably manage a baseball club, regardless of his being afflicted by a nagging virus. Like his pitcher, Boudreau told the press he felt just fine. Petersen commented, "The Braves are hoping [Boudreau] is not feeling as well as he was on Monday when his two home runs, two singles and a base on balls in five trips to the plate led Cleveland to the playoff victory [over the Red Sox]."[4]

Writer Jack Hand expressed a degree of caution in describing Feller's chances for success in the Series opener. He wrote in his Associated

7. Game One Scuttlebutt

Bob Feller, the most famous fireballer of his time. A fan favorite, Feller was the face of the Cleveland franchise for most of his illustrious career (courtesy Boston Public Library, Leslie Jones Collection).

Press column, "Rapid Robert will have to go hard to top the performance of young Gene Bearden in [Monday's] 8–3 victory over the Boston Red Sox in the sudden-death playoff."[5]

The Braves' late-season loss of Jeff Heath to a grisly leg injury weighed on many scribes' minds—especially those located in Canada as the quick-tempered but skillful Heath hailed from Ontario. Deprived of a fellow Canadian to follow in the Fall Classic, prideful and nationalistic sportswriters from north of the American border ruefully predicted that Heath's absence from Boston's lineup would certainly spell doom for the NL champs against the powerful Cleveland Indians. A World Series preview article in the *Calgary Herald* was typical. "The Braves are short on power hitters," it noted. "This is especially true since the unfortunate injury to Jeff Heath, the Fort William boy."[6] Heath's replacement, minor leaguer Marv Rickert, was skeptically viewed as a huge question mark by the sporting press on both sides of the border.

Although they were the visiting team in Game One, Cleveland was listed by bookmakers as a 5:7 betting favorite to take the Series opener. That they were to face Boston's formidable Johnny Sain seemed to make no difference to the prognosticators. The Indians were expected to bludgeon the Braves as decisively as they had pounded the Red Sox in the playoff game at Fenway Park two days before. If the mighty Cleveland bats were somehow held in check by Sain, the prevailing opinion was that Feller's strong right arm could be counted on to stifle those swung by the Braves. Overall, the Indians were considered solid 1:5 favorites by the oddsmakers to win the Fall Classic.

— 8 —

World Series Game One
Picked Off? No, Ticked Off!

Date: Wednesday, October 6, 1948
Site: Braves Field, Boston, Massachusetts

> "It's been said many times in jest that the country could, or should, be given back to the Indians. Well, today that quip has taken on an aura of reality for America truly has been taken by the redskins: The Cleveland Indians and the Boston Braves."[1]—Radio announcer Mel Allen before Game One

> "Feller and Boudreau have been working the same play all season. They probably have nipped at least ten runners off base en route to Cleveland's first pennant since 1920."[2]—Associated Press, on Cleveland's superb, timed pickoff play at second base

The 1948 World Series opened on the afternoon of Wednesday, October 6, at Braves Field in Boston. The largest ballpark in the Hub had been sold out well in advance.

Heavy rain had been predicted throughout most of Massachusetts that day, prompting more than a few morning newspapers across North America to predict a postponement of the first contest. Hy Hurwitz of the *Boston Globe* feared the worst. He wrote, "The weatherman will probably win the opening game of the World Series. He is not listed in the official lineups, but he is the man of the moment."

The dampness luckily held off, however. The sun shone for most of the morning. By game time at 1 p.m., clouds had rolled over Boston to darken the sky somewhat. Nevertheless, they were not especially threatening. Thus, there was very little chance of Game One being disrupted by inclement weather. However, overcoats were commonplace among the huge and excited crowd to see the Braves' first World Series game in this ballpark. (The Red Sox had commandeered Braves Field during the 1915 and 1916 World Series for wholly for financial reasons. It had a greater seating capacity than Fenway Park, so more tickets could be sold, and more revenue gained. The reverse had occurred during the 1914 World Series when the Braves borrowed Fenway Park for their World Series home games as Fenway dwarfed the Braves' tiny South End Grounds.)

"A wan sun peeked from behind the gray clouds today," a poetic United Press report began, "and as early as 10 a.m. fans began straggling through the blue and gold gates of Braves Field.... On the emerald green playing field, workmen were busy rolling up the huge nylon tarpaulin which had covered the greensward since yesterday."[3]

As was often the case at Braves Field, there was a strong east wind blowing into the ballpark from the Charles River. Jim Britt, who would call the first half of Game One on the Mutual Broadcasting System, noted that it would take a mighty clout for any lefthanded hitter to connect for a home run on this day. As Boston's premier baseball announcer, Britt spoke from experience about such things. He would share the Fall Classic's radio duties with Mel Allen on the Mutual Broadcasting System. In 1948, the emerging medium of television would carry the World Series to a large audience for the first time—although TV sets were not yet common in the typical American home. Red Barber and Van Patrick jointly had the television gig. (Remarkably the TV coverage would be split over four networks: NBC, CBS, ABC and DuMont.) Times were certainly changing, but for a few years more the radio

Broadcaster Mel Allen was known as the "Voice of the Yankees," but for a generation he was the voice of the World Series too. He called all but one Fall Classic from 1947 through 1963 (Library of Congress).

8. World Series Game One

audience for the World Series would surpass television's, thus the audio medium was considered the plum assignment for baseball broadcasters.

Thirty-seven-year-old Jim Britt was easily the most popular sportscaster in Boston in 1948—and for good reason. In an era when most broadcasters did not venture from their home cities to cover road games, Britt called the action for the home games for both the Braves and the Red Sox beginning in 1940—with time off for two and a half years of military service during the Second World War. He was therefore a familiar voice to both AL and NL fans in Boston. In the golden age of radio sports broadcasting, Britt was both smooth and articulate at the microphone, able to skillfully paint vivid pictures of sports events with words alone. In 1970, Wells Twombley of *The Sporting News* amusingly recalled that when he was a 13-year-old listening to ballgames from Boston, he thought Jim Britt made "baseball sound better than red-haired girls with freckles."[4] Britt also hosted a nightly, 15-minute sports roundup show on Boston's WNAC radio. His signature line to end each broadcast was this: "Remember, if you can't take part in a sport, be one anyway, will ya?"

For old time's sake, Tris Speaker, the manager of the Indians' World Series championship team of 1920, was in attendance for the first game of the 1948 World Series. As a direct link to the last pennant-winning club from Cleveland, the 60-year-old Speaker was granted the special privilege of being permitted on the field before Game One. Speaker chatted amiably with Lou Boudreau, the present player-manager of the Tribe. To add to the festivities, there were plenty of Braves' alumni on hand, too. All the living members of the 1914 Boston Braves had been invited to witness the World Series by club owner Lou Perini. A large number accepted the offer. Among the ex-Braves in attendance were Rabbit Maranville and Hank Gowdy. The son of George Stallings, the team's fiery 1914 manager, was present in place of his late father who had died of heart disease on May 13, 1929, at age 61.

Members of the Trenton, New Jersey, American Legion team, national youth champions, were also permitted onto the field before game time. The youngsters relished the opportunity and eagerly acquired autographs from both teams' players. (Jim Britt noted in his broadcast that there were 31 participants in the 1948 World Series who had played in an American Legion baseball program at one time or another.) To cap off the traditional pregame duties, James F. Byrnes, the former secretary of state, threw out the ceremonial first ball from Commissioner Albert (Happy) Chandler's box seat.

George Barr, who had been a National League umpire since 1931, had the honor of working the plate for Game One. Twenty-five months earlier, Barr had collapsed from a heart attack while umpiring a game at the Polo

Grounds, ending his 1946 season—but not his life. He was back calling NL games in 1947. As was his custom, after he dusted off home plate following the national anthem, Barr meticulously erased the vertical chalk lines in both batter's boxes closest to home plate. It was both a superstition and a courtesy to the pitchers. He did not want the hurlers to think the lines were part of the plate.

Three of Barr's colleagues shared the same first name: Bill. Bill Summers, an American League umpire since 1933, was assigned to first base. (He had also worked first base in the Indians-Red Sox playoff game two days earlier.) The versatile Bill Stewart, who had both *refereed and coached* in the National Hockey League, was stationed at second base. A member of the NL's staff of arbiters, Stewart had also been umpiring in the majors since 1933. At third base was Bill Grieve of the AL, who had been working MLB games since 1938. As had been the case in 1947, two "alternate umpires" were stationed on the field too. They would only work the outfield lines during the World Series unless one of the other four men in blue became incapacitated in some way. They were Ralph (Babe) Pinelli of the NL and Joseph (Joe) Paparella of the AL. They would alternate foul lines each game. Pinelli had been a major league third baseman on and off from 1918 through 1927 and had worked as an umpire in four previous World Series. The 39-year-old Paparella was the youngest member of the officiating crew by far. It was only his third year in the majors. The other five arbiters had all been born in the 19th century.

The pitching matchup for the opener was excellent. Two dominant righties would face each other: Cleveland's Bob Feller and Boston's Johnny Sain. The popular Feller won 19 games for the Tribe in the regular season. Sain's record was even better. "The rubber-armed righthander with the fancy curveball,"[5] as he was described by an Associated Press correspondent, won 24 times for the NL champions in 1948. He was the 17th NL pitcher since 1900 to record three consecutive 20-win seasons. Leo H. Petersen, a reporter from United Press International declared, "Two of baseball's greatest pitchers, an Arkansas hillbilly and an Iowa farmer, carried the championship hopes of the Boston Braves and Cleveland Indians into the first game of the World Series today."[6]

One light-hearted pregame story said that Doris Sain, Johnny's nervous wife, had already spent a chunk of his World Series share in advance on an updated wardrobe. Upon learning that her husband was going to start Game One, Sain's better half told reporters, "I was just so jittery, I just had to go out and get some new clothes."[7]

Celebrities from all walks of life had made their way to Boston to witness Game One. They included Benny Goodman, Jack Benny, Lou Costello, Joe Louis, Betty Hutton, and a large assortment of high-ranking politicians—including Fuller Warren, the governor of Florida. Grace Coolidge, the widow of former U.S. president and Massachusetts governor Calvin Coolidge, was a special guest of American League president Will Harridge. She was said to be a huge baseball fan.

According to one report, Lou Costello and an unnamed friend had traveled from California to see the World Series opener but had neglected to purchase tickets in advance—and probably could not. Facing the real possibility of not being able to see the game, they were trying to gain access to sold-out Braves Field by whatever means necessary. According to one scribe, Costello encountered Braves owner Lou Perini in a hotel lobby the day before Game One and offered to do his famous "Who's on First?" routine for the crowd in exchange for admission to the ballpark. Perini reiterated that no tickets were available. Costello pleaded, "All you have to do is get me in! I'll sit on the roof! Just get me in!"[8] Unmoved, Perini just walked away. It was unclear if Costello and his unidentified buddy were eventually successful in their desperate efforts to watch Game One.

Perhaps Costello managed to get a standing-room ticket when the Braves began selling 2,500 of them at 7 p.m. the day before the game. [Authors' note: In 2020, a 1948 World Series program from Braves Field—autographed by both Bud Abbott and Lou Costello—was sold via an online auction for $250, strongly indicating that the comedians were able to see at least one game in Boston.] He would have been waiting in a long queue that included a pair of dedicated Canadian baseball fans who, after a long international journey, had been standing in an unofficial line outside the Braves Field ticket office since 5 a.m. on Tuesday. Fourteen hours later, Hank Dean of Ottawa and Ernie Churchill of Toronto got their cherished passes. Each cost $4.

The enormous crowd was allowed into the ballpark beginning at noon. Pregame entertainment was provided by the Baron Hugo Band who were clad in old-style uniforms "still popular with circus bands," according to the *Boston Globe*. Their audience was mostly standees and bleacher occupants as the majority of grandstand ticketholders leisurely took their time to file in. Many were not seated until the first pitch of the game was thrown.

Oddsmakers liked the Indians' chances, both long-term and in the Series opener. Cleveland was listed as solid 5:13 favorites to win the World Series and 5:9 front-runners to take the first game. The Associated Press reported, "The Braves do not relish the tag of underdogs to the power-laden Indians."[9]

The dangerous Dale Mitchell, a left-handed hitter from Oklahoma, led off for Cleveland in Game One of the 45th World Series of the modern era. Johnny Sain, with his trademark wad of tobacco lodged in his left cheek, coaxed him to hit a harmless fly ball to center fielder Mike McCormick. The home crowd loudly cheered the Series' first out. Sain then threw three straight balls to Cleveland's number-two hitter Larry Doby, causing the Braves fans to groan, before getting the count to 3-2. Doby also flied out to McCormick, who comfortably hauled in the ball in right-center field. Cleveland's player-manager Lou Boudreau got a surprisingly boisterous cheer from the Boston fans when he came to bat. His trip to the plate was for naught, though; Boudreau flied out to left fielder Marv Rickert in the vast tracts of foul ground at Braves Field. Rickert made a fine running catch on the play. The top of the first inning produced neither hits nor runs for the favored Indians.

In the bottom of the first inning, Bob Feller—who was often referred to as Bobby by the media in 1948—took the mound for his much-awaited, first-ever World Series start. The famed fireballer, who was a month away from his 30th birthday, made short work of the first three Braves he encountered. Right fielder Tommy Holmes was the first Boston batsman to face Feller. Holmes was an excellent ballplayer, having been named the 1945 NL MVP by *The Sporting News*. He promptly flied out to Cleveland center fielder Larry Doby. Alvin Dark then grounded to first baseman Eddie Robinson. Eschewing a routine toss to Feller who was heading to cover the bag, Robinson instead decided to engage Dark in a footrace. Robinson barely won the sprint—and he required a dive to the base to record the unassisted putout. AL umpire Bill Summers decisively made the out call. (Jim Britt noted that Summers got no arguments from anyone in the Braves' dugout.) Earl Torgeson, Boston's first baseman, then struck out looking. With Sain and Feller both appearing sharp in the first inning, it was promising to be a difficult day for both teams' hitters.

Cleveland's cleanup hitter, second baseman Joe Gordon, led off the top of the second inning for the visitors. He was called out on strikes by plate umpire George Barr. The first hit of the 1948 World Series came when the next Cleveland batter, Ken Keltner, lined a clean single off Johnny Sain that fell into left field. He did not advance any farther than first base, however. With a full count, Wally Judnich, a San Francisco native, lined out to right fielder Tommy Holmes. (Keltner, who had run on the pitch, had to scamper back to first base quickly to avoid being doubled up.) Eddie Robinson then ended the inning by sharply grounding out to fellow first baseman Earl Torgeson. Torgeson knocked down the ball, retrieved it quickly, and made the unassisted putout at the bag to retire the Indians. The score was still 0-0, but Keltner's single had at least provided evidence to his Cleveland teammates that Johnny Sain was hittable.

Bob Elliott, the 1947 NL MVP, led off the bottom of the second inning for the Braves. He flied out to Wally Judnich in right field. Marv Rickert quickly became the second out of the frame when he flied out to Larry Doby in center field. Catcher Bill Salkeld struck out swinging on a Feller fastball. Rapid Robert was doing well in his long-awaited World Series debut.

Cleveland catcher Jim Hegan, who hailed from Massachusetts, led off the top of the third inning for the Indians. He reached first base when third baseman Bob Elliott misplayed a ground ball that rolled up his arm. The play was properly scored as an error by a panel of three prominent newspapermen assigned to the World Series: Ed Burns of the *Chicago Tribune*, Burt Whitman of the *Boston Herald*, and Ed McAuley of the *Cleveland News*. Pitcher Bob Feller was the next man up for Cleveland. Not especially great with the bat—he had just nine hits in 95 at-bats in 1948—Feller tried to move Hegan to second base on a sacrifice. Feller fouled off two bunts. He then took a full cut at a Sain offering and missed for a strikeout. Dale Mitchell popped up to third baseman Elliott in foul territory for the second out. With Larry Doby batting, Hegan stole second base comfortably. Jim Britt, calling the game on Mutual radio, made a point of saying the base had been swiped due to the deliberate delivery of Sain rather than catcher Bill Salkeld's reaction time. The stolen base mattered little, however, as Doby grounded out to Boston shortstop Alvin Dark to end the frame.

Center fielder Mike McCormick, a .299 hitter in 1948, led off the bottom of the third inning for the hometown Braves. He became the seventh consecutive Brave to fail to reach base off Bob Feller, hitting a high infield pop-up to shortstop Lou Boudreau that was easily snagged. Eddie Stanky, the number-eight batter in the Braves' order, also popped up; his was caught by third baseman Ken Keltner. Pitcher Johnny Sain batted next. He also failed to do anything productive. In keeping with the established trend of the inning, Sain popped out to Cleveland first baseman Eddie Robinson in foul territory near the stands. Through the first three innings of Game One, Feller had been perfect, retiring all nine Braves he had faced.

Lou Boudreau, who batted from an unusual crouch, was the first Cleveland man to bat in the top of the fourth inning. He struck out swinging on a letter-high curve ball from Johnny Sain. It was a rare sight. It was only the tenth time that Boudreau had fanned in 1948. (In his report on Game One, baseball writer Hugh Fullerton duly noted, "Lou is the type of guy who remembers such figures."[10]) Sain got ahead of the next batter, Cleveland second baseman Joe Gordon, but Gordon hit an 0–2 pitch past the reach of shortstop Alvin Dark into left field for a single. For the Indians, it was their second hit of the afternoon. Ken Keltner batted next and put up a good battle versus Sain. He missed an extra-base hit to left field that landed foul by a few inches. Keltner eventually struck out swinging, but Gordon stole second base on the same pitch. Gordon was stranded there as Wally Judnich flied out to Tommy Holmes in right field for the second time in Game One. The score remained tied, 0–0.

In the bottom of the fourth inning, Tommy Holmes knocked a ground ball back to Bob Feller. The Cleveland hurler calmly took his time and still easily threw out Holmes at first base. "Feller is an artist—a baseball-pitching artist, whose coordination is beautiful to watch. He's a magnificently conditioned athlete,"[11] said Jim Britt to his large Mutual radio audience. The next Boston batter, Alvin Dark, grounded out sharply to Joe Gordon who deftly fielded it and threw the Braves shortstop out at first base. The following Boston batter was first baseman Earl Torgeson. He drew a base on balls, ending Feller's streak of 11 consecutive Braves retired. Torgeson was a base-stealing threat, having swiped 18 bases in 1948 with only one caught-stealing on his record. Feller threw twice to first base to prevent Torgeson from taking a large lead. Still, Torgeson broke toward second base on a 1-2 pitch to Bob Elliott and slid safely into the bag. There he remained, however. On the next pitch, Elliott gently lofted an easy fly ball to Cleveland left fielder Dale Mitchell for the third out of the inning. Torgeson was stranded as Game One remained scoreless after four tightly contested frames.

Eddie Robinson, a tall, husky Texan, was the first batter for the Indians in the top of the fifth inning. He blooped a fly ball into right field that was tracked down by Tommy Holmes who hurriedly made a running grab for the out. The Braves Field crowd enthusiastically applauded the fine defensive play. Jim Hegan, the Cleveland catcher, batted next and ripped a single into left field. It was Cleveland's third base hit of the game. This time Bob Feller successfully laid down a sacrifice bunt to advance Hegan to second base with two outs. Dale Mitchell came to the plate next, batting for the third time in Game One. He hit a fly ball to left fielder Marv Rickert who made the routine catch. The pitching duel continued. Halfway through the first World Series contest of 1948, the score remained deadlocked, 0–0.

Mel Allen took over the radio broadcasting duties from Jim Britt as Boston prepared to bat in the home half of the fifth inning. (It was the second time in 1948 that Allen had paired with Britt for a major baseball broadcasting assignment: The twosome had jointly called the All-Star Game from Sportsman's Park in St. Louis on July 13.) Allen noted that Game One had lacked fireworks thus far, but, as in any ballgame, that could change in an instant.

Marv Rickert batted first against Bob Feller to lead off the bottom of the fifth inning. He wasted no time in ripping a single past Eddie Robinson

8. World Series Game One

into right field. It was Boston's first hit of the World Series. Bill Salkeld, a lefthanded hitter who batted .244 in 1948, was the next Brave to bat. His sacrifice bunt, fielded by catcher Jim Hegan, successfully advanced Rickert to second base. The crowd at Braves field began to stir in anticipation of a Boston rally. It never came. Mike McCormick came to bat with Rickert in scoring position. McCormick's at-bat was wasted as he popped out to second baseman Joe Gordon in short center field. Rickert was forced to stay put at second base. Next up was Eddie Stanky who dribbled a check-swing grounder back to the mound. Bob Feller grabbed the ball and quickly threw to first baseman Eddie Robinson for the third out of the inning. Game One remained in a swift-moving, 0–0 deadlock.

Lefthanded Larry Doby led off the top of the sixth inning for Cleveland. He was fortunate as he flared a broken-bat single off Johnny Sain that dropped into center field. Lou Boudreau came up next for the Indians. A hit-and-run play was called and Doby took off on the first pitch. Boudreau slapped a ground ball to Boston second baseman Eddie Stanky whose only play was to first base. Doby advanced to second base with one man out. Joe Gordon flied out to Marv Rickert for the inning's second out. Doby could not advance on the play. Rickert also recorded the third putout of the inning by chasing down Ken Keltner's deep fly ball in right field. Rickert was proving to be a valuable late addition to the Braves' roster, both from an offensive and a defensive standpoint.

Pitcher Johnny Sain grounded out to Cleveland shortstop Lou Boudreau to begin the bottom of the sixth inning. Tommy Holmes followed Sain to the plate. Bob Feller fell behind in the count 3–0 to Holmes, but then worked it to 3–2. Holmes eventually flied out to Dale Mitchell in left field. On the first pitch he saw, Alvin Dark flied out to Larry Doby in left-center field to end another fruitless inning for the home team. Nevertheless, with both teams' offenses being held in check, the score of Game One remained level at 0–0.

Wally Judnich, who had yet to get a hit, led off the seventh inning for the visitors. He quickly flied out for the third time in the game to Tommy Holmes in right field. Eddie Robinson was the next Cleveland batter. Robinson lofted an easy fly ball to Holmes who leisurely made the catch for the second out. The lack of offense in Game One prompted Mel Allen to say to his radio audience, "I don't know how much longer this can go on, but as long as it goes on, we'll be here."[12] The third out of the inning was made by Mike McCormick in center field who made a fine running catch on Jim Hegan's fly ball. The Braves received a loud ovation—perhaps for motivational purposes—when they trotted back to their dugout and prepared to bat in the home half of the seventh inning. The scoreless tie remained intact.

On the first pitch he saw from Bob Feller in the bottom of the seventh, Earl Torgeson tried to bunt his way to first base. He fouled it off. On the second pitch, Torgeson swung away. He hit a hot grounder that first baseman Eddie Robinson had to venture far away from the bag to field. Robinson pivoted and made an accurate throw to Bob Feller who had raced over to cover first base. On the best defensive play of the game, Torgeson was out by a hair—and he accidentally spiked Feller's foot. Next up was Bob Elliott who hit a bounding ball on the third-base side of the mound. Feller, showing no ill effects from the spiking, hustled to field it and threw to Robinson at first base for the second out. Marv Rickert then lofted a high fly ball that shortstop Lou Boudreau chased down in the left-field grass. After seven full innings of Game One, no run had yet been scored by either club. Those innings had been rapidly played in just 80 minutes as the clock on the giant Braves Field scoreboard read 2:20 p.m.

Bob Feller got a courteous round of applause from the Brave partisans as he stepped into the batter's box to lead off the top of eighth inning for Cleveland. He struck out swinging. Johnny Sain's strikeout total for the afternoon was now at five. Dale Mitchell followed Feller to the plate. The native of Oklahoma had not managed a hit in three previous at-bats in Game One. He was 0-for-4 after flying out to Mike McCormick in center field. Larry Doby put a scare into the crowd by launching a long fly ball down the left-field line, but Marv Rickert chased it down in foul territory for the third out. The edgy spectators were still waiting for the game's first run to be scored.

Catcher Bill Salkeld was the first Boston batter to come to the plate in the bottom of the eighth inning. Looking for any edge they could get, after the second pitch, several members of the Indians loudly made it known to plate umpire George Barr that Salkeld's back foot was out of the batter's box. Barr dismissed the complaints, ruling that Salkeld's batting stance was legal. Salkeld eventually drew a base on balls. It was only the second base on balls that Feller had surrendered in Game One, but it would have an enormous effect on the outcome.

With baserunners a rare commodity, Boston manager Billy Southworth made the first substitution of Game One. It would be a noteworthy one: Phil Masi entered the game as a pinch runner. Masi was a fleet-footed catcher—at least he was swifter than Selkeld. He had appeared in 113 games for Boston in 1948. The next Boston batter, Mike McCormick, laid down an excellent bunt that Feller fielded halfway between home and first base. McCormick did some creative baserunning, stopping short of where Feller was going to tag him—and then retreated toward home plate. Instead of chasing McCormick, Feller simply and smartly just threw to first baseman

8. World Series Game One

Eddie Robinson for the out, but Masi moved easily to second base on the sacrifice bunt. Lou Boudreau asked for time and went to the mound to tell Feller to intentionally walk the next Brave batter, Eddie Stanky. Feller did not like the strategy. He told Boudreau he was confident he could retire the eighth man in Boston's batting order without too much trouble. Boudreau was unconvinced. He wanted to set up a potential inning-ending double play, and he was worried by Stanky's well-earned reputation as a gritty player who could find ways to win games for his team. Stanky got a free pass to first base.

Southworth's maneuvers continued as another pinch runner, Sebastian (Sibby) Sisti, ran for Stanky. Johnny Sain was the next Brave to bat. He was better than average at the plate for a pitcher, having once compiled an impressive 14-game hitting streak. He did not hit into a double play as Boudreau had hoped. Instead, Sain drove Feller's first offering into right field, exciting the home crowd for a moment, but the ball was deftly snagged by a retreating Wally Judnich for the second out of the inning. Both Masi and Sisti stayed put.

Tommy Holmes, who had finished third among NL batters in 1948, strode to the plate for Boston. Both baserunners took leadoffs from their respective bags. Feller glanced back toward Masi and noticed that Boudreau's glove was positioned below his knee—the signal for the Indians' deadly timed pickoff play. Before Holmes saw even one pitch, Feller wheeled toward second base and fired an accurate throw to shortstop Boudreau who had moved to the bag. Amazingly, the Braves were unaware that Cleveland had a terrific pickoff play in their bag of tricks. However, some savvy observers knew Cleveland's pickoff play was coming. Nelson Potter, sitting in the Boston dugout, who had pitched in the AL for a decade, tried to yell a warning to Masi to be alert—but his shout was a smidgen late. Likewise, Tris Speaker, who had seen plenty of Cleveland ballgames in 1948, told reporters in the press box that if Masi strayed too far off second base, Boudreau and Feller would likely catch him napping.

To most observers, the Indians' pickoff play had worked to perfection and had caught another snoozing baserunner; Masi had apparently slid directly into Boudreau's tag. However, second-base umpire Bill Stewart, positioned about 10 feet from the base on the first-base side, quickly and emphatically indicated that Masi's slide had gotten him safely back to second base. "They almost had Masi!" exclaimed Mel Allen to his vast Mutual radio audience. "Boudreau is arguing. Bill Stewart signals that Boudreau tagged him [Masi] on the arm above the elbow, meaning, of course, that the hand had the bag before Boudreau put on the tag. But it was beautifully executed."[13]

Newsreel footage of the play shows Boudreau looking skyward in disgust as he slammed the baseball into his glove. Nevertheless, the Indians' argument about Stewart's call on Masi was a short one—for the time being. The game quickly resumed with Bob Feller pitching to lefthanded Tommy Holmes with two out. Holmes made the most of what may have been a second chance gifted to his team in the bottom of the eighth: He lined a base hit into left field just beyond the reach of third baseman Ken Keltner. Masi, running hard on the play and clutching his cap in his right hand, scored easily. The throw from the outfield came toward third base where it was cut off. Sisti slid safely into third base as Holmes alertly moved up to second base. Baseball scribe Gayle Talbot described the reaction of the home team's supporters: "A partisan crowd … sent up a roar that must have raised ripples on the nearby Charles River."[14]

It was just the second hit that Feller had allowed—but it was a hugely costly one. (Feller would later tell reporters that his game plan was to work to the outside corner of the plate when lefties were batting to prevent them from aiming for the short right-field fence that was only 319 feet down the line. Holmes, however, often struck base hits to the opposite field, as he did versus Feller.) Any further hopes the Braves had about adding to their lead vanished when the next batter, Alvin Dark, grounded out to third baseman Ken Keltner. Still, the breakthrough in the scoreless pitchers' duel had been achieved. Boston led 1-0 at the end of eight complete innings. With Sain doing so well on the mound for the Braves, the lone run posted on the scoreboard appeared to be a huge one.

Tommy Holmes received a huge ovation for his batting heroics as he took his position in the outfield for the top of the ninth inning. The two Boston pinch runners from the previous inning stayed in the game defensively: Phil Masi replaced Bill Salkeld as catcher; Sibby Sisti replaced Eddie Stanky at second base. Suddenly the Indians were facing defeat, and were down to their final three outs in Game One. Johnny Sain was still on the mound for Boston, aiming to toss a World Series shutout.

On an 0-1 pitch, leadoff batter Lou Boudreau hit a long blast off Sain into left-center field that was chased down by Mike McCormick for the first out. Sensing impending victory, the partisan Braves Field crowd roared its approval. Joe Gordon, who was 1-for-3 on the afternoon, was the next Indian to bat. On a full count, Gordon hit a high pop-up that was hauled in by shortstop Alvin Dark in foul territory near third base. The din of the crowd became louder as the Boston Braves seemed poised to win their first World Series game in 34 years.

Ken Keltner was the last hope for Cleveland. He hit an infield grounder to third base. He caught a break when Boston third baseman Bob Elliott, who was playing deep, made a poor throw to first base that sailed high over the glove of first baseman Earl Torgeson and out of play.

8. World Series Game One

By rule, Keltner advanced to second base on the throwing error, which was properly assigned to Elliott by the trio of official scorers. Boston had made two errors in Game One. Both of them had been committed by Bob Elliott.

Wally Judnich was the next Cleveland batter. If Elliott's error had unnerved Sain, he did not show it in the slightest. He struck out the overmatched Judnich on three pitches. Sain's sixth strikeout had cinched his 25th victory of the season—and the first World Series triumph of his career. He had done a superb job; no Indian had gotten past second base. Game One had zipped by in a swift 102 minutes. Including their famous four-game sweep of the Philadelphia A's in the 1914 Fall Classic, the Boston Braves were now a perfect 5–0 in World Series play.

The Indians were used to inflicting shutouts on their opponents in 1948. Seldom were the Indians on the receiving end of one. It was the first time Cleveland had suffered a shutout defeat since absorbing a 5–0 whitewash on Saturday, August 7, versus the New York Yankees at Municipal Stadium. Bob Lemon had been the losing pitcher for the Indians that day two months before.

The 1–0 result in Game One marked the first time there had been such a low-scoring tilt in a World Series contest in a quarter century. The most recent previous one occurred when Art Nehf of the New York Giants squeaked by Bullet Joe Bush of the New York Yankees in the third game of the 1923 Fall Classic. (The only scoring in that game came via an inside-the-park home run by Casey Stengel. Stengel was still making news in 1948. He had just led the Oakland Oaks to the championship of the Pacific Coast League. Now he was about to be hired by the Yankees as their new manager to replace the fired Bucky Harris. In his travels through organized baseball, Stengel had been the manager of the Boston Bees/Braves for five and a half seasons from 1938 to 1943.) The only previous time a World Series opener had ended 1–0 was back in 1918. The winning pitcher that afternoon was a crafty 23-year-old lefthander named Babe Ruth. The unlucky Bob Feller became just the second pitcher in World Series history to lose a complete-game two-hitter. Mort Cooper had last achieved the dubious feat for the St. Louis Cardinals four autumns before in 1944.

During his postgame radio commentary of Game One, Mel Allen sympathetically likened Bob Feller to Walter Johnson, the famed and popular smoke-thrower for the Washington Senators, a man who never got into a World Series until late in his career—and then struggled mightily to win a game once he got there. (Johnson finally won Game Seven of the 1924 World Series in a relief role in a 12-inning thriller versus the New York Giants. He won a game as a starter versus Pittsburgh the following October, but this time he also lost the dramatic seventh game. The 1948

Indians had a link to the 1924 Senators: Muddy Ruel, who scored the World Series-winning run for Washington, was now a coach for the Tribe. He had managed the St. Louis Browns in 1947.) One journalist expressed sourness about Feller. Still apparently dwelling on the Cleveland hurler's refusal to participate in the All-Star Game in July, Frank Graham unkindly wrote, "No one [in the press box] seemed to care that Feller had lost. Apparently, they thought it served him right."[15] Graham was not alone in wanting to see Feller fail in his first attempt to win a World Series game. Some MLB players found Feller to be off-putting. More than half a century later, in an interview for SABR's oral history collection, Warren Spahn said, "Feller was a bit past his prime in 1948. He'd still strut around the mound—arrogance personified."[16]

On the Mutual Broadcasting System, Jim Britt gushed that Game One had to be considered one of the greatest Fall Classic games ever contested. His broadcasting partner, Mel Allen, was not nearly as enthralled by the opener and was therefore decidedly more subdued in his assessment. Allen opined that the low-scoring Sain-Feller pitchers' duel was probably best appreciated by baseball connoisseurs. Grantland Rice, arguably America's foremost sports scribe, sided with Britt. The 68-year-old wrote that Game One had exhibited the finest Fall Classic pitching since the 1905 "shutout series" when the New York Giants (mostly Christy Mathewson) and the Philadelphia Athletics tossed nothing but whitewashes in all five games. Rice eloquently opined that those lucky fans who saw 1948's opener had the privilege of witnessing two masters on the mound.

Despite the home team's victory, some reporters preferred to dwell on how poorly the Braves batting was. One of them was an unnamed writer for the *Daytona Beach Morning Journal*. He stated that the winners' hitters had provided very little help for Sain—even during the bottom of the eighth inning when they mustered the game's only run. The writer harshly described Boston's batters as being "weak with the willow." He further panned Bob Elliott and Earl Torgeson, "the nearest thing [the Braves] have to power hitters," for giving their Arkansas pitcher "no help whatever."

With the two teams combining for just six hits, there was, of course, only one major talking point among baseball fans after Game One was entered into the books. Associated Press scribe Jack Hand wrote afterwards, "Arguments sprouted up all over town last night after publication of pictures of the vital play of the opener—an attempt by Bobby Feller to pick pinch runner Phil Masi off second base in the eighth inning of a 0–0 tie. Eventually Masi came home on Tommy Holmes' single."

Those four photos indicated that Masi had slid directly into Boudreau's tag and the Boston pinch runner should have been called out by umpire Bill Stewart. That out would have ended the Braves' threat in the bottom of the eighth and the score would have remained 0–0 entering the top of the ninth inning.

Hand continued, "Of course, there will be no official protest by anybody connected with the Cleveland club. All agreed it was just one of those things about which nothing could be done."[17]

Indians owner Bill Veeck issued a brief comment when he was shown the photographic evidence of the alleged missed call: "These are very interesting pictures, but the game is over,"[18] he said without displaying any emotion at all.

Manager Lou Boudreau did not wish to overly dwell on the play, but he did make a few carefully constructed comments to the press. "It's a shame to ruin such a masterful pitching performance by one decision," Boudreau grumbled. "I thought I had him. I tagged him on the shoulder. But that's just my opinion; Stewart has his." To avoid the wrath of Commissioner Happy Chandler, Boudreau felt compelled to add this coda: "It isn't a complaint."[19]

AL president Will Harridge said even less about the controversy. "Officially, Masi was safe,"[20] the prexy stated—and then diplomatically said no more.

MLB Commissioner Chandler wisely offered no opinion about Stewart's contentious call except to presciently comment, "Those fellows [the umpires] have to use their judgment out there. That's the best we can do until we get an electric eye."[21]

During his radio pregame commentary before Game Two, Jim Britt commented, "The fact that that one play was the main subject of the post-mortems that followed the game is proof—if you need proof—of the fact that yesterday's opener was close and hard-fought every single pitch of the way."[22]

Others were not so willing to let the controversy die so quietly. New York sports journalist Carl Lundquist, covering the World Series for United Press, wrote that Stewart "was as popular in Cleveland as the Mad Butcher of Kingsbury Run."[23] That was an allusion to a violent serial killer, still on the loose, who was terrorizing the Ohio city.

It was later learned that Lou Boudreau had approached the umpires prior to Game One to politely alert them to his team's terrific pickoff play—a deft maneuver that had successfully nabbed eight sleeping runners off second base during the 1948 regular season. After Boudreau was out of earshot, Bill Stewart openly scoffed at the idea that he would not be prepared for such a play.

After the game Bob Feller told reporters, "Take a look at the pictures of it. We thought we had him on the trap."[24] Decades later, Feller remarked in his 1990 autobiography, "We caught Masi napping. Unfortunately, we caught Bill Stewart napping too. Lou tagged out Masi by two feet. It wasn't even close. Everybody in the ballpark saw that Masi was out—except one—the umpire. We hadn't just picked off Masi. We had picked off Stewart too."[25]

It was to be the most memorable play of the entire 1948 World Series—and, according to Feller, it set a tone for the remaining games. "[It] started a scrap that ran through the Series and was picked up lustily by the fans in Cleveland,"[26] he wrote.

When the final out was made, Bill Stewart was given a police escort to the umpires' room. However, after he got into his civilian clothes, Stewart left the ballpark and quickly blended into the lingering crowd without being recognized.

Boudreau's decision to issue the intentional walk to Eddie Stanky with one out in the bottom of the eighth also got a few tongues wagging. Opinions varied. In his World Series column, Rogers Hornsby supported the Cleveland skipper's strategy. However, former pitcher Dutch Ruether who had pitched for Cincinnati in the 1919 Fall Classic and was now working as an MLB scout, was adamant that giving a free pass to the eighth man in the batting order defied logic. He told a gathering of baseball scribes that he never would have walked Stanky in a million years.

Unfortunately, Stewart's controversial call on the pickoff play somewhat overshadowed Johnny Sain's brilliant hurling for Boston in Game One. Joe Gordon was among the Indians who were openly impressed by Sain's array of accurate off-speed pitches. He said he had not seen such control and variety of curveballs from any AL hurler all season.

Journalist Jack Hand heaped praise on the victorious Brave pitcher too. "Sain's four-hit performance was a precision masterpiece," declared the veteran baseball scribe. "Cleveland could do nothing with his roundhouse curve, except hit easy pop flies."[27] Indeed, the Boston infielders combined for only three assists in the game to tie a Series mark for inactivity. The Braves outfielders had by far the bulk of the defensive work, making 15 putouts. Sain exhibited masterful control, too. He faced 33 batters in Game One and did not issue a single walk to the Indians. (Feller, who only pitched eight innings, faced just 29 Braves.)

Billy Southworth offered a few kind words about the defeated Cleveland starter. "Bob Feller was sensational and so was our Johnny Sain," gushed the Boston manager. "This is the first time I've seen Feller go nine innings. What impressed me most was the remarkable control he had over his curve."[28] Statistics showed that Feller, on nine occasions in the game, had retired Brave batters on a single pitch.

As was his custom, Game One's winning pitcher was not very

8. World Series Game One

Tommy Holmes (left) and Johnny Sain, two Boston heroes from Game One, jointly answer questions from the gentlemen of the press (courtesy Boston Public Library, Leslie Jones Collection).

talkative afterward. Bill King of the Associated Press wrote, "[Johnny] Sain, an unusually silent type, had little to say about his well-earned triumph. He let a beaming smile serve as his words when his grateful teammates showered him with their congratulations."[29]

Tommy Holmes, who got the game's lone RBI was more talkative. "We knew Feller was going to be tough as soon as he started," Holmes said. "With Johnny Sain matching him pitch for pitch we knew it was going to be a 1–0 game. We concentrated on getting that run in every inning until we got it."[30]

In Sain's small hometown of Belleville, Arkansas—a rural village at the foot of the Ozark Mountains—his World Series victory was duly noted and celebrated by the proprietor of the community's only drug store. At precisely 2:43 p.m., a sign advertising cigars and soda water was removed from the front window of the Main Street business. In its place was a hand-made placard that read, "Johnny Sain 1, Bob Feller 0."

At the start of the following day's radio broadcast, Jim Britt relayed this amusing anecdote involving Sain and an inquisitive reporter—who got Sain to open up to him just a little bit—regarding his efficient, three-pitch strikeout of Wally Judnich in the ninth inning to end Game One:

> "Was the last one a curveball?" asked the newspaperman.
> "Yeah, it was," replied Sain.
> "Well, what was the second pitch?" the scribe pressed.
> "Look," said Sain, "the word will get around soon enough what I'm throwing. Let's let the Cleveland players find out for themselves."

Bill James, who had pitched a 1–0 shutout for the Boston Braves in Game Two of the 1914 World Series, was one of the honored guests of the club for the opening game. He had traveled from his home in California to be feted once again as a Boston baseball hero. The 56-year-old righthander—described in his youth as "a hulk of a man with the arms of a village blacksmith"—was besieged by curious reporters who wanted to know how his whitewash from 34 years earlier compared to Sain's Game One shutout in 1948. James absolutely reveled in the unexpected attention and happily spoke at length to all and sundry about his accomplishment in that famous Fall Classic from yesteryear. (*The Sporting News* reported that six of the players from the 1914 Braves—and the team's manager—were deceased.) During the First World War, James made patriotic use of his strong pitching arm: He instructed American troops in basic training on how to accurately throw grenades.

Another still active old-timer who attended Game One at Braves Field was Philadelphia Athletics manager Connie Mack whose underdog team threatened for a while to win the AL pennant in 1948 before fading to a fourth-place finish. The 85-year-old Mack admitted he had underestimated the capabilities of the 1948 Braves—much like his players had done in the 1914 Fall Classic. He said Game One had forced him to re-evaluate the Series, especially after witnessing Sain's terrific outing. "I was fooled by Johnny Sain. I always thought he was just [an ordinary] pitcher," Mack confessed to a reporter. "He was great today ... and now I have to change my mind about the Braves. I thought Cleveland would take them easy [sic]."[31]

Leo H. Petersen of United Press lamented Feller not getting his cherished World Series victory despite tossing a complete-game two-hitter in Game One. Conversely, he saw Boston's triumph as a springboard to a possible Fall Classic title. He wrote, "There was no doubt what Sain's performance gave the Braves: a great lift in morale."[32]

Lou Boudreau did not seem especially worried about his club dropping Game One. The Cleveland player-manager told reporters, "Naturally, we felt badly about not getting Feller a run out there. But I'm still sure

8. World Series Game One 99

we'll win the Series. Bobby will go again in Cleveland on Sunday—if not before—and we'll do better by him then."³³

Feller was not especially impressed by the Boston lineup he had faced (and lost to) in game One—and he said so to reporters. "I had pretty good stuff out there," he told one scribe, "but it wasn't nearly so good as against Detroit and Boston Red Sox recently. I might not have given up as many hits [in Game One] as in the other games, but I pitched against better hitters on the Tigers and Red Sox."³⁴

Boston's outfielders quietly tied a single-game World Series record by making 15 putouts, a mark that had been set on October 14, 1912, by another NL club—the New York Giants—but had not been equaled in all the years since. In his World Series column, Rogers Hornsby wrote, "It was a perfect day for a 1–0 game. The wind was blowing in steadily, which took all the power away from the Indians."³⁵

One of the surprise stars of the game for Boston was Marv Rickert who was replacing the injured Jeff Heath only by special permission granted by MLB Commissioner Happy Chandler. One unnamed scribe noted that it was Rickert who got the first hit for the home team off Bob Feller, in the fifth inning, and had made five putouts in the outfield, "three of which were very nifty." (Another reporter disagreed, opining that every fly ball the Indians hit to the outfield was a routine catch.) Although Rickert had modestly said that he was not quite sure if he should unpack his bags yet, the writer commented, "It may take an act of Congress or a Supreme Court decision"³⁶ to get Rickert out of the Braves' lineup.

Something of an October custom, wherever the World Series stopped, so did unemployed baseball figures who were on the lookout for new jobs. The 1948 Fall Classic was no different. According to one report, three noteworthy baseball figures had been seen lingering around the hotels where the baseball magnates were staying, hoping to find new bosses. They were Bucky Harris, the recently deposed manager of the New York Yankees; Specs Toporcer, the former director of farm teams for the Red Sox; and Rip Collins, no longer working as the manager of the San Diego Padres of the Pacific Coast League.

AP scribe Jim Calorgero amusingly wrote in his summary of the first game, "Both the Boston Weather Bureau and Cleveland rooters are alibiing [the] World Series opener. The bureau had predicted rain." Undaunted by its miscalculation for Game One, the Hub's professional meteorologists predicted warmer temperatures for Game Two—around 60 degrees. An official statement said, "We can look forward to pleasant weather that will last long enough for the second game to be played under comfortable conditions."³⁷

In what was likely the first public outdoor "watch party" for a major sports event, about 5,000 curious people were drawn to Boston Common to view Game One on about 100 television sets specially installed for the World Series. Each screen was surrounded by a wooden box to reduce glare and maintain contrast. The following day's *Boston Post* described the scene as "a vast and unique experiment." The newspaper positively noted, "The action on the baseball field was clearly visible."[38] (Comedian Bob Hope, who was also penning his thoughts about the World Series for a Cleveland daily, joked that Indians second baseman Joe Gordon had made a spinning defensive play in order to show his best side to the television cameras.) Gillette officially sponsored the event, but the *Post* distributed free souvenir scorecards—bearing the newspaper's logo, of course—to anybody who wanted them. Not everyone was entranced by the TV pictures, however. According to reporter Jim Calorgero, a noticeable group of men in the Commons showed no interest whatsoever in the tight pitching duel at Braves Field; they were instead intently enthralled by a game of checkers being contested on one of the park's benches. "They had their backs to the screens, too!"[39] one incredulous baseball devotee remarked.

Future sportswriter George Sullivan attended Game One as a 14-year-old. Nearly 64 years later, in an interview for a Boston University publication, Sullivan's most vivid memory of the game had nothing to do with the terrific pitching duel or the contentious pickoff play, but a glimpse of the unthinkable: He saw Satchel Paige stealthily puffing on a cigarette behind a fence next to the Cleveland bullpen! Although Braves Field was replete with billboards advertising tobacco products, beer and whiskey, Sullivan recalled Paige's smoking as "an eye-popping sight for an impressionable [youth] who saw major leaguers as role models."[40]

The overflow crowd at Braves Field was a mostly civil bunch. It was reported that one standee spent the entire game perched atop a ballpark water dispenser to better view the action on the diamond. He was an accommodating chap, however, obligingly repositioning his feet anytime someone desired a drink.

The *Boston Globe* reported that a probate judge in Suffolk, Massachusetts, had his priorities straight. Judge Robert G. Wilson Jr. opened the October 6 proceedings by noting, "We've got to move right along this morning. The Court has to take a view out along Commonwealth Avenue this afternoon."[41] Braves Field was located there.

During Game One, there was a conspicuous killjoy present at the ballpark. A stern-looking man was busily interrogating school-age fans and jotting down their names in a notepad. He identified himself as "an employee of the Boston School Department."

8. World Series Game One

Game One Box Score
Cleveland Indians 0, Boston Braves 1
Game played on Wednesday, October 6, 1948, at Braves Field

Cleveland Indians	ab	r	h	rbi	Boston Braves	ab	r	h	rbi
Mitchell lf	4	0	0	0	Holmes rf	4	0	1	1
Doby cf	4	0	1	0	Dark ss	4	0	0	0
Boudreau ss	4	0	0	0	Torgeson 1b	2	0	0	0
Gordon 2b	4	0	1	0	Elliott 3b	3	0	0	0
Keltner 3b	4	0	1	0	Rickert lf	3	0	1	0
Judnich rf	4	0	0	0	Salkeld c	1	0	0	0
Robinson 1b	3	0	0	0	Masi pr,c	0	1	0	0
Hegan c	3	0	1	0	McCormick cf	2	0	0	0
Feller p	2	0	0	0	Stanky 2b	2	0	0	0
Totals	32	0	4	0	Sisti pr,2b	0	0	0	0
					Sain p	3	0	0	0
					Totals	24	1	2	1

```
Cleveland  0 0 0 0 0 0 0 0 0 --  0 4 0
Boston     0 0 0 0 0 0 0 1 x --  1 2 2
```

Cleveland Indians	IP	H	R	ER	BB	SO
Feller L (0–1)	8.0	2	1	1	3	2
Totals	8.0	2	1	1	3	2

Boston Braves	IP	H	R	ER	BB	SO
Sain W (1–0)	9.0	4	0	0	0	6
Totals	9.0	4	0	0	0	6

E—Elliott 2 (2). **SH**—Feller (1, off Sain); Salkeld (1, off Feller); M McCormick (1, off Feller). **Team LOB**—6. **IBB**—Stanky (1, by Feller). **Team**—4. **SB**—Hegan (1, 2nd base off Sain/Salkeld); Gordon (1, 2nd base off Sain/Salkeld); Torgeson (1, 2nd base off Feller/Hegan). **IBB**—Feller (1, Stanky). **U**—George Barr (NL), Bill Summers (AL), Bill Stewart (NL), Bill Grieve (AL), Babe Pinelli (NL), Joe Paparella (AL). **T**—1:42. **A**—40,135.

— 9 —

Game Two Scuttlebutt
Pressure Now on Cleveland

"Only three more to go, Billy!"[1] shouted an enthusiastic well-wisher at Boston manager Billy Southworth after his team's surprising Game One victory over the favored Cleveland Indians.

Fully realizing that one game does not decide a World Series, Southworth acknowledged his admirer with a slight smile. However, he quickly became realistic when speaking with a collection of reporters. "I'm not going to make any predictions about a final outcome [of the Series]," Southworth insisted. Relying on a hackneyed sports adage, the Braves manager said, "We're going to play each game as it comes up."[2]

Still, the outcome of Game One changed the dynamics of the Series. Cleveland, still the favorite to win the Fall Classic, would be in a daunting hole if Boston could do the unexpected and go two games up by winning the second contest at Braves Field on Thursday.

The Indians' hopes to level the World Series fell to Bob Lemon—and everyone knew it. This included an unnamed Associated Press correspondent, who wrote, "The former outfielder who won 20 games in Cleveland's pennant drive [is manager Lou] Boudreau's choice to try to tie up the World Series and send the two clubs into the third battle at Cleveland all even." The same scribe added, "Lemon will have to do a lot of chucking to beat what Feller turned in on Wednesday."[3]

Fans who were hoping the ageless Satchel Paige might get a World Series start for Cleveland were unlikely to get their wish, according to manager Boudreau. "We started with Feller," he noted. "Today comes Lemon, and after that Bearden. I haven't decided on my fourth starting pitcher yet."[4]

Paige himself was saddened by the situation, insisting that starting a World Series game was his "life's ambition." Still, Paige remained hopeful of getting some work versus the Braves, perhaps via the bullpen. He told a

9. Game Two Scuttlebutt

reporter he had an influential friend who just might have some say in the matter., "Mr. Veeck says it's his ambition to see me out on the mound."[5]

Esteemed sports scribe Grantland Rice liked Boston's Warren Spahn's chances to give the NL champions a 2–0 Series lead. He optimistically wrote in a preview piece for Game Two, "It's in pitching that the Braves are likely to upset the experts' idea that the Indians have all the tomahawks and arrows. If Spahn comes even fairly close to Sain's performance, the Braves can throw even more poisoned arrows into the Indians than Bill Veeck and Lou Boudreau can absorb."[6]

Despite the Indians' surprising loss in Game One, Cleveland was still the favored team to win the 1948 World Series—but the bookmakers' odds had noticeably narrowed over the course of 24 hours. Having dropped the opener, the AL tribe was now listed at 7:10, meaning bettors would now only have to wager $10 to win $7 if they put their money on Lou Boudreau's club to win the Fall Classic.

Indeed, most observers (and the Indians themselves) still liked the AL champs' overall chances. In his pregame commentary for Game Two, Jim Britt told the Mutual Radio audience,

> Any hint that Boudreau and his Indians might be discouraged as a result of Feller's defeat yesterday would be misleading. They saw a pennant slip almost from their grasp last Sunday when the Detroit Tigers beat Feller. Following that, they had to endure a long train ride to Boston. Once there, before a hostile crowd, they [won] the flag going away. This Cleveland club is in no sense on trial. That they can come back, not even Billy Southworth has any doubt.

It was now up to the vaunted visitors to meet the expectations foisted upon them by the leading baseball experts.

Baseball history was against the AL Tribe, though. The 1948 Fall Classic pitting the Braves against the Indians was the 45th of the modern era. Excluding the 1922 Series (which featured a tie in the opening game), in the other 43 previous meetings between the AL and NL champions, only 17 of the teams that lost Game One had managed to capture the World Series.

— 10 —

World Series Game Two
Cleveland Gets Some Lemon-Aid

Date: Thursday, October 7, 1948
Site: Braves Field, Boston, Massachusetts

> "The two most important things in life are good friends and a strong bullpen."[1]—Bob Lemon

Despite a positive weather forecast for the Boston area, a rainstorm did descend on the Hub before Game Two began. However, it stopped well before the teams took the field. Despite wet weather and two recent football games played at the venue, Braves Field was in excellent condition for its second World Series contest in as many days.

In what promised to be another excellent pitching matchup, Boston's Warren Spahn, a superb lefthander, and Cleveland's Bob Lemon, a crafty righthander, were given starting assignments by their respective managers. Coincidentally, the two pitchers each wore uniform #21.

The quick-witted Spahn could be counted on to make both amusing quips and thoughtful insights about baseball. In discussing how to pitch, Spahn once explained, "You don't throw the ball, you propel it."[2] On resuming his baseball career after the war, Spahn said, "What a great way to make a living. If I goof up, there's going to be a relief pitcher come in there. Nobody's going to shoot me."[3] Spahn knew what he was talking about. During the war, Spahn was awarded the Bronze Star and a Presidential Citation for his part in helping to seize, secure and repair the famous bridge at Remagen, Germany in March 1945 where he was nicked by an enemy bullet that zipped by his head. Spahn's most prominent physical feature was his permanently disfigured nose that came courtesy of a teammate's wild throw in 1941. Teammates took to jokingly calling Spahn "The Great Profile"—a cruel moniker that he loathed. Spahn was famous

10. World Series Game Two

Tickets for the first two games of the 1948 World Series were precious commodities. Here a seasoned fan gets his reward for enduring a long lineup at the Braves Field ticket office (courtesy Boston Public Library, Leslie Jones Collection).

for his abnormally high leg kick when he delivered a pitch, readily admitting it was designed to distract hitters and disguise where the ball was being released. Upon being called up to the majors in June 1946, the soldierly Spahn told manager Billy Southworth, "This is the first time in years I've reported to anybody without saluting."[4]

Cleveland made one change in its lineup from Game One. Allie Clark, a 25-year-old righthanded hitter, was placed in the second spot and would play right field for the AL Tribe. He had played 81 games for the Indians in 1948, had batted .310, and had driven in 38 runs. Clark was replacing lefthanded-hitting Wally Judnich. Larry Doby was dropped from second to sixth in the Cleveland batting order. Not wishing to tamper with success, the Braves opted to use the same eight players behind Spahn that they employed with Johnny Sain in their unexpected opening-game victory.

Unlike the Braves, the Mutual radio broadcasting duo changed their batting order—so to speak—for Game Two. This time Mel Allen led off to call the first 4½ innings from Braves Field with Boston announcer Jim

Britt stepping to the microphone to describe the game's second half. The 35-year-old Allen was already a well-known voice in broadcasting by the time the 1948 World Series was played. Born Melvin Allen Israel, he first became prominent when, as a CBS radio announcer in May 1937, he informed the nation of the fiery crash of the German airship Hindenburg in Lakehurst, New Jersey. A graduate of the University of Alabama's law school, Allen was just beginning his heyday as a baseball broadcaster and would soon become forever associated with both the New York Yankees (his main employer) and the Fall Classic. Remarkably, Allen called 16 of the 17 World Series played between 1947 and 1963.

The dangerous Dale Mitchell led off the game for Cleveland against Warren Spahn of Buffalo, New York. Mel Allen noted that Spahn had been born when Warren Harding occupied the White House and his parents had named him after the 29th American president. Mitchell popped out to third baseman Bob Elliott in foul territory near the Boston dugout. Allie Clark, who had played in the 1947 World Series for the New York Yankees, struck out swinging on a letter-high fastball. Lou Boudreau followed Clark to the plate. He hit a slow roller toward third base. Bob Elliott played the ball well and just nipped the Cleveland player-manager at first base with an excellent throw. Spahn had successfully set down the first three Indians he had faced in Game Two as the vaunted AL champions continued to fail in generating any offense whatsoever against the NL champs from Boston.

Gangly 28-year-old Bob Lemon, who had thrown 10 shutouts and a no-hitter in 1948, took the mound for Cleveland. Jim Britt told his radio audience that Lemon had looked to be a cinch to win 22 or 23 games in 1948 after reaching the 20-victory plateau, but he had visibly tired by September. Britt said Lemon had received his "comeuppance" in his final few appearances on the mound during the regular season. Lemon had been signed by the Indians in 1941 as a third baseman, but reliable Ken Keltner was a fixture there. The Indians then shifted Lemon to the outfield where he struggled mightily to hit MLB pitching. "I could hit anything else they threw at me, but not the changeup, and word got around pretty quick," he recalled years later. "Pretty soon that's all I saw. Fastball out of the strike zone. Curveball out of the strike zone. Then the damned changeup."[5]

Lemon's task in Game Two was to make up for Bob Feller's loss the previous day. Two-and-a-half years earlier, Lemon had also come to Rapid Robert's rescue—but in an entirely different way. On Opening Day 1946 versus the Chicago White Sox, Lemon was patrolling center field for the Indians. With one out and the tying run on second base in the bottom of the ninth inning, Feller was struggling to preserve a tenuous 1–0 lead. Chicago pinch-hitter Jake Jones launched a drive to right-center field. Lemon madly sprinted to his left as the ball tailed away from him. At the

10. World Series Game Two

last instant he dived and fully extended his left arm to make a spectacular catch. Aware of the White Sox baserunner, Lemon sprang to his feet, threw accurately to second base, and doubled off a shocked Bob Kennedy who had already rounded third base. Remarkably, it was Lemon's first MLB game as an outfielder, and he sported bruises on his elbow, chin, and chest as souvenirs. In a 1947 autobiography, Feller recalled Lemon's catch as the greatest play by an outfielder that he had ever seen to that point in his baseball life.

Lemon had pitched on service teams while in the navy during the Second World War, so the Indians gave him a try on the mound stating in 1946. They liked what they saw. During the 1948 season, Lemon unexpectedly blossomed into one of the best hurlers in the AL. Coach Bill McKechnie wryly commented, "[Lemon] began to enjoy himself and decided it's better to be a great pitcher than maybe a mediocre outfielder."[6]

Tommy Holmes was the first Brave whom Lemon faced in Game Two. Holmes was retired on a ground ball that softly bounced back to the mound. Lemon made the easy throw to first baseman Eddie Robinson for the putout. It was a harbinger of the busy day Lemon would have as a fielder. Next up was Boston shortstop Alvin Dark. First-base umpire Bill Stewart found himself the center of controversy once again when Cleveland second baseman Joe Gordon bobbled Dark's ground ball. Gordon eventually corralled the ball and hastily flung it to Robinson. Stewart called Dark safe at first base on a very close play. The decision was protested vehemently by both Gordon and Lou Boudreau. Gordon was charged with an error—and the Indians began squawking from the dugout. Reporter J.C. O'Leary of the *Boston Globe* sympathized with the visitors, humorously noting, "Umpire Stewart must have anticipated the [outcome]. He called Dark safe before the play was completed." Earl Torgeson was the next Boston batter. During Torgeson's at-bat, plate umpire Bill Summers removed his mask and authoritatively strode toward the agitated Cleveland dugout. He had heard enough disparaging remarks from the visitors and ordered the complainers to cease their criticisms about Stewart's call at first base.

When the game resumed, Torgeson promptly smacked a single into right field. Dark speedily advanced to third base with just one out. Although it was just the first inning, activity began in the Cleveland bullpen. Bob Elliott, the next Boston hitter, looped a single into left field, scoring Dark and moving Torgeson up to second base. Boston had jumped out to a quick 1–0 lead over the favored visitors from Cleveland and looked for a big inning. Marv Rickert batted next for the Braves. During his plate appearance, the Indians once again tried their deadly pickoff play at second base. This time it resulted in an out—according to second-base umpire

Bill Grieve—as Torgeson was clearly tagged by Boudreau before getting back to the bag. Lemon struck out Rickert shortly thereafter for the third out. The Indians had escaped a tricky situation with minimal damage. In a February 1982 interview for the Baseball Hall of Fame's oral history collection, Lemon noted, "I was on the ropes in the first inning. The bullpen was warming up. I could hear them. Another hit and I'd have been gone. I picked off [Torgeson] at second base and the game turned around."

Before the top of the second inning began, plate umpire Bill Summers had a further discussion with the dissatisfied Indians to try to squelch the bickering from the visitors' dugout. Summers was also alerted by the Indians to several photographers who had allegedly improperly positioned themselves in the field of play near Braves Field's huge outfield scoreboard. They were summarily chased away—but only briefly. Unbeknownst to the men in blue, those photojournalists had been given special dispensation by the Commissioner's office to take pictures from that particular locale. They were permitted to return once the misunderstanding had been straightened out—and they did.

Joe Gordon led off the top of the second inning for the Indians who found themselves trailing Game Two by a run. Gordon hit a ground ball to shortstop Alvin Dark who threw to first baseman Earl Torgeson for the first out. Third baseman Ken Keltner was the next Indian batter to face Warren Spahn. He hit a fly ball to Mike McCormick in center field for the second out. Lefthanded hitter Larry Doby followed Keltner to the plate. He fared much better than the two Indian batters who preceded hm. Doby slapped a double to left-center field that required him to slide into second base. It had taken 11 innings, but it was the first extra-base hit in the World Series by either club. Doby's two-bagger may have rattled Spahn momentarily as he lost his fine control long enough for Cleveland first baseman Eddie Robinson to draw a walk. Jim Hegan had a chance to tie the score with a base hit, but he flied out to Mike McCormick in center field to make the anxious home crowd happy. Doby and Robinson were stranded on base. Boston kept its 1–0 lead heading into the bottom of the second inning.

Catcher Bill Salkeld was the first Boston batter in the home half of the second inning. He knocked a solid single into right field to start things off. Mike McCormick, a righthanded hitter, was next up for the Braves. "Lemon hasn't seemed as sharp as we've seen him in the regular season,"[7] Mel Allen noted in his commentary. McCormick attempted to bunt for a base hit, but he popped it up between home and third base. Lemon hustled off the mound to make the catch and quickly threw to first base to try to double off Salkeld, but the Boston catcher made it back to the bag safely without expending too much effort. Pesky Eddie Stanky then drew a walk

10. World Series Game Two

off Lemon. Pitcher Warren Spahn, not an especially skilled batter, was the next man up for the Braves. He got the count to 3–2 before grounding out to Joe Gordon. With the runners on the move, the Indians second baseman had no other play than to toss the ball to first base to retire Spahn. There were now two outs with Braves occupying third and second base. The dangerous Tommy Holmes batted next. The man who had fashioned a 37-game hitting streak in 1945 failed to do anything productive with his turn at bat. As he had done in the first inning, Holmes grounded harmlessly back to Lemon who made the simple toss to first baseman Eddie Robinson to retire the side and escape the jam.

The top of the third inning saw Cleveland pitcher Bob Lemon come to bat first. Lemon, who batted lefthanded but pitched with his right arm, was an excellent hitter for his position. But in his first World Series at-bat he flied out softly to Marv Rickert in left field. Dale Mitchell followed Lemon. He also flied out to Rickert who caught the ball in foul territory this time. Allie Clark was the third Indian to bat. He grounded out to third baseman Bill Elliott. The Indians had surprisingly not scored in the first 12 innings of the 1948 World Series. They trailed in Game Two by a 1–0 score.

Alvin Dark, who scored the Braves' run in the first inning, led off the bottom of the third for Boston. Dark lined a Bob Lemon pitch over the head of shortstop Lou Boudreau into left field for a single. Dark considered trying for second base for a moment, but he thought better of it and scampered back to the safety of first base. Dark's hit was already the fourth one attained by the home team in Game Two. Next to bat was Boston first baseman Earl Torgeson. He lofted a fly ball into shallow right field. Three Indians converged on it. Right fielder Allie Clark took charge, calling off his teammates, and made the routine catch. Bob Elliott struck out on a Bob Lemon curveball for the second out. Marv Rickert batted next. He dribbled a ground ball to Lemon who threw to first baseman Eddie Robinson for the final out of the frame. Dark was stranded at first base. Boston still led Game Two by a narrow 1–0 score.

Warren Spahn faced Lou Boudreau to start the top of the fourth inning. Boudreau made good contact and doubled down the right field line. With Boudreau at second base, the next Cleveland batter, Joe Gordon, scared the home team's fans by whacking a solid line drive that slammed into the left field wall—but it was about three feet foul by Mel Allen's estimation. On the very next pitch, though, Gordon knocked a base hit into left-center field. Boudreau had no intention of stopping at third base. He rounded the bag and headed for home. Left fielder Marv Rickert tried to gun him down, but Boudreau was safe when Spahn chose to cut off the throw. Spahn did not do an especially good job of corralling the ball as Gordon still was able to advance to second base on the play. The Indians had finally scored their first World Series run of 1948. Game Two was level at 1–1—and the AL version of the Tribe was threatening to score more runs to take the lead.

Ken Keltner was the next Cleveland batter to face Spahn in the top of the fourth. He failed to produce anything positive, flying out in foul territory to Boston left fielder Marv Rickert. Gordon remained at second base. Larry Doby batted next for the Indians. He slashed a single into right field. Gordon charged toward the plate intent on breaking the tie score. Right fielder Tommy Holmes' throw to the plate was cut off by first baseman Earl Torgeson, but Doby's speed still allowed him to beat Torgeson's relay throw to second base. Gordon scored the go-ahead run. Cleveland now led 2–1 thanks to Larry Doby's third hit of the World Series. Eddie Robinson, the next Indian batter, swung at the first pitch he saw and harmlessly flied out to Marv Rickert in left field. Jim Hegan was intentionally walked by Spahn so he could instead pitch to Bob Lemon. The strategy worked as Lemon weakly tapped a slow grounder to the pitcher's mound. Spahn fielded it without difficulty and threw the ball to Torgeson to conclude the inning without any further damage being inflicted on the Braves. Still, it had been a productive one for Cleveland. Game Two had flipped completely; now the visitors led by a run.

In the last half of the fourth inning, Bill Salkeld batted first for Boston, who were now trailing for the first time in the World Series. He patiently worked Bob Lemon for a walk. Mike McCormick batted next for the Braves. On the first pitch he saw, McCormick drove a base hit into left field. Salkeld moved to second base as the home crowd cheered the positive development. A Boston rally seemed imminent. Eddie Stanky dropped a perfect sacrifice bunt down the first-base line. Eddie Robinson fielded it and tossed the ball to second baseman Joe Gordon who was alertly covering first base on the play. The Braves now had runners at second and third with only one out. Warren Spahn came up and promptly hit a hard grounder directly at Lemon who fielded it deftly. Salkeld, the Boston runner at third base, made a couple of steps toward the plate, but he abruptly halted and went back to his bag when he saw Lemon in firm possession of the ball and staring menacingly at him. Lemon threw to first baseman Eddie Robinson for the second out. Tommy Holmes then came up and flied out to Dale Mitchell in left field. The Braves' promising fourth inning amounted to nothing. Cleveland still held its 2–1 lead and also retained the game's momentum.

Dale Mitchell led off the top of the fifth inning for the visitors. He ripped a single into left field. It was his first hit of the World Series. On Billy Southworth's orders, 33-year-old Red Barrett began warming up in the Boston bullpen. Allie Clark was the next Indian to face Spahn. Clark

10. World Series Game Two 111

bunted the ball toward first base. Earl Torgeson fielded it and threw to Eddie Stanky who covered the bag on the play. Lou Boudreau—who batted .355 during the regular season to finish runner-up in the AL behind Ted Williams—was the next Indian batter. He slapped a single up the middle. (The ball passed through Spahn's legs.) The base hit drove home Mitchell for Cleveland's third run of the game. With second baseman Joe Gordon coming to bat, Boston manager Billy Southworth had seen enough and made the slow stroll to the mound to remove Spahn from the game.

With the home team now trailing the AL champions by a pair of runs, righthander Charlie (Red) Barrett, a Californian, was summoned from the bullpen by Southworth to replace Spahn. While a member of the St. Louis Cardinals, Barrett appeared, unidentified, on the cover of *Life* magazine on April 1, 1946. On August 10, 1944, Barrett tossed a complete-game two hitter versus Cincinnati in which he threw just 58 pitches! (The game took just 75 minutes to play.) Mel Allen referred to Barrett as "a chunky righthander" who was undoubtedly the best singer on the Braves' roster—whatever that meant to a baseball team. During one offseason, Barrett had a two-week gig singing for the Sammy Kaye Orchestra when it appeared in Boston. The versatile pitching vocalist was known to warble country music, too, as a means of padding his income.

On the first pitch Barrett threw to Gordon, Cleveland executed a hit-and-run play. It did not quite produce the desired result for the Indians. However, it did prevent a double play as Gordon slapped a ground ball to first baseman Earl Torgeson. He made an unassisted putout, but he had no chance to get Boudreau, the lead runner, who advanced to second base. Ken Keltner followed Gordon to the plate. He failed to drive home another Indian run as he grounded out to third baseman Bob Elliott for the third out of the inning. The game moved to the last half of the fifth inning with the visiting Indians holding a 3-1 lead in Game Two and looking strong.

Shortstop Alvin Dark led off the Boston fifth inning. Jim Britt, now calling the game for Mutual radio, mentioned that a delegation from Dark's hometown of Lake Charles, Louisiana, had made the long journey to Boston to present Dark with a silver tea service and an engraved scroll honoring him for his participation in the World Series. In a flattering piece about Dark prior to Game One, baseball writer Oscar Fraley described the Braves shortstop as "a deceptively built young man who doesn't look his six feet and 180 pounds [who has] all the poise of a longtime star even though he's just finishing his first year in the majors."[8] (Dark's ascension to the major leagues was interrupted by a four-year stint in the Marines during the war where he had a mostly quiet military career. He was supposed to be shipped out from Pearl Harbor as part a machine-gun crew when someone in high places recognized Dark as a star collegiate athlete.

His orders were abruptly changed so he could stay put and play on the Marine Corps football team.) Lemon, apparently unimpressed with Dark's celebrity status, struck him out. That gave Lemon three whiffs in the game.

Earl Torgeson batted next for Boston. The lefthanded-batting first baseman tried to lay down a bunt, but it went foul. With a count of two strikes, Torgeson swung away. He bounced a ground ball to Cleveland first baseman Eddie Robinson. Robinson tossed the ball to Lemon who covered the bag and got the putout. (Lemon was becoming a defensive stalwart in Game Two. He had been involved in seven putouts in the field one way or another with the contest only about halfway completed.) Third baseman Bob Elliott was the next Brave to come to the plate. He lofted a high foul ball back of home plate. Catcher Jim Hegan had plenty of time and space to make the routine catch for the final out of the frame. The Braves had been set down in order for the first time in Game Two. The home team still trailed Cleveland, 3–1.

There was a slight delay before the top of the sixth inning began as first base needed to be replaced by members of the Braves Field grounds crew. A broken strap had caused it to become detached from its mooring. When play began, Red Barrett continued his good relief work for Boston as he struck out Larry Doby, the first Indian batter of the inning. Eddie Robinson batted next for the visitors. A bit of levity broke the tension of Game Two as a fan nearly fell awkwardly headfirst onto the field from his box seat trying to snare a foul ball that was enticingly bounding down the right field line in front of him. Robinson eventually knocked a base hit—Cleveland's seventh of the game—into center field. Jim Hegan, Cleveland's catcher, came up next and launched a drive deep to right field. Robinson was convinced the ball was going to drop to the outfield grass and ran at full speed. However, Boston right fielder Tommy Holmes made a fine leaping catch—perhaps assisted by a friendly strong wind that kept the ball inside the park. Robinson was nearly halfway to third base when the ball was caught. He was easily doubled off at first base to end the inning. It was the first double play of the World Series turned by either team. Jim Britt told his radio listeners, "That is, by all odds, the standout defensive play of the Series."[9] The score remained 3–1 in Cleveland's favor after five and a half entertaining innings of World Series play.

The bottom of the sixth began with Marv Rickert lofting a high infield pop-up to Cleveland shortstop Lou Broudreau who caught it directly behind the pitcher's mound for an easy out. Catcher Bill Salkeld was the next Brave to bat. He reached base for the third time in Game Two by drawing a walk, snapping Lemon's run of seven consecutive batters retired. It was the third base on balls issued by Lemon. Mike McCormick, who had played in all seven games for Cincinnati in the 1940 World

10. World Series Game Two

Series, was the next Boston batter. He blooped a hit into center field as the Braves were threatening to rally. Salkeld advanced to second base. He was not there very long. Boston manager Billy Southworth opted to replace Salkeld with pinch runner Phil Masi. (It was later revealed that Salkeld was struggling with a bad knee.) Eddie Stanky batted next for the Braves. Stanky slapped a ground ball to shortstop Lou Boudreau who began a timely 6–4–3 double play to end the inning. Jim Britt was initially surprised the Indians had time to get Stanky at first base to complete the twin killing, but then he remembered Boston's second baseman had been considerably slowed by an ankle injury he had suffered in July. Another promising Boston inning concluded with a zero on the scoreboard. "This is the Braves' day, apparently, to fail in the clutch,"[10] Britt opined as the Indians confidently trotted to their dugout. Cleveland retained its 3–1 lead after six full innings of Game Two.

Phil Masi stayed in the game as Boston's catcher. Red Barrett coaxed Bob Lemon to fly out to Tommy Holmes to begin top of the seventh inning. Dale Mitchell hit an infield grounder that seemed to be heading into right field, but Eddie Stanky covered plenty of ground for a man with a bad right ankle to field the ball and throw out Mitchell at first base. Allie Clark got a break when his check-swing grounder was mishandled by Alvin Dark. Clark reached first base safely on what was ruled an error on Boston's outstanding rookie shortstop. Shortly thereafter, with Lou Boudreau batting, Boston third baseman Bob Elliott also botched a fielding chance. The ball struck him on the leg. The second consecutive error by Boston meant that Cleveland now had two runners on base with two out. Joe Gordon was the next Cleveland batter. He failed to take advantage of the home team's largesse. Gordon knocked another ground ball to Elliott. He redeemed himself by fielding it cleanly and making the throw to Earl Torgeson at first base with no trouble at all this time. Despite being gifted two baserunners on a pair of Boston errors, the Indians were retired without adding to their advantage. The visitors still led Game Two, 3–1.

Frank (Buck) McCormick, a 37-year-old righthanded batter, entered the game to pinch hit for Red Barrett to lead off the bottom of the seventh inning of Game Two. (He was not related to teammate Mike McCormick, who was six years younger, but the two men had been teammates on the 1940 Cincinnati Reds, the World Series winners that season. His first name led to his nickname: Frank Buck was a noteworthy big-game hunter who had attained some esteem as an author and a film director in the 1930s.) McCormick was at the tail end of his career, but it had been a noteworthy one. As a member of the Cincinnati Reds, he led the NL for three consecutive years in hits (1938 through 1940), averaging 203 over those seasons. No other NL player has achieved that feat since then and only two had done it before McCormick. Eight times he was the NL's All-Star first baseman. At one point he played in 682 consecutive games for the Reds—the longest such streak in MLB since Lou Gehrig's retirement. In 1940 McCormick was the NL MVP. During the 1941 season, McCormick injured his back while attempting a fancy dive into a hotel swimming pool and had to wear a brace for the rest of the season. "This may have exempted him from military service,"[11] speculated one biographer. Indeed, McCormick was one conspicuous prewar baseball star who did not end up in any branch of the armed forces during the Second World War. His MLB career continued uninterrupted.

Game Two was moving along far slower than the opener. As Frank McCormick batted, Jim Britt told his radio listeners that the time elapsed thus far in Game Two was the same amount that had been needed to complete Game One. Bob Lemon began the frame by striking McCormick out swinging. It was Lemon's fourth whiff of the afternoon. Tommy Holmes batted next for Boston. He hit a fly ball to shallow center field. It was caught by backpedaling Indian shortstop Lou Boudreau. Alvin Dark also went down meekly, flying out to Allie Clark in right field. Cleveland still held a two-run edge at the end of seven complete innings.

Nels Potter was the new Boston pitcher in the top of the eighth inning. The 37-year-old righthander had played for three MLB teams in 1948: the St Louis Browns, Philadelphia A's and Boston Braves. (His short tenure with the Athletics ended sourly when Connie Mack fired him on the spot for blowing a three-run, eighth-inning lead in the space of five batters in a June 13 game versus the Browns. The Braves picked up Potter shortly thereafter as a free agent.) He was given a warm reception by the crowd who likely remembered his pitching heroics in a late-season 13-inning game in Philadelphia where he escaped unscathed from a bases-loaded jam with nobody out in the 12th inning. (Potter must have enjoyed thwarting Mack's team that day!) The aging Potter's specialty was an effective screwball that complemented a better-than-average fastball. Ken Keltner was the first Indian batter he faced. Keltner was retired on a ground ball to shortstop Alvin Dark. Potter struck out Larry Doby for the second out of the inning. Eddie Robinson looked overmatched on a couple of wild swings before he grounded out to Eddie Stanky at second base to end the inning. Potter received a huge cheer as he headed to the home team's dugout following the third out. His team still trailed by two runs, however.

Cleveland made a defensive substitution in the bottom of the eighth inning. Bob Kennedy, who possessed an excellent throwing arm, was sent in by Lou Boudreau to play right field, replacing Allie Clark. Earl Torgeson led off the frame for Boston. He fell behind in the count to Bob Lemon, but he singled into center field. It was Torgeson's second hit of the game.

10. World Series Game Two 115

The baserunner enlivened the home team's supporters—but not for very long. Bob Elliott was the next Boston batter. On a 1-2 count Elliott hit into a 4-6-3 double play. Torgeson tried to upend shortstop Boudreau with a well-placed body block, But Boudreau was able to make an accurate throw to first base to nip Elliott despite the physical contact. Marv Rickert, who was 0-for-3 in the game, batted next for the Braves. He slapped a ground ball directly to first baseman Eddie Robinson—who flipped the ball to Bob Lemon covering the bag. The out was made. Cleveland still held their 3-1 edge over the NL pennant winners in Game Two heading into the ninth inning at Braves Field.

In the visitors' half of the ninth inning, Jim Hegan batted first for Cleveland. His ground ball to Alvin Dark was misplayed by the Boston shortstop. By the time Dark made the throw, Hegan was safe at first base. Dark was tagged with his second error of Game Two. In recognition of his fine pitching thus far, Cleveland's Bob Lemon received some polite applause from the hometown Brave fans when he strode to the plate. With the count full, Hegan attempted to steal second base, but Lemon fouled off Potter's pitch. On the next pitch, Lemon grounded to Earl Torgeson. Torgeson's only option was to make an unassisted play at first base to retire Lemon. Hegan advanced to second base on the fielder's choice. Dale Mitchell batted next for Cleveland. Another fielder's choice on a grounder to second baseman Eddie Stanky moved Hegan to third base with two out. Bob Kennedy had his first at-bat of the World Series. He blooped a Texas Leaguer that dropped quickly into short right-center field that drove in the fourth Indian run as Hegan scored. (Because of Alvin Dark's error, it was an unearned run.) Lou Boudreau followed Kennedy to the plate. The Indians player-manager grounded out to third baseman Bob Elliott to end the top of the ninth inning. Cleveland now had a three-run lead to protect for just one inning to even the World Series at a game apiece.

Down to their final three outs, Phil Masi was the first Boston batter in the bottom of the ninth inning. Masi hit a high, foul pop-up that was caught by Cleveland's catcher Jim Hegan about 40 feet from home plate for the first out. "Bob is pitching about the best game he has pitched in a month's time,"[12] said Jim Britt. Mike McCormick followed Masi. A foul ball rattled off the leg of plate umpire Bill Summers causing him to do something akin to an Irish jig which amused the crowd. Lemon struck out McCormick swinging on a 2-2 pitch. Lemon's strikeout total was now five. Eddie Stanky was the last hope for Boston. On a 2-2 pitch, Stanky hit a double to left-center field—the first extra-base hit for Boston in the 1948 World Series. Ray Sanders entered the game as a pinch hitter for Nels Potter. On the first pitch Sanders saw, he grounded back to the mound. Bob Lemon, quite fittingly, snagged the ball and made the toss to first base for the final out of Game Two. With a 4–1 victory secure in the books, the Indians happily departed the field having evened the 1948 Fall Classic at a game apiece.

Having won all four games of the 1914 Fall Classic and the first one in 1948, Boston's loss in Game Two was the first time the Braves had ever dropped a World Series game.

Most of the postgame plaudits went to Bob Lemon who survived a shaky first inning to throw an impressive and dominant complete game. A Canadian Press correspondent succinctly noted, "Lemon, accomplishing what his more famous pitching mate failed to do, came through with a Series win in his first start."[13]

Renowned baseball scribe Hugh Fullerton accurately wrote of Game Two's winning pitcher, "Lemon didn't look especially strong in the early innings—in fact manager Lou Boudreau had relievers warming up in the very first inning. But when things looked bad, Lemon usually managed to make someone top the ball toward the mound and then he'd throw out the guy himself."[14]

Fullerton was not exaggerating. During the game, both Mel Allen and Jim Britt wondered aloud if Bob Lemon was on the verge of setting a World Series fielding record for total chances in a game by a pitcher. (He ended up with nine: three putouts and six assists.) Lemon fell short of the longstanding mark by two. Nick Altrock of the 1906 Chicago White Sox had handled 11 chances during the fourth game of that year's Fall Classic. Altrock had three putouts and eight assists during his busy day 42 years before. Altrock did better than Lemon on the scoreboard too. He threw a 3–0 shutout against the Cubs in the only all-Chicago World Series ever contested.

Lemon readily admitted he had gotten off to a rocky start. He told the press, "I couldn't control my breaking stuff in the early innings, but it turned out all right because after men got on base, my control seemed to return. [It's] one of those things you can't explain."[15]

Praise was also showered on Lou Boudreau for his all-round excellent work for the winners throughout Game Two. An Associated Press story, written by Jack Hand, declared, "Boudreau, held hitless in [Game One], led the Indians. His double started a two-run splurge in the fourth. He drove in a run in the fifth. He started one double play, was in the middle of another, made a fine catch in short center, and picked a man off second."[16]

A Canadian Press story about Game Two showed just how superstitious baseball people can be. A pool of writers was assigned to get stories from the Cleveland clubhouse, so that's where most of them stayed for the entire game. When they tried to turn on a radio to follow the action they were missing on the field, the Indians' traveling attendants quickly turned it off and put on a music station instead. They steadfastly believed in not knowing anything about how the game was progressing until it was over. Any violation of that protocol would surely inflict bad karma to the AL Tribe, they earnestly told their restless guests from the Fifth Estate.

Communications technology was advancing rapidly in the late 1940s—and it took riders on a commuter train between Washington and New York City by pleasant surprise. Its passengers were amazed—and generally delighted—to be able to see live television coverage of Game Two of the World Series as they relaxed in their railroad cars. The 1948 World Series was only the second to be televised. The previous year's Fall Classic's TV audience was limited to certain small areas along the east coast of the country. Be that as it may, most Americans got their live baseball broadcasts from radio as only about three percent of the country's households had television sets. TV owners who did not live near the Atlantic coast were generally out of luck if they wanted to see the action on their screens. The television coverage of the World Series encompassed most of the eastern United States, but it was far from being fully available on a national level. It would be coming soon, though.

As was the case in 1947, when two New York clubs were vying for baseball's top honor, there was no travel day set aside in the World Series. (However, there had been two travel days scheduled in 1946 when the Boston Red Sox played the St. Louis Cardinals.) Both teams caught a train from Boston to Cleveland that was supposed to arrive at its destination in the wee hours of the morning and hoped for the best. At least that was the plan. Unexpected delays, however, kept both teams in Boston long past the scheduled hour of departure. Accordingly, there was some doubt whether Game Three would begin at the appointed hour of 1 p.m. Trains carrying members of the media fared even worse in getting their passengers to the ballpark on time. (Many weary scribes sent their pregame stories to their editors by telephone or telegram from stops along the way. Several writers' bylines were prefixed by the notation "en route to Cleveland.") At least MLB players in 1948 had long gotten used to sleeping on the trains that shuttled them to their destinations.

Bookmakers were impressed by the performance of the victors of Game Two. The odds for Cleveland winning the World Series had now shifted drastically to 5:14 in the AL Tribe's favor. (If you liked Cleveland to win the Fall Classic, you had to wager $14 to win just $5.) The Indians were 9:20 favorites to take the third game in their familiar home ballpark on Friday.

The Braves, Eddie Stanky, Alvin Dark and Bob Elliott, were all displeased with the infield of their home ballpark. The threesome claimed the infield was in substandard condition because of two recent football games held at Braves Field.

"Cleveland beat us fair and square [in Game Two]," Stanky admitted, "but that infield is stinking to play." All three Braves considered the area between second and third base to be the worst portion of the diamond.

"It's spongy as a powder puff along the bases," claimed Bob Elliott. "And the holes...."

"When that ball's coming at you," Stanky insisted, "you never know if you're going to get smacked in the teeth or have it bounce in your eyes. Bob's too good a ball player to boot 'em like that. Look at how Joe Gordon fumbled that easy one. He's the best in the business."[17]

Attendance at Braves Field for Game Two dropped a bit from Game One to 39,633 ticket-buyers. Hugh Fullerton thought he knew the reasons why this had happened: "A cold wind and the $4 price of standing room apparently discouraged customers. Perhaps some folks [learned from a Game One] standee who quit trying to see over folks and was listening to the radio [broadcast] by a concession stand. 'It's almost as good as being at home,' he said."[18]

Another newspaper giant was thoroughly unimpressed with the action in Game Two. Despite a healthy parade of baserunners to keep things interesting in the second Braves-Indians clash, the esteemed 67-year-old Grantland Rice, who seemingly had been covering major American sports events forever, penned in his World Series column, "Cleveland won between yawns. Yes, I'm afraid it was a dull game for all involved, except the Indians." Rice held almost the entire Boston team in low esteem. He wrote, "I doubt that even two Braves could make the Indians' [roster]. Maybe Elliott—who has been sour this Series. Always Sain—the star of one job so far. The Indians have most of the stars, topped by Boudreau—the most valuable shortstop since Honus Wagner—the greatest of them all."[19]

After displaying it twice in the World Series, Lou Boudreau was asked to explain how his club's sneaky pickoff play at second base worked. Here is the description provided by Cleveland's shortstop/manager to the press:

> Just before the pitcher is ready to pitch, I flash the sign to catcher Jim Hegan from my normal position. I wait for Hegan to relay the signal to the pitcher. As soon as he does, I take three strides toward the bag. The pitcher counts to three to match my strides. Then he whirls and fires—not to me but to the bag. Of course, it takes split-second timing and a quick break to get it down to perfection. I acquired that from my basketball-playing days.[20]

The Indian players announced their World Series money would be divided into 34 equal portions. Who exactly those recipients were was a

10. World Series Game Two

private matter between the Cleveland club and the Commissioner Chandler's office. However, it was widely rumored that two midseason acquisitions by the Indians—Satchel Paige and Sammy Zoldak—were voted full Series shares although neither was entitled to such a large cut. Manager Lou Boudreau told reporters, "I think the boys have been pretty generous."[21]

Several writers openly wondered whether Warren Spahn would make another appearance in the 1948 World Series for the Braves, so disappointing was his outing in Game Two. One unnamed scribe, in an Associated Press story, wrote off Spahn entirely. He penned, "Off his marked failure Thursday, Spahn might not be given another start by Billy Southworth unless he runs very short of pitchers."[22] Spahn certainly had other ideas.

Game Two Box Score
Cleveland Indians 4, Boston Braves 1
Game played on Thursday, October 7, 1948, at Braves Field

Cleveland Indians	ab	r	h	rbi	Boston Braves	ab	r	h	rbi
Mitchell lf	5	1	1	0	Holmes rf	4	0	0	0
Clark rf	3	0	0	0	Dark ss	4	1	1	0
Kennedy rf	1	0	1	1	Torgeson 1b	4	0	2	0
Boudreau ss	5	1	2	1	Elliott 3b	4	0	1	1
Gordon 2b	4	1	1	1	Rickert lf	4	0	0	0
Keltner 3b	4	0	0	0	Salkeld c	1	0	1	0
Doby cf	4	0	2	1	Masi c	1	0	0	0
Robinson 1b	3	0	1	0	McCormick M. cf	4	0	2	0
Hegan c	3	1	0	0	Stanky 2b	2	0	1	0
Lemon p	4	0	0	0	Spahn p	2	0	0	0
Totals	36	4	8	4	Barrett p	0	0	0	0
					McCormick F. ph	1	0	0	0
					Potter p	0	0	0	0
					Sanders ph	1	0	0	0
					Totals	32	1	8	1

	1	2	3	4	5	6	7	8	9		R	H	E
Cleveland	0	0	0	2	1	0	0	0	1	--	4	8	1
Boston	1	0	0	0	0	0	0	0	0	--	1	8	3

Cleveland Indians	IP	H	R	ER	BB	SO
Lemon W (1-0)	9.0	8	1	0	3	5
Totals	9.0	8	1	0	3	5

Boston Braves	IP	H	R	ER	BB	SO
Spahn L (0–1)	4.1	6	3	3	2	1
Barrett	2.2	1	0	0	0	1
Potter	2.0	1	1	0	0	1
Totals	9.0	8	4	3	2	3

E—Gordon (1), Dark 2 (2), Elliott (3). **DP**—Cleveland 2, Boston 1. **2B**—Cleveland Doby (1, off Spahn); Boudreau (1, off Spahn), Boston Stanky (1, off Lemon). **SH**—Clark (1, off Spahn); Stanky (1, off Lemon). **IBB**—Hegan (1, by Spahn). **Team LOB**—8. **Team**—8. **IBB**—Spahn (1, Hegan). **U**—Bill Stewart (NL), Bill Grieve (AL), George Barr (NL), Bill Summers (AL), Babe Pinelli (NL), Joe Paparella (AL). **T**—2:14. **A**—39,633.

— 11 —

Game Three Scuttlebutt

*Bearden's Boast, Puzzled Paige,
and Bickford Under Pressure*

Baseball scribes noted that Cleveland's Indians did not spend much time celebrating their Series-tying victory in Game Two in the visitors' clubhouse. That display of professionalism was absolutely fine with manager Lou Boudreau, who understood the true goal. He said, "It was a good win, but don't forget we need three more. That's what we're after."[1]

Certainly, the bookmakers' faith in the AL champions had been restored after Game Two. Updated odds, which always moved slightly, now listed the Indians as 1:3 favorites to win the World Series with 9:20 odds to take Game Three at their home ballpark on Friday afternoon.

Cleveland's surprise pitching hero of 1948, Gene Bearden, fresh off his win against the Red Sox in Monday's one-game playoff at Fenway Park, raised a few eyebrows by dismissing any possibility that the Braves would beat him in Friday's Game Three. According to some reports, the happy-go-lucky Bearden classified the NL champions as mere "pushovers"[2] who should present him with no troubles whatsoever. Certainly, neither club had been an offensive juggernaut through the first two games of the Fall Classic—and Boston had scored a mere two runs in two games—but such immodest comments from pitchers were rarely heard in advance of World Series contests.

To try to generate more offense, it was expected that Boston manager Billy Southworth would make a few changes in his team's lineup. It would also follow strategic norms as right-handed hitters Frank McCormick and Mike McCormick would see action versus southpaw Bearden, while Marv Rickert and Earl Torgeson—both lefthanded batters, would be benched.

Satchel Paige was still generating conversation even though he had not yet thrown a single pitch for Cleveland in the World Series. Some writers were amused to see Paige leave the Indians' bullpen following Game

Two with a magazine tucked under his arm, having apparently passed the time reading instead of watching the ballgame. Before Game Three, Paige commented to journalists that the complexity of catchers' signals to pitchers in MLB were something new to him. He noted, "Down where I come from, when my catcher signaled with one finger, I threw a fastball. When he put two fingers down, I threw a curveball. These fancy major league signals have me a little confused. I don't understand all that fancy wig-wag stuff."

Despite the occasional miscommunication, Paige nevertheless praised Cleveland's backstop Jim Hegan's excellent work behind the plate. "He's one good catcher; I like to have him working with me," Paige said. "I cross him up all the time. I don't throw what he calls for, but he catches the ball all the same."[3]

Grantland Rice wrote that the Braves' hopes to win the Fall Classic now largely fell to Game Three starter Vernon Bickford. Rice declared, "There are sufficient suggestions of brimstone in young Bickford's name and hometown to indicate trouble for Gene Bearden and the Indians."[4] Bickford hailed from Hellier, Kentucky.

Still, Rice fully acknowledged that Bickford might have a "rough afternoon" in front of him, pitching in Cleveland's ballpark against the hero of Monday's AL playoff game. "Beating Bearden is no soft assignment," Rice conceded. "But unless Bickford can give Johnny Sain some help, the pride of Belleville, Arkansas, will be sunk—and, with him, the Braves."[5]

— 12 —

World Series Game Three
Bearden Blanks the Braves

Date: Friday, October 8, 1948
Site: Municipal Stadium, Cleveland, Ohio

> "'Spahn and Sain and Pray for Rain' is a popular refrain when baseball fans think back to the late-1940s Braves. But from 1948 through 1950, Vern Bickford was a strong number-three hurler, accumulating 46 wins, throwing a no-hitter, and leading the league in innings pitched one year."[1]—Vern Bickford biographer Les Masterson

> "When a fellow such as [Gene] Bearden can smack out a double and a single and score his team's first run, in addition to pitching sensational ball and fielding superbly, it doesn't leave anybody else much of a chance to take bows."[2]—Whitney Martin, Associated Press

Once again, iffy weather cast serious doubt about the 1948 World Series staying on schedule. Rain was falling at Cleveland's Municipal Stadium on Friday, October 8 until just a few minutes before the 1 p.m. game time for Game Three. Mel Allen noted in his pregame comments that heavy showers were falling steadily all the way from Boston to Cleveland as he rode an overnight train from one World Series venue to the other. (Rain or no rain, some 15,000 excited fans were waiting to warmly greet the Indians as they detrained at the railroad station. The team had not been back in Cleveland since clinching the AL pennant four days earlier.) Despite the less-than-ideal weather, about 20,000 fans lined up in 22 separate queues to buy the remaining available tickets. One stalwart Cleveland rooter, 24-year-old Steve Banyard, arrived five hours in advance of the box office opening. He certainly came fully prepared to make the best of a long wait. He arrived with five boiled eggs, four sandwiches, a quart of milk, a banana, an apple, and a slice of pie. For personal comfort he came equipped with a homemade oilcloth tent to keep him dry, an alarm clock, two candles and a portable radio.

There was no opportunity for either club to take batting practice or fielding practice as the showers fell. Luckily, for the more than 70,000 baseball fans who flocked to the huge ballpark to see the first World Series game in Cleveland since 1920, the murky weather subsided almost on cue. The tarpaulin was only lifted from the infield a few minutes before the teams and umpires strode onto the diamond. To the surprise of many people, Game Three would proceed precisely as scheduled.

The start of Friday's game was almost delayed for a reason unconnected with the weather. Overnight trains from Boston carrying many journalists and ticketholders had been slow getting into Cleveland. Originally it was announced by Commissioner Happy Chandler that the starting time would be pushed back half an hour to 1:30 p.m. to accommodate

Red Barrett (left), Johnny Sain (center) and Warren Spahn combined for 56 wins for Boston in 1948. Eight different pitchers won at least five games for the Braves during that memorable season when the club won 91 of 153 NL games (courtesy Boston Public Library, Leslie Jones Collection).

them. Not long afterwards, a second announcement from Chandler was made to cancel his first one. Fans, players, and everyone else connected to the World Series were understandably unsure of what was going on and why. Journalist Leo H. Petersen, one of the annoyed reporters, described the situation as "the greatest confusion in the history of the Fall Classic."[3]

There was only one change in Cleveland's lineup. Wally Judnich returned to the AL Tribe's starting nine in right field where he had played in the opener. Allie Clark, who had patrolled that field in Game Two, was back on the bench. Speedy Larry Doby was promoted back to the number-two spot in the Indians' lineup that Clark had occupied.

Boston made more substantial changes for the first Fall Classic game in Cleveland in 1948. The most noticeable was the insertion of first baseman Frank (Buck) McCormick into the Braves' starting nine—which meant there were two men named McCormick in Boston's Game Three batting order. Clint Conatser would play center field instead of Marv Rickert and bat second in place of Earl Torgeson. It was part of manager Billy Southworth's plan to overload his lineup with righthanded hitters against Cleveland's lefty starter.

Cleveland owner Bill Veeck made his presence known after the national anthem was played by launching several noisy skyrockets into the air. The unexpected bangs startled most everyone in the ballpark—including Mel Allen who was trying to run through the two teams' batting orders for his radio audience when the explosions occurred. He had not been told to expect fireworks—at least in the literal sense of the word. "That's a typical Bill Veeck demonstration," Mel Allen stated once he refocused. "[Veeck is] one of the greatest showmen in baseball."[4]

During the pregame introduction of the six umpires, only Bill Stewart was roundly booed by the partisan Cleveland crowd who were not about to let him forget about his controversial call on Bob Feller's pickoff play in Game One. The other two NL umpires garnered no noticeable reaction from the fans. League partisanship even extended to the trio of AL umpires, however, as they were politely applauded. The unpopular Stewart was the plate umpire for Game Three.

The starting pitchers were both rookies—an unusual occurrence in World Series play. They were Gene Bearden for Cleveland and Vern Bickford for Boston. Both men had served in the military during the Second World War which probably slowed down the development of their professional baseball careers.

Bearden was still reveling in his performance versus the Red Sox four days earlier at Fenway Park when he won his twentieth game to give the Indians the AL pennant. In the Mutual radio broadcast booth, Jim Britt predicted the Braves would have their hands full with Bearden in Game

Three because it would be the first time in the entire 1948 season that they would be facing a lefthanded knuckleball pitcher. Bearden was also Cleveland's hottest starting pitcher at the moment. He had not lost a game since Labor Day.

Vern Bickford was a 28-year-old rookie. Born in Hellier, Kentucky, Bickford spent his formative years in West Virginia. He was playing Class D baseball in the Mountain State League when the Second World War interrupted his rise through the lower ranks of the professional game. Bickford would later claim that the war oddly helped accelerate his career as he was able to interact with several MLB pitchers in the military who gave him valuable tips. He started the 1948 season as a Braves reliever but was quickly shifted to a starting role. It was a very successful transition. Bickford finished the 1948 regular season with a solid 11–5 record and a passable 3.27 ERA. Overall, he was a pleasant surprise for an ascending Boston club. Bickford's unexpected good showing, after struggling in the

Vern Bickford had an excellent campaign for the Boston Braves in 1948. As a 27-year-old rookie, Bickford posted an 11–5 record with a 3.27 ERA. He was Boston's starting pitcher in Game Three of the World Series (courtesy Boston Public Library, Leslie Jones Collection).

12. World Series Game Three

American Association in 1947, earned him a mid-season raise from his club in 1948. It was described by *The Sporting News* as "a four-figure boost in pay."[5]

Tommy Holmes led off Game Three for the visiting Boston Braves. Gene Bearden coaxed Holmes to hit a ground ball to shortstop Lou Boudreau who efficiently fired the ball to first baseman Eddie Robinson for the first out of the contest. Alvin Dark followed Holmes to the plate and struck out swinging. First baseman Mike McCormick of Ventura, California, who was 2-for-6 in the World Series, batted next. Bearden struck him out too as the Braves swiftly went down in order in the first inning as the Cleveland crowd roared its approval.

In the home half of the first inning, Dale Mitchell was the leadoff batter for the Indians and promptly flied out to Mike McCormick in left field. Larry Doby, a lefthanded batter, faced Bickford next. He drew a base on balls. Lou Boudreau, the number-three hitter for the Indians, got a huge cheer when he stepped into the batter's box. He did not live up the home crowd's expectations, though—far from it. Boudreau grounded into a textbook 6-4-3 double play that was perfectly turned by the NL champs. The second out was not even close at first base; Eddie Stanky's relay throw beat Boudreau to first base by about 20 feet. There was no score after one inning of Game Three.

Gene Bearden faced Bob Elliott to start the top of the second inning. On the first pitch to him, the Boston third baseman dribbled a slow ground ball. It rolled toward his counterpart, Indian third baseman Ken Keltner, who had to hustle to make the play. His strong throw to first base just nipped Elliott. Frank (Buck) McCormick was the next Brave to bat. He did better than Elliott. McCormick slapped a single up the middle. The number-three hitter, Clint Conatser, a 27-year-old rookie from Los Angeles, came to bat for the first time in the World Series. He hit another slow roller toward third base. Bearden, a capable glove man, quickly came off the mound to field it and make the out at first base. McCormick advanced to second base on the 1–3 fielder's choice. With a runner in scoring position, catcher Phil Masi batted. He solidly knocked the ball to the left-field warning track where Dale Mitchell retreated and confidently snared it for the third out. McCormick was stranded at second base when the top of the second inning ended.

Second baseman Joe Gordon—who, predictably, was given the nickname Flash by his teammates—was the leadoff man for the Indians in the bottom of the second inning. His at-bat ended in a flash as he was not up for very long. He lofted an easy fly ball to Mike McCormick in left field for the first out. Ken Keltner, who was 1-for-8 in the Series, followed Gordon to the plate. (The popular Keltner had been feted with his own night at Municipal Stadium earlier in the 1948 season; he and his family were presented with a new station wagon and a pet collie by Bill Veeck.) He hit a ground ball that was easily fielded by first baseman Buck McCormick for an unassisted putout. With two out, Wally Judnich, Cleveland's right fielder, next faced the righthanded Vern Bickford. He drew a walk. Lefthanded batter Eddie Robinson, who was 1-for-6 thus far in the World Series, flied out to shallow left field to Mike McCormick—meaning that Braves named McCormick made all three of the putouts in the bottom of the second inning. As in the first two World Series contests, good pitching was stifling the offenses of both teams again. Game Three was still scoreless after two frames.

Eddie Stanky, the number-eight hitter in the Braves' lineup, led off the third inning, possessing the only extra-base hit for Boston thus far in the World Series. Jim Britt noted that Stanky, as a member of the Brooklyn Dodgers, established the NL's single-season record for bases on balls with 148 in 1945. Stanky did not walk this time. He drove a hit into right field that just eluded the glove of Cleveland first baseman Eddie Robinson. Pitcher Vern Bickford, a righthanded batter, laid down what was supposed to be a routine sacrifice bunt. Catcher Jim Hegan picked up the ball in front of home plate and subtly tagged Bickford before throwing to shortstop Lou Boudreau covering second base for an attempt at an unusual double play. Stanky was safe at second, however, causing the Indian supporters to groan. Unaware that he had been tagged out, Bickford continued to run to first base. First-base umpire Bill Grieve checked with plate umpire Bill Stewart to confirm that Bickford had been tagged out and then sent him to the Boston dugout. The play went into the books as a sacrifice (Hegan unassisted). Next up was Tommy Holmes who grounded back to Gene Bearden. The Cleveland pitcher had no play on Boston's lead runner, so he threw to first baseman Eddie Robinson for the second out of the inning. Stanky advanced to third base. The next Brave batter, shortstop Alvin Dark, then belted a sharply hit fly ball to right field. Wally Judnich caught it about 300 feet from home plate to end the Boston threat in the top of the third.

Jim Hegan led off the bottom of the third inning for the Indians. He quickly popped out to Phil Masi behind home plate. Gene Bearden, who hit two home runs and batted .256 in 1948, came up next for Cleveland. He lived up to his reputation as a better-than-average batter for a pitcher by hitting a long double to right field. Jim Britt told his radio audience, "That would have been a home run anytime at Braves field; it would have been long gone."[6] It was the Indians' third two-base hit of the World Series. Bearden completed the play by aggressively sliding into second base. This greatly pleased Rogers Hornsby. The superb batsman from yesteryear was

12. World Series Game Three

writing a World Series column for the *Chicago Daily News* that was being nationally syndicated. "It warmed the cockles of an old-timer's heart," declared the delighted Hornsby (or perhaps his ghostwriter). "I haven't seen a pitcher do that in 20 years. He hit the dirt like a Cobb or a Speaker."[7]

Bearden's unexpected double may have shaken Vern Bickford's confidence. The Braves hurler struggled with the next Indian batter, Dale Mitchell. Mitchell drew a walk on five pitches, after which Boston catcher Phil Masi walked toward the mound to offer encouragement to the rattled Bickford. With Larry Doby batting, Cleveland got a break. Doby hit a hard ground ball to second baseman Eddie Stanky that should have been an inning-ending double play. Mitchell was forced out at second base, but shortstop Alvin Dark's relay throw to first base ended up sailing past first baseman Frank McCormick and into the Cleveland dugout. Bearden was awarded home on the overthrow (giving the AL Tribe the first run of the game) while Doby was waved by the umpires toward second base on the Braves' sixth error of the World Series. Lou Boudreau batted next and drew a base on balls, Bickford's fourth walk of the game. There was no further scoring in the bottom of the third inning as Joe Gordon flied out to Boston center fielder Mike McCormick for the final out. Nevertheless, Cleveland had jumped out to a 1–0 lead. It was the first time that Cleveland had scored the opening run in a 1948 Fall Classic game.

As Mike McCormick batted in the top of the fourth inning, there was an audible clamor in the crowd as comedian Bob Hope was spotted entering the ballpark. Hope was one of the Indians' owners. He probably disapproved when McCormick slapped a single that bounced by second base into the outfield. Bob Elliott flied out to Larry Doby in shallow center field for the second out. Doby had to sprint to make a running catch. Buck McCormick was the next Boston batter. McCormick hit a ground ball back to the mound. Bearden fielded it deftly and started a 1–4–3 double play to retire the side. Boston, who trailed 1–0, had not scored since the first inning of Game Two.

To start the bottom half of the fourth inning, Vern Bickford walked his fifth batter of the game, Ken Keltner, on four pitches. Wally Judnich was the next Indian to bat. He struck out swinging. It was Bickford's first whiff of the game. Eddie Robinson followed with a base hit—his second of the World Series—into left field. Keltner stopped at second base. Jim Hegan wasted no time in his at-bat. On the first pitch he smashed a single into center field. Keltner scored from second base to increase the AL Tribe's lead to 2–0 as Robinson stopped at second base. Gene Bearden kept the Cleveland rally going by getting his second hit of the game. This one fell into left field to load the bases. Boston manager Billy Southworth had seen enough and pulled Vern Bickford. Bill Voiselle was brought in from the bullpen to try to squelch the Cleveland rally. He succeeded. Dale Mitchell was set down on a foul pop-up caught by Bob Elliott near the Braves dugout along the third-base line. Larry Doby then grounded to Buck McCormick at first base. He tossed to Voiselle who alertly covered the bag. Heading into the top of the fifth, Boston was somewhat fortunate to only be trailing by two runs.

Boston center fielder, Clint Conatser, the first batter to face Gene Bearden in the top of the fifth inning, hit a hot grounder to Ken Keltner, Cleveland's third baseman. Keltner had a difficult time getting the ball out of his glove, but he found the handle in time to retire Conatser at first base. The next Brave hitter, Phil Masi, also challenged Keltner's fielding abilities. Keltner took the bounding ball in front of Lou Boudreau and nipped Masi with another accurate toss to first base for the second out. Eddie Stanky hit a long fly ball down the left-field line that just drifted foul. Umpire Joe Paparella correctly made the appropriate signal. Stanky then hit a routine fly ball to Cleveland leftfielder Dale Mitchell who scarcely had to move to make the catch. Halfway through Game Three, Boston's offensive woes continued as Cleveland still led, 2–0. The Braves had only scored a pair of runs in the Series.

Mel Allen took over the broadcasting duties for Mutual radio as the home half of the fifth inning started. Lou Boudreau popped out to Bob Elliott at third base. Joe Gordon stepped into the batter's box. He tapped a slow roller to Elliott who had to hustle, but he successfully made the throw to teammate Frank McCormick at first base. Ken Keltner was fooled on a Bill Voiselle changeup, but he still managed to hit a sinking fly ball that left fielder Mike McCormick ran down. It was a fine defensive play that even drew applause from the Cleveland rooters.

Pitcher Bill Voiselle led off the top of the sixth inning. His ground ball to Lou Boudreau resulted in the first Boston out of the inning. Tommy Holmes batted next against Gene Bearden. His only hit so far in the World Series was an RBI single that won the first game for Boston. He failed to get his second hit. Instead, Homes grounded out to Cleveland second baseman Joe Gordon. Alvin Dark batted next. He solved Gene Bearden by connecting for a double. His drive off the left field fence missed being a home run by about three feet. Mike McCormick's pop out to shallow left field almost created chaos. Four Indians converged on the ball with second baseman Joe Gordon eventually making the catch—and then nearly dropping it. With Dark sprinting toward the plate, Gordon's play certainly saved a run as the side was retired. Boston was still behind in Game Three by a 2–0 score.

Bill Voiselle remained on the mound for Boston. He set down the home team efficiently. Wally Judnich flied out to Clint Conatser in

12. World Series Game Three

left-center field to start the bottom of the sixth inning. With Eddie Robinson batting, Eddie Stanky made an over-the-shoulder catch in shallow right field that also earned him a round of applause from the Cleveland crowd. Catcher Jim Hegan followed by flying out to Tommy Holmes in right field. The score remained unchanged: It was still 2–0 for the home team after six innings.

The top of the seventh inning began promisingly for the Braves. Bob Elliot slammed a single into left field. It went for naught, however. Frank McCormick struck out swinging on a Gene Bearden knuckleball. Clint Conatser followed by bouncing into a 5–4–3 double play. Boston had now gone 15 innings without scoring a run.

Gene Bearden, the star of the game thus far, led off the bottom of the seventh inning for the home team. He grounded out to Boston shortstop Alvin Dark. Dale Mitchell faced Bill Voiselle next. He hit a pop-up to Alvin Dark who made the catch in the outfield grass for the second out. Larry Doby may have caught a break when plate umpire Bill Stewart called a borderline 1–2 pitch a ball. On Voiselle's next pitch, Doby singled into right field. That hit broke a skein of 10 straight Indians retired by Voiselle. Doby, who was the only man on either team to get a hit in each of the first three games, got no farther than first base, however. Lou Boudreau hit another pop fly that was hauled in by Dark. Cleveland still held a 2–0 advantage after seven full innings of Game Three.

The top half of the eighth inning began with Phil Masi trying to bunt for a base hit off Gene Bearden. Masi's bunt looked like an effective one, but Bearden still managed to field the ball and throw to first baseman Eddie Robinson in time to record the out. With Eddie Stanky batting, plate umpire Bill Stewart stopped play momentarily because he noticed the Braves, improperly, had two men standing in their on-deck circle. Stewart shooed one of them away. With that technicality settled, Stanky hit a hot grounder back to Bearden who initially had trouble with it, but he still managed to retire the Boston second baseman with an accurate throw to Robinson. Boston manager Billy Southworth opted to lift Bill Voiselle for a pinch hitter—Connie Ryan, a righthanded batter. Gene Bearden whiffed Ryan when, on a two-strike pitch, umpire Stewart ruled that Ryan had not checked his swing. The Indians left the field still ahead, 2–0. Mel Allen remarked that Game Three was progressing at a "sparkling pace."[8]

The new Boston pitcher in the bottom of the eighth inning was Red Barrett who had seen action as a reliever in Game Two and had done well. Using mostly off-speed tosses, Barrett proceeded to swiftly retire the Indians in order: Joe Gordon flied out on a long blast to left center field, Ken Keltner flied out to right field, and Wally Judnich grounded out to Braves second baseman Eddie Stanky.

Boston was down to their final three outs in Game Three. Lefthanded hitter Tommy Holmes, 0-for-3 on the afternoon, led off the frame for the Braves against Gene Bearden who was trying to earn a complete-game shutout. The tension was broken momentarily when a fan in a box seat lost his hat trying to field a foul ball—and had to plead with a stadium attendant to retrieve it from the playing field for him. When the action resumed, Holmes grounded to Bearden who made the easy play to first base for the out. Joe Gordon made a terrific play for the second out, snagging an Alvin Dark grounder behind second base and making a fine pivot and throw to first baseman Eddie Robinson. Mike McCormick was Boston's last hope as he batted with two outs. McCormick worked Bearden for a full count but, after a foul ball, he lofted a popup to shortstop Lou Boudreau. He made the simple catch to end the battle with the Indians on top, 2-0. Game Three had taken just 96 minutes to play. It was six minutes shorter than Game One.

With the final out in the books, two shutout streaks remained intact. The Braves had not scored in their last 17 times at bat. Baseball scholars also noted that Cleveland had now recorded three consecutive home shutouts in World Series play as Brooklyn had failed to score in the final two games of the 1920 World Series played at League Park 28 years before.

The Indians jogged off the field without showing too much emotion. Journalist Fritz Howell wrote in his report of Game Three, "The Cleveland Indians were about as excited after winning today's World Series game as a veteran poker player after winning a small pot on a pair of jacks."[9]

Gene Bearden—the feel-good baseball story of 1948—continued to be nothing short of fantastic on the mound for Cleveland. Jim Britt referenced Bearden's military record when he noted to his radio listeners, "He [Bearden] has a silver [sic] plate in his head and several silver plates in his legs. He also has ice water in his veins and iron and steel in his heart. He was just too good for Boston today."[10]

Cleveland catcher Jim Hegan glowingly assessed Bearden's performance this way: "There was one game I could have caught from a rocking chair. This guy was terrific today." A Canadian Press correspondent concurred, calling the Indians' triumph "a heart-warming victory for the loyal Cleveland fans."[11]

In writing about Game Three, Jack Hand of the Associated Press duly noted, "Bases on balls ruined rookie Vern Bickford on Friday along with jittery infield play. No matter what Bickford did, he would have found Bearden tough to beat. [Bearden] appeared to take his first Series start as just another game. He was under more pressure [versus] the Red Sox on Monday."[12]

Hand further reported that Boston never had more than one hit in

12. World Series Game Three

any inning in Game Three, and when the Braves got the leadoff hitter on base in both the fourth and seventh innings, they were each summarily erased by timely Cleveland double plays. Rogers Hornsby concurred in his column. He wrote, "The big problem with the Braves is that they can't get more than one hit in the same frame. As long as the Cleveland pitchers don't walk anybody, those scattered Boston hits are wasted."[13]

When the final out was made in the ninth inning, Bill Veeck's ballpark band serenaded the victorious Bearden with the song "My Hero." Whitney Martin, an Associated Press reporter, humorously wrote, "It was not announced to whom the piece was directed, but it was assumed it wasn't Bill Stewart." Martin also unleashed this zinger in his Associated Press column: "The press was tardy. Trains bearing the typewriter caravan from Boston were three hours late, so many scribblers were straggling in around the second inning. It still was 0–0, so they hadn't missed anything. The Braves themselves could have missed those two innings—and the other seven for that matter."[14]

Jim Britt said in his postgame radio remarks that if the Braves were looking for anything positive to take from Game Three, it would be from the fine showing of their relief corps who superbly held the Indians in check after Vern Bickford departed during the fourth inning. They could hardly be faulted for their team dropping the game. Conversely, losing hurler Bickford came under some criticism for his short outing as the Braves starter. Al Abrams of the *Pittsburgh Post-Gazette* opined, "Billy Southworth's choice of Vern Bickford as his starting pitcher ... proved an unhappy one. The youngster was wild and unsure of himself."[15]

Baseball scribe Gayle Talbot wrote, "Through today's tussle, the impotent Braves had scored exactly twice in three times against Cleveland's great mound staff. When Bearden finished with Billy Southworth's boys today, they looked as though they may never score again."[16]

Talbot thought that Bearden's busy week of pitching was one for the books:

> An amazing feature of Bearden's great performance was [he] was pitching his third vital game in seven days.
>
> His control was so superb that he issued no walks. Toward the last, the Braves were so desperate for any hit that they were bunting. That worked no better than anything else.[17]

Bearden was also the offensive stalwart for Cleveland in Game Three. He was the only player on either team to register more than one hit. Since Bearden scored the first run of the game for the Indians on Alvin Dark's third-inning throwing error—the only run they required—he conveniently provided his own margin of victory.

Dark's bad throw was magnified by Jerry Nason of the *Boston Globe*. His report on Game Three began with this zinger: "Two players were throwing knuckleballs here today. One was Gene Bearden, lefthanded pitcher for the Cleveland Indians. The other was Alvin Dark, rookie shortstop for the Boston Braves."

Al Abrams of the *Pittsburgh Post-Gazette* figured the Braves had plenty to worry about as the rest of the Series unfolded—namely, the unfulfilled potential of the betting favorites. He wrote, "While the supposedly more powerful Indians have not been any balls of fire themselves on the attack, their superiority in practically every phase of the game stands out in such bold relief that it is frightening to contemplate what might happen if Cleveland ever starts hitting."[18]

When the turnstiles stopped clicking at Municipal Stadium on October 8, a grand total of 70,306 customers had paid their way into the vast ballpark. Gate receipts totaled nearly $346,000. The Game Three attendance figure, enormous as it was, was still somewhat disappointing. It was believed that the pregame downpours in and around Cleveland had scared many fans away who likely anticipated a rainout. (It was also possible that speculators had purchased far more tickets to resell at a profit than the demand warranted. Al Abrams reported, "Scalpers ... were forced to sell $6.25 ducats for as low as $2 to get rid of the excess baggage at a loss."[19] Other reports had tickets going for as little as 50 cents to patient fans who controlled their buying impulses until after the game began.) The World Series single-game attendance record, set just the previous October at Yankee Stadium, still stood: 74,065.

Rogers Hornsby noted in his column that the 1948 World Series was very reminiscent of Fall Classics from the distant past with its dominant pitching by both teams effectively stifling offensive outbursts. "There hasn't been a triple or a home run in three games,"[20] he pointed out. The dearth of home runs was indeed unusual. Not until 2014 would there again be three consecutive World Series games without a homer being hit. As of 2021, no Fall Classic since 1948 has been homerless in the opening three contests.

The Braves were a sullen lot in their clubhouse after Game Three. They were conversing among themselves and to numerous reporters in low, unenthusiastic tones. Finally, Mike McCormick raised his voice loud enough to be heard across the room. He bellowed, "We're going to score some runs pretty soon!" He then lowered his voice again to softly add, "We'll have to wait for next spring if we don't."[21]

Two men who were absent from the World Series due to medical issues were coping with being sidelined as best they could. It was reported that Cleveland's Don Black had watched the first three Series games on television, as had Jeff Heath of the Braves. "It doesn't feel too good to sit and watch them play,"[22] Heath said of his Boston teammates. The power hitter with the broken ankle also rued not being able to take advantage of the enticing temporary fence at Municipal Stadium.

Cleveland's baseball fans got their chance to experience a viewing party too. At the city's Central Armory, six large-screen receivers were installed courtesy of Philco for the locals to watch Game Three. There was no admission charge to get into the building, but the operators of nearby parking lots cagily raised their price to $2 per vehicle to take advantage of the situation. The folks in charge of one local watering hole, the bar at the Hotel Atherton, were irked that the game had just taken 84 minutes to play. Its management had installed TV sets for their customers' pleasure. Furthermore, an enormous ballpark menu of soft drinks hot dogs and peanuts had been prepared for the viewers. The brevity of Game Three, however, left much of the food and beverages unsold.

Journalist Hugh Fullerton recalled that before the World Series began that Mel Ott had picked the Braves to win in an upset based on the strength of their bullpen. Fullerton noted, "Mel had a right smart idea, but he failed to allow for the fact that Billy Southworth's boys can't score enough runs to make their reliefers [sic] useful."[23]

Game Three Box Score
Boston Braves 0, Cleveland Indians 2
Game played on Friday, October 8, 1948, at Cleveland Stadium

Boston Braves	ab	r	h	rbi	Cleveland Indians	ab	r	h	rbi
Holmes rf	4	0	0	0	Mitchell lf	3	0	0	0
Dark ss	4	0	1	0	Doby cf	3	0	1	0
McCormick M. lf	4	0	1	0	Boudreau ss	3	0	0	0
Elliott 3b	3	0	1	0	Gordon 2b	4	0	0	0
McCormick F. 1b	3	0	1	0	Keltner 3b	3	1	0	0
Conatser cf	3	0	0	0	Judnich rf	3	0	0	0
Masi c	3	0	0	0	Robinson 1b	3	0	1	0
Stanky 2b	3	0	1	0	Hegan c	3	0	1	1
Bickford p	0	0	0	0	Bearden p	3	1	2	0
Voiselle p	1	0	0	0	**Totals**	28	2	5	1
Ryan ph	1	0	0	0					
Barrett p	0	0	0	0					
Totals	29	0	5	0					

```
Boston     0 0 0 0 0 0 0 0 --  0 5 1
Cleveland  0 0 1 1 0 0 0 0 x  -- 2 5 0
```

Boston Braves	IP	H	R	ER	BB	SO
Bickford L (0–1)	3.1	4	2	1	5	1
Voiselle	3.2	1	0	0	0	0
Barrett	1.0	0	0	0	0	0
Totals	8.0	5	2	1	5	1

Cleveland Indians	IP	H	R	ER	BB	SO
Bearden W (1–0)	9.0	5	0	0	0	4
Totals	9.0	5	0	0	0	4

E—Dark (3). **DP**—Boston 1, Cleveland 2. **2B**—Boston Dark (1, off Bearden), Cleveland Bearden (1, off Bickford). **SH**—Bickford (1, off Bearden). **Team LOB**—3. **Team**—7. **U**—Bill Stewart (NL), Bill Grieve (AL), George Barr (NL), Bill Summers (AL), Joe Paparella (AL), Babe Pinelli (NL). **T**—1:36. **A**—70,306.

— 13 —

Game Four Scuttlebutt

*Boudreau Cautious,
Gromek Disrespected,
Absent Offense*

Even with his club now leading the 1948 Fall Classic two games to one, Cleveland manager Lou Boudreau figured upcoming Game Four to be the critical contest of the entire World Series. "Tomorrow is the big one,"[1] he succinctly told the reporters. Boudreau opined that a victory by his club on Saturday would place the Braves in a discouraging 1–3 deficit and set up a Series-clincher for the Indians in Game Five in front of what was certain to be a huge and charged-up Sunday home crowd at Municipal Stadium.

Bookmakers seemed more confident of an eventual Cleveland triumph than Boudreau was. After the result of Game Three was official, odds-makers swiftly listed the Indians as 5:9 favorites to win the World Series.

An Associated Press story that appeared in newspapers on the morning of Game Four noted that, with the Indians now in the driver's seat, Boudreau had the luxury of starting Steve Gromek on the mound that Saturday. It unkindly declared the pitcher to be an "undistinguished righthander."[2] (Boudreau himself gave Gromek something akin to a lefthanded compliment, labeling him the team's "fourth-best pitcher."[3]) That same AP article painted Boston's Saturday starter in a better light. "Billy Southworth" it said, "has little choice than to come back with [Johnny] Sain, his big, tobacco-chewing righthander in the fourth game."[4]

Jack Hand, also writing for AP, opined that Johnny Sain was now the most important figure of the World Series for either team. "If Sain, a 1–0 conqueror of Bobby Feller in the opener, can stop the [AL] Tribe again, this [World Series] may turn out to be a seven-game marathon. If Sain fails," Hand continued, "Cleveland is expected to rack up the National Leaguers by Sunday night."[5]

Hand had some faith in Gromek's ability to win Game Four,

reminding his readers that the pitcher had been excellent in his last outing of the regular season—a shutout victory over the Philadelphia Athletics on September 19. If the unheralded Cleveland starter could earn a win in Game Four, Hand believed, "the Indians will be ready to swarm in for the kill. A well-rested Feller is due to pitch on Sunday."[6]

Grantland Rice's columns continued to lament the lack of offense the 1948 World Series had thus far provided through its first trio of contests. He wryly wrote, "It might be suggested that all three games have been extremely dull from an entertainment angle, unless you care for pop-ups and easy outfield flies."[7] Rice's colleague, Hugh Fullerton, also injected a bit of levity about the NL champions' lack of scoring punch. Fullerton kiddingly wrote, "The Braves aren't in a hitting slump, [manager Billy] Southworth insists, but they're in a heck of a runs-batted-in slump."[8]

Still, Rice held out hope that things would change for the benefit of those fans who preferred high-scoring ballgames over pitchers' duels. "It's about time for this Series to develop some action," Rice wrote. "It has been mostly slow motion so far. We need some class that isn't attached to pitching arms."[9]

— 14 —

World Series Game Four
Doby's Homer Does It

Date: Saturday, October 9, 1948
Site: Municipal Stadium, Cleveland, Ohio

> "[Steve] Gromek's stout heart and strong right arm combined to prove him the better man in a nerve-tearing pitching duel with Johnny Sain, who won the first Series game for Boston."—1948 World Series film commentary

The inclement weather had stopped, but a driving rain pelted most of Cleveland just after the completion of Friday's Game Three, leaving the outfield at Municipal Stadium in subpar condition for Game Four. There were several soggy spots in the grass that had the potential to cause trouble for both teams' outfielders. The infield, which had been protected by a tarpaulin all night, was in absolutely fine shape.

During his pregame commentary on Mutual radio, Jim Britt reported that Boston catcher Bill Salkeld had incurred a groin injury and would likely be out of action for the rest of the World Series. Phil Masi would be behind the plate for Boston in Game Four—and, presumably, for all the remaining games of the Fall Classic.

Britt also recounted an amusing anecdote from earlier in the day. A few hours before Game Four began, Boston relief pitcher Red Barrett stopped Britt in a hotel coffee shop to complain about a headline he had seen in a Cleveland newspaper that disparaged the Braves as "Humpty Dumpty hitters." The irked Barrett concurred that the Braves were indeed batting just .166 as a team—but the Indians were not faring too much better with their poor .167 average.

The Indians starter for Game Three was the well-rested Steve Gromek who hailed from a suburb of Detroit. The 28-year-old righthander, who pitched with a sidearm motion, had not started a game since September 19. His specialty pitch was a knuckle-curve. Early in his career, Gromek was thought to be nearly on par with Bob Feller in importance to the Indians' pitching staff. By 1948, however, he was something of a forgotten man. In limited use, Gromek recorded a solid 9–3 record and won a couple of key games when four clubs were still vying for the AL pennant. However, manager Lou Boudreau preferred to use the already overworked trio of Feller, Lemon and Bearden down the stretch rather than hand the ball to Gromek. Boudreau had basically lost confidence in him. It was in part because he considered Gromek to merely be a one-pitch pitcher. "I had a good rising fastball but not much of a curve," Gromek readily admitted. "Boudreau told me he'd fine me $250 if I ever threw a curve."[1] When the World Series was about to begin, Gromek quietly told his family he did not expect to see much action—perhaps none at all. Accordingly, when Boudreau told Gromek that he would be Cleveland's starting pitcher for Game Four, it came as a huge surprise to him. "I almost fell off my chair,"[2] he recalled years later.

Cleveland's starting lineup was the same as it had been for Game Three, but Billy Southworth—an apostle of platooning—inserted Marv Rickert and Earl Torgeson back into Boston's batting order for Game Four. Frank McCormick and Clint Conatser were relegated to the Braves' bench.

Tommy Holmes led off the top of the first inning for Boston against Gromek. He had had just one hit in 12 official at-bats thus far in the World Series. He lofted a fly ball to shallow right field that was routinely caught by Wally Judnich. Alvin Dark then popped out to sure-handed Cleveland catcher Jim Hegan. It was caught near the home team's on-deck circle. The next Brave to bat, Earl Torgeson, drove a Gromek pitch to left field that got by Larry Doby and rolled to the wall. Torgeson reached second base easily and intended to try for a triple, but he stumbled halfway to the bag. He had to hustle back to second base to avoid being put out. There he stayed as Bob Elliott fouled out to Hegan to end the top of the first.

Johnny Sain, pitching on just two days' rest, took the mound for the Braves. Cleveland's leadoff hitter, Dale Mitchell, greeted him rudely by slapping a base hit into center field. Larry Doby, batting a lofty .364 in the World Series thus far, batted next. He hit what Mel Allen described as a "vicious bounder"[3] toward first base. Boston first baseman Earl Torgeson made a splendid defensive play. He knocked the ball down, recovered in time to grab the ball and flip it to Johnny Sain who was covering the bag. Mitchell, however, moved to second base on the fielder's choice. Lou Boudreau followed Doby to the plate. He connected for another drive off Sain. The ball landed in fair territory in the right-field corner near the foul line. It was chased down by Tommy Holmes. Mitchell scored easily. Boudreau

14. World Series Game Four   141

reached second, but he was thrown out at third base trying to greedily extend his hit to a triple. The putout was 9-6-5: Holmes to shortstop Alvin Dark to third baseman Bob Elliott. "The play was very close at third,"[4] insisted Mel Allen. The umpire at third base who made the out call was the omnipresent Bill Stewart! (Years later Bob Feller humorously wrote that Stewart had completed something of an infield tour: He had made controversial calls against the Indians at all three bases!)

Boudreau, who was credited with an RBI double, threw a fit over being called out and had to be restrained by Cleveland coach Bill McKechnie. Two other umpires intervened in the dispute as "the stadium quivered with boos" according to the next day's *Pittsburgh Press*. (Newsreel footage of the play seems to indicate that Stewart's out call was correct.) When order was restored, Joe Gordon grounded out to shortstop Alvin Dark. The bottom of the first inning ended with the crowd still in an uproar over umpire Stewart's out call at third base and the hometown Indians leading Game Four by a 1-0 score.

To start the top of the second inning, Marv Rickert lined the first pitch he saw from Steve Gromek to Cleveland first baseman Eddie Robinson for a quick out. Center fielder Mike McCormick, who was batting .300 in the Series, was the next Boston batter. He lofted a fly ball to left field that required Dale Mitchell to make a running catch for the putout. Phil Masi followed with a similar at-bat. This time shortstop Lou Boudreau backpedaled into left field to make the catch. With the Braves going down in order, the score remained 1-0 in Cleveland's favor after one and a half innings of Game Four.

Johnny Sain faced Cleveland's third baseman Ken Keltner to start the home half of the second inning. Keltner smacked what Mel Allen called a "low, mean liner"[5] that temporarily handcuffed shortstop Alvin Dark. However, Dark coolly recovered in time to pick up the loose ball and throw out Keltner by a step at first base. Wally Judnich, who was hitless thus far in the World Series, batted next. He remained without a hit as he grounded to Boston first baseman Earl Torgeson, who efficiently made the unassisted putout. Cleveland's first baseman, Eddie Robinson, came up next and hit a 3-1 pitch into right field for a single. He stayed at first base as Jim Hegan popped out to shortstop Alvin Dark. The Boston shortstop, moving far to his right, snared it in fair territory, about 10 feet behind third base, to conclude the inning. The Indians still led by just a single run after two full innings.

Boston's second baseman, Eddie Stanky, led off the top of the third inning by depositing a base hit into left field. Pitcher Johnny Sain came to the plate with sacrificing on his mind. His bunt was a competent one. It was fielded by catcher Jim Hegan who made the throw to first base to retire the Boston pitcher. Sain's sacrifice advanced Stanky to second base. Tommy Holmes failed to move Stanky as he grounded out to Ken Keltner, Cleveland third baseman. Keltner smartly looked Stanky back to second base before making his throw to first baseman Eddie Robinson. Alvin Dark popped out to second baseman Joe Gordon in shallow right field for the final out of the top of the third inning. Despite having a baserunner, Boston again failed to score.

The home half of the third inning began with pitcher Steve Gromek batting. The lefthanded hitter, who had just six hits in 1948, struck out on five pitches. Dale Mitchell, another lefthanded hitter, followed Gromek. He made contact, grounding out on a slow roller that Boston third baseman Bob Elliott successfully fielded and fired to first base in time for the out. Larry Doby batted next for Cleveland. His at-bat was highly productive. Doby launched the first home run of the World Series by either team. It came off a high fastball delivered by Johnny Sain. It was a long, soaring drive that majestically cleared the 380-foot sign in right-center field. (Estimates put its distance traveled at about 410 feet.) Doby's solo homer doubled the Indians' advantage to 2–0. Moments after Doby had circled the bases, Lou Boudreau quietly made the third out of the inning by grounding out to Boston shortstop Alvin Dark.

The top of the fourth inning began with Boston's Earl Torgeson grounding out to Eddie Robinson at first base. Robinson booted the ball momentarily, but he recovered in time to corral it and make the necessary toss to Steve Gromek who was alertly covering the base. Bob Elliott then grounded to Ken Keltner at third base. Keltner's throw to Robinson nearly pulled him off the bag, but the first baseman's stretching ability helped him make the out as the crowd let out a worried gasp. Marv Rickert, batting lefthanded, came up next for the Braves. Rickert blooped a hit that dropped untouched into shallow center field. Mike McCormick then hit a ground ball to shortstop Lou Boudreau. He threw to Joe Gordon to force out Rickert at second base to conclude the inning. "The Braves are finding it impossible to bunch their hits together,"[6] noted Mel Allen, as Boston put yet another zero on the scoreboard despite once again having a base runner. The Braves had not scored a run since the first inning of Game Two—a streak of 21 consecutive frames. Cleveland still held its 2–0 advantage in Game Four after three and a half innings.

Joe Gordon hit a check-swing roller to Johnny Sain to start the home half of the fourth inning for Cleveland. Sain made the routine throw to first baseman Earl Torgeson for the easy out. Ken Keltner then popped out to Bob Elliott in foul territory near third base. Wally Judnich struck out swinging for the third out of the inning. It was Sain's second whiff of the ballgame. The 2–0 score remained unchanged. The first four innings of

14. World Series Game Four

Game Four had been contested at a rapid pace, taking just 40 minutes to complete.

To begin the top of the fifth inning, Boston's Phil Masi slapped a ground ball to shortstop Lou Boudreau on the first pitch he was offered by Steve Gromek. Boudreau fielded it easily and retired Masi with a strong throw to first baseman Eddie Robinson. Boudreau also retired the next Boston batter, second baseman Eddie Stanky, in precisely the same manner. Pitcher Johnny Sain kept the inning alive by slapping a single into left field. It was Boston's fourth hit of Game Four. Next up was Tommy Holmes. On the first pitch, Holmes hit a high pop-up to second baseman Joe Gordon who, moving to his left, caught the ball in foul territory near the right-field line. Holmes was now hitless in three at-bats in Game Four. Halfway through the game, Cleveland was still holding fast to its 2–0 lead.

Cleveland first baseman Eddie Robinson batted first in the home half of the fifth inning. He reached first base because of an embarrassing miscommunication between pitcher Johnny Sain and his first baseman Earl Torgeson. Sain backed away and let Torgeson field the ground ball near the mound—but no Brave thought to cover first base as the home crowd hooted at Boston's defensive confusion. "There's the first out-and-out mental lapse of the Series,"[7] declared Jim Britt to his Mutual radio listeners. As there was no error, Robinson was credited with a chintzy base hit on the play. Catcher Jim Hegan batted next, bunting Sain's first pitch. Third baseman Bob Elliott fielded the ball and made an on-time throw to first base. Robinson moved to second base on the successful sacrifice. Pitcher Steve Gromek got a warm round of applause from the Cleveland crowd when he strode to the plate. However, Gromek did nothing productive with his at-bat. He popped out in foul territory near third base, a ball that was easily caught by shortstop Alvin Dark. Robinson stayed put at second base. Dale Mitchell, the next Cleveland batter, softly grounded back to Sain. The Boston pitcher made the throw to Torgeson at first base to retire the Indians. The two-run advantage for the home team remained unchanged after five full innings.

Before the top of the sixth inning began, Cleveland third baseman Ken Keltner returned to his team's dugout to get a pair of sunglasses as shadows started to become a factor at Municipal Stadium. With Alvin Dark batting, third-base umpire Bill Stewart was booed loudly when he briefly stopped play to pick up a piece of paper that had blown onto the infield near him. Dark flied out to Larry Doby in center field for the first out of the frame. On a full count, Earl Torgeson drew a walk off Steve Gromek to become Boston's fifth baserunner of the game. Again, a Boston runner was wasted as Bob Elliott, the next Brave batter, grounded into a routine 6–4–3 double play. Cleveland still led Game Four by a 2–0 score.

Larry Doby, the batting hero thus far in the World Series, led off the bottom of the sixth inning against Johnny Sain. This time Doby grounded out to second baseman Eddie Stanky. Stanky's throw was slightly off the mark. Nevertheless, it was still caught comfortably by Earl Torgeson to complete the out. Lou Boudreau followed Doby by flying out to Mike McCormick in center field. Joe Gordon flied out to Marv Rickert in foul ground in left field as Cleveland failed to add to their 2–0 lead.

Marv Rickert led off the top of the seventh inning for the Braves. On a 2–0 pitch from Steve Gromek, Rickert homered to right field to cut the Indians' advantage in half to just 2–1. It was the first run for Boston after the Braves endured 23 consecutive scoreless innings, and it was their first home run of the World Series. The Cleveland bullpen was called into action and began to buzz with activity after Rickert's home run. The next Boston batter, Mike McCormick, connected for a base hit to left field as a worrisome murmur swept through the large, pro-Cleveland crowd. Braves catcher Phil Masi hurt his hand as he fouled a bunt down the third-base line. The also-injured Bill Salkeld prepared to bat in Masi's place, but Masi convinced manager Billy Southworth that he was healthy enough to continue. Masi got a polite round of applause for his overt display of pluck, but he quickly popped out to third baseman Ken Keltner to calm the ticket-holders for a moment. Eddie Stanky put another scare into the paying customers when he flied out to left field. The ball was struck well but it was caught 350 feet from home plate by Dale Mitchell for the second out of the inning. The next batter was pitcher Johnny Sain. He grounded out to his counterpart, Steve Gromek, for the inning's third out. The Braves had suddenly made a game of it, but they were still down by a run entering the bottom of the seventh inning of Game Four.

After the seventh inning stretch, Cleveland's Ken Keltner flied out to Marv Rickert who passed in front of Mike McCormick to make the grab in right-center field. Wally Judnich struck out looking for the second out of the frame. Eddie Robinson knocked a hard ground ball to Boston first baseman Earl Torgeson, who grabbed it with little difficulty and tossed the ball to pitcher Johnny Sain who was alertly covering first base. The putout ended the unproductive Cleveland seventh inning. The Indians still led Game Four, 2–1.

Before Steve Gromek threw his first pitch of the top of the eighth inning, Bob Kennedy entered the game defensively for Cleveland. He became the new right fielder as Wally Judnich was taken out of the game. (Kennedy was the superior fielder of the two.) Tommy Holmes flied out to center fielder Larry Doby, followed by Alvin Dark popping out to shortstop Lou Boudreau. With two outs, Earl Torgeson gave the Braves some hope by smacking a double to left field. It nicked third baseman Ken Keltner's glove which caused the ball to come to rest in shallow left field. A near catastrophe almost befell the Indians as there was some confusion on a subsequent infield pop-up by Boston third baseman Bob Elliott. With Torgeson running on contact, catcher Jim Hegan and third baseman Keltner nearly collided at the base of the pitcher's mound. It was an adventure, but Hegan made the catch—an awkward, juggling one. It undoubtedly prevented the tying run from scoring. Torgeson's double was wasted. Boston still trailed Game Four, 2–1.

The first out of the bottom of the eighth inning occurred when Jim Hegan popped out to Boston's second baseman Eddie Stanky. Steve Gromek got a rousing cheer as he stepped into the lefthanded batter's box. Gromek dribbled a fair ball in front of home plate. Catcher Phil Masi—still in the game despite playing with a painful hand—fielded it and made an accurate throw to first base for the second out. Dale Mitchell ended the inning by grounding out to Alvin Dark. The Boston shortstop made an excellent defensive play, snagging the ball behind second base and making an off-balance throw to first baseman Earl Torgeson. Johnny Sain had only permitted one Cleveland hit in his last five and a third innings of work to keep his club very much in Game Four.

Boston was down by a run as they batted in the top of the ninth inning. Marv Rickert was called out on strikes on a 2–2 fastball. Remarkably it was Gromek's first strikeout of the game. (This fact startled both Jim Britt and Mel Allen who each double-checked their individual scorecards to make sure the stat was correct. It was.) Mike McCormick came up next for Boston. The second pitch McCormick saw from Gromek sent him sprawling. "He has a good deal of Cleveland Municipal Stadium all over the back of him,"[8] joked Britt. McCormick also struck out looking for out number two. Down to his last out, Boston manager Billy Southworth went to his bench. Bill Salkeld batted for Phil Masi in Boston's last gasp in Game Four. On a full count, Salkeld flied out to right field. Bob Kennedy hardly needed to move to make the catch that sealed the Indians' hard-fought 2–1 victory in Game Four, giving them a commanding 3–1 lead in the 1948 World Series. A marching band merrily struck up two college fight songs, "Across the Field" followed by the "Notre Dame Victory March," to salute the winning AL Tribe players as they happily departed the diamond and headed into their clubhouse.

Game Four was another swift-moving contest, taking just 91 minutes to play. It was just six minutes longer than the shortest World Series game on record. (That one occurred 40 years previously, in the 1908 Fall Classic between the Detroit Tigers and Chicago Cubs.) Along with providing fans with the first two home runs of the World Series, Game Four also featured flawless fielding. It was the first errorless game between the Braves and the Indians.

The official attendance figure for Game Four was not available until long after the game ended. At various times during their radio broadcast, Mel Allen and Jim Britt both said they expected it would surpass 80,000. They were correct. When the attendance was finally announced, it was a new World Series record: 81,897. It eclipsed the old high-water mark by more than 7,000 that had been set on October 5, 1947, at Yankee Stadium. There was every expectation that a new attendance record would be set at Game Five the next day. Regardless of that game's outcome, it definitely would be the last MLB contest played in Cleveland in 1948.

The Indians' bullpen was not getting a lot of exposure in the World Series. In fact, it was getting none at all. Game Four marked the fourth time that Cleveland's starting pitcher recorded a complete game. In going the distance, Gromek threw just 98 pitches to get the necessary 27 outs. According to an Associated Press report, Gromek's great day on the mound was attributed to his "sneaking a weird assortment of curves and screwballs past the bewildered Bostons."[9] Gromek admitted to reporters that he had felt nervous early in the game but was able to quickly settle down. Not surprisingly, he rated his Game Four victory as the greatest thrill in his entire baseball career.

Boston's Johnny Sain was widely praised for his efforts in a game he lost. Chester L. Smith of the *Pittsburgh Press* sympathetically wrote the next day, "Sain was all Billy Southworth had left to checkmate the buoyant Indians, and although he gave it a magnificent try, it wasn't enough."

Cleveland's Lou Boudreau got high praise from a former manager of the club: Tris Speaker. Prior to 1948, Speaker was the last man to manage a pennant winner in that city. Speaker thought Boudreau was the best shortstop he had ever seen—even better than Honus Wagner. "I never saw Wagner play until the twilight of his career," Speaker admitted. "But from what those who saw him tell me, he must have been a wonder. However, I doubt whether he could field any better than Boudreau."[10]

Speaker, a Hall of Famer, however, politely declined to judge how his 1920 Indians would rate against their 1948 counterparts. "How can you compare teams of different generations?" he asked in rhetorical fashion. "The times were different. The ball was different. Even the style of play differed in those days." Speaker then felt obligated to add, "But we sure had a great ball club."[11]

While Lou Boudreau was receiving verbal bouquets from many admirers, he was getting quite a few raspberries from the Braves who thought his complaints about being tagged out at third base in the bottom of the first inning were ridiculous. Third baseman Bob Elliot bluntly told reporters, "Sure, he was out. I got a perfect throw from Al Dark and I tagged him on the left shoe as he slid in. I don't know what he was squawking about. He squawks on every play anyway."[12] When asked for his opinion of that play, Boston manager Billy Southworth politely declined, diplomatically stating he had less than an ideal view of third base from where he was sitting in the visitors' dugout.

After Game Four concluded, a bit of American social history unexpectedly occurred: A smiling Steve Gromek was photographed in the Indians' clubhouse happily embracing Larry Doby, the man whose home run had provided him with the necessary margin of victory. The picture was printed in hundreds of newspapers the next day. (It was prominently featured on the front page of the *Baltimore Afro-American,* a publication overwhelmingly focused on black social issues, and on the front page of the *Boston Globe*.) The photo seems to be an utterly innocuous image today, but it was groundbreaking in 1948 as it showed a white athlete showing unrestrained happiness over the achievement of a black teammate—and vice versa. Decades later, long after both Doby and Gromek had died, a 2016 retrospective article in the *New York Times* by Richard Sandomir described the photograph as "a stirring image of baseball's emerging integration."[13]

In an interview years later with the *Cleveland Plain Dealer,* Gromek noted that the moment was truly a spontaneous one. "I was being interviewed in front of my locker, and somebody asked Larry to come over. He put his arm around me and squeezed me so hard I thought he was going to break my ribs. We were both so happy."

"The picture was more rewarding and happy [sic] for me than actually hitting that home run," Doby would relate to his biographer. "It was such a scuffle for me until that picture. The picture finally showed a moment of a man showing his feelings for me. I think enlightenment can come from such a picture."[14] A little more than a year earlier, in 1947, when Veeck had signed Doby to an AL contract not long after Jackie Robinson began playing with the Brooklyn Dodgers, the Indians received more than 20,000 negative letters regarding the club's acquisition of Doby—solely because of his pigmentation. Veeck claimed to have patiently answered every one of them that contained a return address. In 1998, during his Hall of Fame induction speech, Doby spoke of what the famous photo had captured. "That was a feeling from within, the human side of two people, one black and one white," Doby noted. "That made up for everything I went through. I would always relate back to that whenever I was insulted or rejected from hotels. I'd always think about that picture. It would take away all the negatives."

Gromek received mixed reactions about the photograph. According to his SABR biography, when Gromek returned home to Hamtramck, Michigan, once the 1948 season had ended, he strolled into a favorite neighborhood bar to buy a drink. He quickly recognized a few familiar faces. "I saw a guy I had known for more than ten years, a guy I had played ball with," Gromek recalled. "I said hello—and he ignored me."

The bartender quickly deduced the reason for the man's decidedly cold reaction to the town's baseball star. "Oh, Christ!" he blurted out with exasperation. "It's that picture you took with Larry Doby."

The man who had snubbed Gromek finally spoke up. "Jesus, you could have just shaken his hand!" But another old friend of Gromek's interjected on his behalf and sided with the Cleveland pitcher. He commented, "If I were in Steve's shoes, and Doby did what he did, I would have kissed him."[15]

A photograph in the October 10 edition of the *Tuscaloosa News* showed a local hardware store proprietor listening to the World Series broadcast from his place of business. There was nothing especially unusual about this common October sight—except that the proprietor was Joe Sewell who had played for the 1920 Cleveland Indians. He was predicting a Fall Classic victory for his former team. "The Indians will win it. They've got the best club," the 50-year-old confidently told a reporter, openly admitting his opinion was biased.

Sewell only had about a month's experience in the majors when he played in the 1920 World Series. He had been elevated to the Indians to replace second baseman Ray Chapman who had been infamously killed in an August 16 game at the Polo Grounds by a wild pitch hurled by Carl Mays of the New York Yankees. Sewell turned 22 years old during that World Series when his club played the NL champs from Brooklyn. He celebrated that personal milestone on October 9 by hitting a double and a single that afternoon.

Sewell recalled the different World Series format in 1920. "In those days you had to win five out of nine—and we won four straight [games] in Cleveland after dropping two out of three in Brooklyn," he accurately noted. Something else had stuck in his memory for 28 years: "You know, a funny thing happened in that Series: Before [Game Six] at Cleveland, our pitcher, Johnny Mails, took a look at the Dodgers in batting practice and said to us, 'Get me one run and I'll win the game.' We did and we won, 1–0. I wonder if Johnny Sain said that the other day."[16]

Just before Game Four, syndicated columnist Red Smith paid a visit to one of Cleveland's unique ballpark amenities just beneath the right-field grandstand: a babysitting service. Patrons who come to Municipal Stadium with children aged two to six have the option of leaving them in the capable hands of guardians such as Elizabeth Fithian, one of the three

14. World Series Game Four

women in charge of "Bill Veeck's moppet preserve." Though quite diligent in her caregiving role, Fithian told Smith she would rather be among the hometown supporters watching the game. "All my life I've rooted for the Indians," she noted, "worried about them and prayed for them to win a pennant." Pointing to the large gathering of children, Fithian lamented, "Now that they're in a World Series, this is what I see." Smith explained that the children are registered by a parent, tagged and numbered "just like hats, umbrellas, and overshoes" and assigned to one of three pens depending on their ages. The kiddies have monkey bars, slides, sandboxes and an abundance of toys for their amusement. Cots are provided for napping wee ones, but Smith only saw two being utilized. Each parent is given a claim check to retrieve his/her youngster from "the juvenile isolation ward" at game's end. Fithian reported that the Indians' babysitting service had cared for about 5,000 "small, squirming bundles of joy" in 1948—and only three parents had mislaid their claim checks. Smith amusingly commented that he saw "no fighting, no such raffish behavior as Lou Boudreau [displayed] when Bill Stewart called him out at third base."[17]

The surging baseball interest in Ohio was having an unforeseen effect on college football. A longtime ban on fans using portable radios at Ohio State's football stadium was suspended for the Buckeyes' Big Nine game versus the Iowa Hawkeyes in Columbus on October 9. Apparently, many gridiron fans wished to watch the football game while simultaneously listening to Game Four of the World Series. Public pressure—and the unusual confluence of two major sporting events in Ohio—forced Ohio Stadium's rules-makers to temporarily waive the restriction for this one occasion. The spectators with radios tuned in to the Indians' victory probably had a more enjoyable afternoon than those who only watched football. Iowa defeated eleventh-ranked OSU in one of many NCAA pigskin upsets that Saturday, 14–7, handing the Buckeyes their first loss of the 1948 season.

Game Four Box Score
Boston Braves 1, Cleveland Indians 2
Game played on Saturday, October 9, 1948, at Cleveland Stadium

Boston Braves	ab	r	h	rbi	Cleveland Indians	ab	r	h	rbi
Holmes rf	4	0	0	0	Mitchell lf	4	1	1	0
Dark ss	4	0	0	0	Doby cf	3	1	1	1
Torgeson 1b	3	0	2	0	Boudreau ss	3	0	1	1
Elliott 3b	4	0	0	0	Gordon 2b	3	0	0	0
Rickert lf	4	1	2	1	Keltner 3b	3	0	0	0
McCormick cf	4	0	1	0	Judnich rf	3	0	0	0
Masi c	3	0	0	0	Kennedy rf	0	0	0	0

Boston Braves	ab	r	h	rbi	Cleveland Indians	ab	r	h	rbi
Salkeld ph	1	0	0	0	Robinson 1b	3	0	2	0
Stanky 2b	3	0	1	0	Hegan c	2	0	0	0
Sain p	2	0	1	0	Gromek p	3	0	0	0
Totals	32	1	7	1	Totals	27	2	5	2

Boston	0	0	0	0	0	0	1	0	0	--	1	7	0
Cleveland	1	0	1	0	0	0	0	0	x	--	2	5	0

Boston Braves	IP	H	R	ER	BB	SO
Sain L (1–1)	8.0	5	2	2	0	3
Totals	8.0	5	2	2	0	3

Cleveland Indians	IP	H	R	ER	BB	SO
Gromek W (1–0)	9.0	7	1	1	1	2
Totals	9.0	7	1	1	1	2

E—None. **DP**—Cleveland 1. **2B**—Boston Torgeson 2 (2, off Gromek 2), Cleveland Boudreau (2, off Sain). **HR**—Boston Rickert (1,7th inning off Gromek 0 on, 0 out), Cleveland Doby (1, 3rd inning off Sain 0 on, 2 out). **SH**—Sain (1, off Gromek); Hegan (1, off Sain). **Team LOB**—6. **Team**—2. **U**—Bill Grieve (AL), George Barr (NL), Bill Summers (AL), Bill Stewart (NL), Joe Paparella (AL), Babe Pinelli (NL). **T**—1:31. **A**—81,897.

— 15 —

Game Five Scuttlebutt
Boudreau Still Cautious, Rickert Gets No Share

After posting their third consecutive loss in Game Four, the Boston Braves were undeniably in dire straits. They were not getting much love from newspaper correspondents who were using unflattering adjectives, such as "anemic," "hapless," and "far from murderous" to describe the NL champions' disappointing offense that again failed to muster much of a threat to the home team.

Chester L. Smith, the sports editor of the *Pittsburgh Press*, believed a Series-clinching Cleveland victory at Municipal Stadium in Game Five seemed almost inevitable for the AL pennant winners. Many fellow baseball writers readily agreed. The most prominent dissenter was Lou Boudreau. Tactfully, he was not inclined to specifically say his club had the Fall Classic in the proverbial bag—and would not do so until a fourth win was secured.

"Yes, I know we're out in front and need only one game," Boudreau said, "but I won't admit we're in the driver's seat yet."[1] The Cleveland player-manager did concede, however, that his charges were in a highly favorable position heading into Sunday afternoon's Game Five. "I will say my pitching aces are in great shape and ready to go. We will go with Feller."[2]

In a bit of a surprise move, Boston manager Billy Southworth announced that Nelson Potter would toe the rubber for the visitors in what might be the final MLB game of the exciting 1948 season. Hy Hurwitz of the *Boston Globe* wrote that Potter had "saved their scalps" during the regular season and would "attempt to prevent a Boston Braves' massacre on the shores of Lake Erie"[3] on Sunday afternoon.

The oddsmakers were more decisive in facing reality than the modest Cleveland pilot. The Indians were now listed as strong 7:20 favorites to win

Game Five and wrap up the 1948 World Series. (One had to wager $20 on Cleveland to win just $7.) Conversely, any bettors who wanted to risk their cash on the Braves could expect enticing 11:5 odds from their bookmakers. Given the circumstances, the latter option was widely deemed to be a foolish investment.

The unquestioned feel-good story of the 1948 World Series was Marv Rickert's fine play in the Boston outfield as a replacement for the injured Jeff Heath. He had done well at the plate for the Braves thus far (having accounted for the lone Boston run in Game Four with a solo homer). Rickert had been flawless in the Boston outfield, too. Accordingly, Rickert's general excellence in the Fall Classic made the startling and sour news of his not being entitled to a World Series share seem grossly unfair.

The attention-grabbing story broke on October 9: The Braves, having clinched the NL pennant well before the regular season had concluded, had already decided upon how their World Series money would be split and who would receive shares. The appropriate paperwork was duly submitted to the Commissioner Chandler's office. That happened before minor-leaguer Rickert got the welcome news to hastily join the Braves late in the 1948 campaign to take Heath's spot in Boston's outfield. Apparently, no amendments in the financial arrangements could be made to account for Rickert's situation. It was really nobody's fault, but it appeared that Rickert might be playing—and performing quite well—in the 1948 World Series *pro bono*.

Rickert himself laughed at the matter when it became public

Overseeing the 1948 World Series was Albert ("Happy") Chandler. He was MLB's Commissioner from 1945 to July 1951. Chandler served a term as Kentucky's governor before he was baseball's top man—and another term after he left the game. Chandler's greatest contribution to MLB was permitting its racial integration (Library of Congress).

knowledge. He outwardly seemed unconcerned by it all. Baseball fans overwhelmingly did not, however. Regardless of one's rooting allegiance, the vast majority of the sports fanciers across the continent strongly believed that Boston's outstanding late substitute deserved at least a portion of a World Series share for his fine postseason contributions. It was hoped that Happy Chandler would use the authority of his position within MLB to rectify the matter so Rickert could head back to his Tacoma, Washington, home with something a bit more tangible for his magnificent efforts beyond merely the gratitude of his teammates, manager, and the Braves' front office.

— 16 —

World Series Game Five
Brave Resistance

Date: Sunday, October 10, 1948
Site: Municipal Stadium, Cleveland, Ohio

> "In this 1948 World Series, in this tribal warfare, it appears that the Clevelands have the Indian sign on their embattled brethren, the Braves. With it, most experts figure they have a bright chance of smoking the peace pipe along about two hours from now because that's all there will be left to do if the Clevelands continue to keep the Bostons penned up on the reservation, so to speak."[1]—Mel Allen's opening remarks on Mutual radio prior to Game Five

> "The series of silent bats is breaking into a rash of booming bats as the big sticks begin to speak."—Official MLB 1948 World Series film's description of Game Five

Much like the previous four games of the 1948 World Series, inclement weather threatened to disrupt Game Five. Thankfully, as was becoming the routine, it once again failed to appear. As Cleveland fans gathered in record numbers at Municipal Stadium in anticipation of their first World Series title in 28 years, the overcast skies slowly but steadily gave way to afternoon sunshine.

On the Mutual radio broadcast, Mel Allen spent the majority of his pregame commentary pointing out how tightly the World Series had been contested over the first four games—if one examined the raw statistics alone. Allen noted that the Braves and Indians were even or nearly even in a great many categories although the Braves were teetering on the verge of elimination. For example, Allen pointed out that both teams had so far managed to connect for 22 hits apiece. Both teams had received seven

16. World Series Game Five

walks. Both teams had struck out 13 times. Both teams also had the same amounts of doubles (four) and home runs (one).

Boston manager Billy Southworth received full marks for bravado after Game Four for not only announcing his Game Five starting pitcher (Nels Potter), but his Game Six starter as well (Bill Voiselle). He fully expected that a return trip to Braves Field would be a requirement.

As was becoming the custom in Cleveland, Bill Stewart was severely booed when he was announced as the second-base umpire. (While Mel Allen insisted the loud catcalls were "good-natured," one scribe referred to the arbiter as "Cleveland's favorite villain.") The four "main" umpires had completed their rotation of the bases after the first four Series games and, for Game Five, were back at the same positions where they had begun their postseason duties in Game One on October 6. Joe Paparella and Babe Pinelli remained stationed along the outfield lines.

Bill Salkeld was in the Game Five lineup for Boston as the Braves catcher, despite earlier reports that a groin injury would surely keep him out of the remainder of the World Series. He had replaced Phil Masi partway through Game Four. Masi was battling blistered hands. Southworth apparently deemed Salkeld to be the most able of his two wounded backstops.

Game Five was delayed for a bizarre reason: In a scenario that could only happen in Cleveland, a duck, released by a clown during the pregame festivities, was steadfastly refusing to leave the field and had amusingly positioned itself on the pitcher's mound. A cagy ballpark security man was called into action. He finally chased the fowl to an area of the infield where a shortstop typically stands and roughly captured it by the neck.

Bob Feller, trying to earn an elusive World Series victory, was making his second start of the Fall Classic, having been a hard-luck 1–0 loser in Game One. He got off to a shaky start in Game Five as Tommy Holmes led off the contest with a single. Alvin Dark came up next and reached base on an infield hit that just struck his bat handle and dribbled slowly toward third base. Cleveland third baseman Ken Keltner had no chance to throw out Dark, so he wisely held onto the ball. After just two batters had faced Feller, Lou Boudreau sensed that his starter was in for a long game. Accordingly, the Cleveland manager ordered action in the Indians' bullpen. Earl Torgeson came up next and hit a fly ball to right fielder Wally Judnich. He caught it about 325 feet from home plate. The two Boston baserunners could not advance on the out. Bob Elliott was the next Brave hitter. He too smashed a drive to right field—but he fared better. It was an opposite-field home run estimated to have travelled 385 feet. The Braves were off to a dream start in Game Five, establishing a quick 3–0 lead. Elliott now had four RBIs in the World Series, the most of any player on either team.

As the smiling Braves celebrated and slapped Elliott on the back in their dugout, Feller regained his poise and methodically struck out Marv Rickert. Catcher Bill Salkeld was the next Boston hitter. He hit a long fly ball to center field that was caught by Larry Doby for the third out of a highly productive inning for the visitors. Remarkably, the Braves' three runs in the top of the first equaled their output for the first four games of the 1948 World Series.

Cleveland's Dale Mitchell, batting a poor .125, led off the bottom of the first inning. Nelson (Nels) Potter of Mount Morris, Illinois, was the Boston pitcher. Apart from his relief work in this World Series, Potter had previous Fall Classic experience, having been on the roster of the 1944 Browns in the one and only all–St. Louis World Series. On Potter's second pitch, Mitchell whittled away at the Boston lead by promptly belting a home run into the throng of right-field standees. The indications were it was not likely going to be a pitchers' duel on this afternoon.

When the cheers for Mitchell's home run began to subside, Larry Doby grounded out sharply to second baseman Eddie Stanky. Lou Boudreau received a huge cheer when he came to bat. He hit the ball directly back to the mound. Potter got his glove on the ball, but it rolled beyond his grasp. By the time Eddie Stanky picked it up, Boudreau was safe at first base with one out. Joe Gordon drew a walk and the crowd grew noticeably louder. Third baseman Ken Keltner, who had just one hit in 14 at-bats in the Series, followed Gordon. He hit a high foul fly that was caught about 20 feet from home plate by catcher Bill Salkeld. Wally Judnich's futility at the plate continued as he whacked a ground ball directly at Boston first baseman Earl Torgeson. The bespectacled Torgeson easily made the unassisted putout at the bag. Judnich was still looking for his first hit of the World Series. After one full inning, Boston held a 3–1 lead.

Mike McCormick, batting a respectable .286 in the Series, led off the top of the second for Boston. His ground ball to third baseman Ken Keltner resulted in an error. It was just the second Cleveland miscue of the entire World Series. McCormick reached first base safely. Eddie Stanky batted next for the Braves. He hit the ball solidly, but it was caught without much difficulty by center fielder Larry Doby. Nels Potter, an excellent hitter for a pitcher, was the next Brave to face Bob Feller. He struck out. (On the radio, Jim Britt commented on the elongated and deliberate manner in which plate umpire George Barr tended to call strikes.) Catcher Jim Hegan squeezed the foul tip for the out. Tommy Holmes batted for the second time in Game Five. Holmes dribbled a ground ball to Cleveland first

16. World Series Game Five   157

baseman Eddie Robinson who made the putout himself. The Braves did not add to their 3–1 lead.

Robinson led off the bottom of the second inning for Cleveland. On a full count, Robinson flied out to Boston center fielder Mike McCormick. Jim Hegan batted next for the Indians. He hit a ground ball to Bob Elliott at third base who threw accurately to Earl Torgeson for the second out of the inning. Bob Feller grounded out to shortstop Alvin Dark as Cleveland went down in order in the frame. The score remained unchanged.

Alvin Dark, who was batting just .176 (3-for-17) in the World Series, made contact with the first Bob Feller pitch he saw and grounded out to third baseman Ken Keltner. Earl Torgeson, batting .400 in the Series, followed Dark to the plate. Torgeson knocked a hard grounder to Cleveland first baseman Eddie Robinson who juggled the ball briefly but still beat Torgeson to the bag by a comfortable margin. With two out, Bob Elliott increased the visitors' lead to 4–1 by smacking his second home run of the game. This one flew down the left-field line. Feller clearly did not have his overwhelming arsenal in Game Five. Marv Rickert grounded to Eddie Robinson who flipped the ball to Feller covering the bag for the third out of the inning. Heading into the home half of the third inning, the Braves surprisingly held a three-run lead. All four of Boston's runs had been driven in by Bob Elliott homers.

Dale Mitchell led off the bottom of the third inning by hitting a sinking line drive to Marv Rickert in left field that was caught but not without a few thrills. Rickert misjudged the ball slightly. He dropped to both knees and ungracefully fell on his face after making the grab. Nevertheless, it was a legal catch for the first out. Larry Doby, batting next, hit a ground ball to Earl Torgeson about 30 feet from first base. Torgeson tossed the ball to Nels Potter who beat Doby in a competitive footrace to the bag. Potter had set down seven consecutive Indians. Lou Boudreau was the next Indian batter. He grounded out to Bob Elliott at third base. Elliott's throw was a little bit off the mark, but Torgeson stretched himself sufficiently to make the catch to retire Cleveland's player-manager for the final out of the inning. With a third of the game entered into the books, Cleveland was still trailing the Braves, 4–1.

The top of the fourth inning started with Boston's Bill Salkeld batting against Bob Feller. Lou Boudreau had ageless Satchel Paige warming up on the sidelines in case Feller faltered further. Salkeld popped out to Joe Gordon at second base. Gordon made the catch on the grass in shallow right field. Jim Britt noted to his Mutual radio listeners that Gordon was covering plenty of ground on Brave popups, sometimes even drifting as far away as left field to make catches. Mike McCormick flied out to Dale Mitchell in left field for the second out of the frame. Eddie Stanky drew a walk—his specialty—off Feller to keep the inning alive. (Britt mentioned that Stanky was one of the few players in the Series who wore a protective liner inside his cap while batting.) Pitcher Nels Potter then knocked a base hit into right field between Gordon and first baseman Eddie Robinson. "Mr. Potter is living up to his press notices as a hitter,"[2] Britt commented. The two Brave baserunners were stranded, however, as Tommy Holmes too flied out to left fielder Mitchell. Heading to the home half of the fourth inning, Boston, fighting to stay alive in the World Series, retained its 4–1 lead.

Second baseman Joe Gordon was the first Cleveland batter to face Nels Potter in the home half of the fourth inning. He launched a line drive into left field for a base hit. (Gordon, playing in his sixth World Series, had now accrued 24 hits in Fall Classic games.) Ken Keltner was the next man up for the Indians. He was struggling with the bat, having had just one hit in 15 at-bats thus far in the series. He drew a base on balls from Potter, which did not improve or harm his batting average, but it did get him stationed on first base. Wally Judnich, still searching for his first Series hit, caught a lucky break when his broken-bat blooper fell into left-center field for an RBI single. Gordon scored on the chintzy hit and Kelter moved up to third base. The Braves lead had been cut to 4–2—and the Indians were mounting a rally.

Eddie Robinson batted next. He too connected for a looper that initially looked promising, but Boston shortstop Alvin Dark skillfully moved backwards on the play and made the catch in shallow left field for the first out of the inning. Jim Hegan, Cleveland's catcher, batted next and smashed a home run over the left-field fence. Cleveland had suddenly vaulted into a 5–4 lead as the overflow crowd roared its approval. Perhaps the baseball season would end on this afternoon after all. Hegan's blast meant that Nels Potter's day was done. The Boston starter was removed from the mound by manager Billy Southworth. Potter was replaced by Warren Spahn, the losing pitcher in Game Two, who was making an unusual relief pitching appearance. (He had made just one during the entire 1948 regular season.) His mound opponent, Bob Feller, was the first Indian he faced. Feller got to a full count, but he bounced the next pitch back to Spahn. The Boston lefthander accurately tossed the ball to first baseman Earl Torgeson for the second out. Dale Mitchell strode to the plate next and drew a base on balls. Larry Doby was the eighth man to bat for Cleveland in the bottom of the fourth. He struck out to end the productive frame for the home team. Doby was the first Indian batter to whiff in the game. For the first time in Game Five, Cleveland held a lead. They were 15 outs away from winning the 1948 World Series.

Shortstop Alvin Dark was the first Boston batter to face Bob Feller in the top of the fifth inning. So far, Dark had connected for three hits in

16. World Series Game Five

Cleveland catcher Jim Hegan was one of the AL's most reliable backstops in 1948. He batted just .248, but he was solid defensively. Hegan made just seven errors all season as he compiled a .990 fielding percentage (courtesy Boston Public Library, Leslie Jones Collection).

18 official at-bats in the World Series, giving him a disappointing batting average of .167. It did not improve as Dark flied out on a 2-0 pitch to center fielder Larry Doby. First baseman Earl Torgeson, who, by comparison, was batting a terrific .364 in the Series, came up next. He lofted a long fly ball to Dale Mitchell in left field. It was caught for the second out. (In his radio commentary, Jim Britt noted it likely would have been a home run in the tighter confines of Braves Field.)

Despite wearing a Boston uniform, Bob Elliott received a polite round of applause from the Cleveland crowd for his batting heroics when he came to the plate after Torgeson with two men out. (In the Mutual broadcast booth, Britt made the faux pas of wondering aloud if Elliott might be approaching a record for World Series home runs in a single game. Mel Allen, a New York Yankee through and through, said looking it up was unnecessary as it was common knowledge that Babe Ruth had twice hit three home runs in a Fall Classic game—and no one else had done it even once. Britt, likely chagrined, made no further comment on the subject.

Elliott had, however, equaled the record of two homers by an NL batter in a single World Series game. It had only been accomplished once before, by Benny Kauff of the New York Giants, in the fourth game of the 1917 Fall Classic. One of Kauff's clouts was an inside-the-park homer.) Elliott did not connect for round-tripper number three to equal the late Bambino who had died of cancer less than two months earlier. Feller struck him out on a curveball. It was Feller's third strikeout of Game Five. Cleveland still held onto the lead, 5–4, and were now 12 outs away from wrapping up the World Series with a five-game victory.

Lou Boudreau grounded out to Boston third baseman Bob Elliott to start the home half of the fifth inning. Joe Gordon batted next against the fast-operating Warren Spahn. The Cleveland second baseman lined out to the Boston third baseman as Elliott reacted quickly to make an excellent reflex catch. Ken Keltner was the third batter of the inning for the AL Tribe. He became the third out after hitting a drive to deep left-center field that Mike McCormick hauled in without any noticeable difficulty. The score was unchanged. Cleveland was still up, 5–4, after five complete innings

Left fielder Marv Rickert led off for the NL champions to start the top of the sixth inning. Rickert struck out, but the ball popped out of Jim Hegan's mitt, requiring the Cleveland backstop to throw to first baseman Eddie Robinson to formally complete the putout. Catcher Bill Salkeld batted next for Boston. He hardly looked the part of someone who was injured as he drove a long blast to right field where Wally Judnich slipped in his pursuit of the ball. The misstep made no difference. The ball descended well beyond the barrier and deep into the standees. The home run—the fifth of the game—tied matters at 5–5. (It was an unexpected display of power from Salkeld who batted .242 with just eight home runs in the regular season.) With the crowd still buzzing about Feller's subpar outing, Mike McCormick hit a sharp ground ball. Cleveland shortstop Lou Boudreau had to make a fine defensive play to stop it from getting by him. Boudreau then made an accurate throw to first baseman Eddie Robinson for the second out of the inning. "That was a very neat play by the Indians player-manager,"[3] Mel Allen commented on Mutual radio. The cheering crowd concurred. Eddie Stanky drew a four-pitch walk off Feller. It was the Cleveland hurler's second base on balls; both had been issued to the elusive Stanky. Pitcher Warren Spahn came to bat next for Boston. During his plate appearance, the official announcement of the attendance at Municipal Stadium for Game Five was made to press row: 86,288. Not long afterward, when the crowd heard the figure was a new MLB record for a single game, the paying customers enthusiastically applauded themselves. Spahn struck out to end the inning, but not before the Braves had

16. World Series Game Five

leveled the score in the most compelling, see-saw game thus far in the 1948 World Series.

Cleveland's right fielder, Wally Judnich, led off against Warren Spahn in the bottom of the sixth inning. He popped out to first baseman Earl Torgeson who was almost standing on the bag when he made the catch. Next, Eddie Robinson hit a hot grounder to Boston second baseman Eddie Stanky who fielded it coolly and threw to Torgeson at first base for the second out of the frame. Jim Hegan, who had driven in three of the home team's runs in Game Five, was the next Indian to face Spahn. He struck out swinging. It was truly anyone's ballgame as the score was still deadlocked, 5–5, after six full innings.

Tommy Holmes led off the top of the fateful seventh inning against Bob Feller. He smacked a solid single into left-center field. It was the Braves' seventh hit of the ballgame. Alvin Dark came to the plate to bunt. He laid one down the first base line. It was fielded by first baseman Eddie Robinson who threw the ball to second baseman Joe Gordon who was alertly covering the bag. The sacrifice advanced Holmes to second base, as intended. With one out, Boston first baseman Earl Torgeson became a hero for the visitors, driving a base hit into center field that scored Holmes from second base. Boston regained the lead, 6–5.

That was the end of the line for the famed Cleveland starter. "Feller is the picture of dejection as he walks to the dugout,"[4] Mel Allen noted, as Feller exited the field realizing he had no chance to be the winning pitcher in Give Five. One scribe, who was apparently still steamed at Feller over his opting out of the All-Star Game in July, penned, "[Holmes' single] decided the fate of Feller who went to the showers—his cocky, arrogant strut giving way to the despondent, slouching gait of a man who had seen his chance to win a World Series game gone for at least another year."[5]

That was not an isolated opinion. Player-turned-writer Moe Berg recalled that loud hooting and jeering were surprisingly widespread in the crowded Municipal Stadium press box as Feller stepped from the pitcher's mound and headed toward the Cleveland clubhouse and its showers.

Ed Klieman, a righthander from Norwood, Ohio, replaced Feller on the mound for the reeling Indians. He answered to the nickname Spec because he wore eyeglasses. Spec did not fare well as Feller's replacement. He worked to only three Boston batters. Klieman walked Bob Elliott, advancing Torgeson to second base. Marv Rickert batted next. He singled into center field, scoring Torgeson, giving the Braves a 7–5 advantage. When Larry Doby threw the ball to third base in an attempt to nail Torgeson, the ball caromed off the sliding Boston first baseman and into the Cleveland dugout. By rule, Torgeson was awarded home and Rickert moved up to third base. Doby was given a tough error on the play, but it was the correct ruling. Boston now led by three runs. After Klieman walked Bill Salkeld, the ineffective pitcher was lifted from the game, having retired none of the three Boston batsmen he had faced.

A righthanded submarine-style pitcher, Russ Christopher, became the third Cleveland hurler of the seventh inning to try to stem the Braves' rally. He fared no better than Klieman. Mike McCormick hit a line drive just beyond the reach of first baseman Eddie Robinson. It dropped into right field, scoring Rickert. Salkeld advanced to third base as Boston's lead climbed to 9–5. Good fortune was shining on Eddie Stanky, the next Boston batter. On a hit-and-run play, Stanky blooped a single into right field after literally throwing his bat at the ball—and connecting. Salkeld scored the Braves' tenth run of Game Five while McCormick moved to third easily because he had been running on the pitch. This was the end of Russ Christopher's day. He also failed to retire any Brave batters. To a great cheer from the crowd, Satchel Paige made history by entering the game to pitch in his first World Series.

Before Paige began, plate umpire George Barr made a point of warning him about balking as his famous "hesitation pitch" had been ruled illegal in the American League if he threw it with a runner on base. (Broadcaster Jack Brickhouse once quipped that Paige "threw a lot of pitches that were not quite legal and not quite illegal."[6]) Warren Spahn connected for what would now be called a sacrifice fly—caught by center fielder Larry Doby—that scored Mike McCormick for Boston's eleventh score of Game Five. Stanky stayed put at first base. Thus, Spahn became the first pitcher of the 1948 World Series to drive in a run. (Spahn, however, was charged with an at-bat based on baseball's scoring rules of the era.) With Tommy Holmes batting for the second time in the seventh inning, first-base umpire Bill Grieve called a balk on Paige. By rule, Stanky took second base. It did not matter. On the next pitch, Tommy Holmes—batting for the second time in the seventh inning—grounded out to Cleveland shortstop Lou Boudreau. The marathon inning ended with the Braves having made five base hits and, more importantly, having scored six runs to take a daunting 11–5 lead over the Indians.

Satchel Paige's day ended abruptly when young Al Rosen batted for him to start the bottom of the seventh inning. Rosen, a promising 24-year-old righthanded hitter, popped out to second baseman Eddie Stanky. Dale Mitchell batted next and he popped out, too. First baseman Earl Torgeson caught the ball near the pitcher's mound. Larry Doby flied out to left fielder Marv Rickert. Spahn, in an unfamiliar relief role, had now retired 10 straight Indians. Boston still led Game Five by six huge runs. A return trip to Braves Field to conclude the 1948 World Series seemed a certainty.

16. World Series Game Five

Satchel Paige chats with Cleveland manager Lou Boudreau. Eyebrows were raised when Bill Veeck signed Paige during the 1948 season, but he proved to be a valuable addition to the Indians' pitching staff and a great box office attraction too (courtesy Boston Public Library, Leslie Jones Collection).

The new Cleveland pitcher in the top of the eighth inning was righthander Bob Muncrief, the fifth pitcher of the afternoon for the home team. (It was quite a change of fortunes for the Indians; in the previous four World Series games, every Cleveland starter had tossed a complete game.) The 32-year-old Muncrief had some World Series experience on his résumé. Four years earlier he had pitched two games in the 1944 Fall Classic for the St. Louis Browns, losing Game Two, a hard-fought 11-inning contest, in relief.

The first Boston batter Muncrief faced was shortstop Alvin Dark. He grounded out to shortstop Lou Boudreau to start the frame. Earl Torgeson singled on a full count into right field on a ball that bounced high over first baseman Eddie Robinson's head. Right fielder Wally Judnich, who corralled the ball, did well to keep Torgeson at first base. Torgeson advanced no further as third baseman Bob Elliott lined out to Dale Mitchell in left field and Marv Rickert followed Elliott by flying out to Judnich in right-center field. Boston failed to increase their lead but still comfortably led the Indians by six runs, 11–5, with time running out for the home team.

Lou Boudreau gave the home fans a glimmer of hope by doubling off Warren Spahn to start the bottom of the eighth. The ball dropped onto the grass in right-center field. That was the first hit that Spahn had surrendered to the Indians since coming into the game in the fourth inning. The quiet Municipal Stadium crowd suddenly became energized. The fans began clapping rhythmically, but Spahn impressively bore down to squelch any hope of a Cleveland rally. The Braves hurler struck out Joe Gordon swinging. Ken Keltner was another victim of a Spahn strikeout; he watched an inside pitch nip the corner of the plate for strike three. Ray Boone, a rookie, entered the game as a pinch hitter in place of Wally Judnich. Boone was retired on strikes too. Like teammate Joe Gordon, he too went down swinging. "Spahn is spinning masterfully!"[7] exclaimed Mel Allen on the radio. More than a few sportsmanlike Cleveland fans politely applauded the Boston pitcher as he headed towards the visitors' dugout. Spahn's only shortcoming on the day was on offense: He was the only Brave of the ten who came to bat who had not gotten at least one hit in Game Five. It mattered little.

Ray Boone did not stay in the game. Hal Peck replaced him as Cleveland's right fielder. Peck, a 31-year-old Wisconsin native, had never lived up to his promise as an MLB player after losing two toes on his left foot in an unfortunate firearm accident in 1942. (He was trying to shoot rats on his farm when he tripped over a vine and the gun he was toting prematurely discharged.) "In a sense, we think it's quite fitting for Hal Peck to get into a portion of a World Series,"[8] stated Mel Allen sympathetically.

Bill Salkeld led off the top of the ninth inning for Boston against Bob Muncrief. He grounded to Joe Gordon. The Cleveland second baseman made an accurate throw to first baseman Eddie Robinson for the putout. Mike McCormick popped out to third baseman Ken Keltner. Eddie Stanky also popped out to the infield. Muncrief himself came off the mound and made the catch to efficiently retire the side. The Braves, holding a six-run lead, were three outs away from forcing a sixth game back in Boston.

Cleveland was down to their final at-bats as they came to the plate in the bottom of the ninth inning. Warren Spahn pitched to Eddie Robinson who swung on the first pitch and connected. It was routinely caught in left field by Marv Rickert for the first out. Next up was catcher Jim Hegan. He struck out swinging. Spahn had struck out six batters since entering the game in a relief role and had whiffed four of the last five Indians who had come to bat against him. As a last gasp, Joe Tipton, a 26-year-old Tennessee native, was put into the game as a pinch hitter for pitcher Bob Muncrief. He too was struck out by Spahn on a swinging third strike. The

16. World Series Game Five

visitors walked off the field as convincing 11–5 winners of Game Five. As Boston manager Billy Southworth had boldly predicted, the 1948 World Series was heading back to Braves Field for at least one more game, perhaps two.

Hy Hurwitz began his coverage of Game Five's upset result for the *Boston Globe* by noting, "Those war whoops off Lake Erie tonight came from a surprising species of Indians. They were the delirious shouts of the Boston Braves."

Some writers saw Bob Feller's poor outing as proof of the general scuttlebutt circulating around the AL for most of the 1948 season that, as an old man approaching age 30, Rapid Robert was no longer the dominant pitcher he once was. "Thank God for Feller," said Boston's Tommy Holmes to an unnamed United Press scribe after the game. The writer commented, "No insult was intended. But it was there just the same." He also wrote,

> One hundred and two pitches burst the Bobby Feller bubble.
> That's how many times the famed Rapid Robert sent his legendary fastball and his once-magnificent curve winging toward the plate in the fifth game of the World Series.
> But this time, instead of burning their way past enemy bats with untouchable speed or cunning manipulation which frustrated the hungry wood, they all too often were temptingly touchable.[9]

The Braves' bullpen was quietly doing an excellent job. In 15 innings they had not surrendered a single run to Cleveland. Warren Spahn was especially masterful in Game Five. Catcher Bill Salkeld noted that Spahn had all but abandoned throwing his curveball against the Indians, the pitch that had not fooled the Cleveland batters very often in Game Two. Instead, Spahn chose to throw an array of mostly fastballs with occasional changeups to baffle the AL champions. According to an anecdote relayed by broadcaster Jim Britt before Game Six, Bob Hope, a passionate Indians supporter, knew the game was over the moment Boston took the lead in the top of the seventh inning. "There's the ballgame," he said to anyone within earshot. "We'll never get a hit off that guy Spahn. He has it today."[10] Spahn had stingily allowed only one Indian hit to the 19 Cleveland batters he faced in relief of Nels Potter.

Spahn modestly credited his excellent relief outing to a special feature of Municipal Stadium. "I wasn't any better than usual," he maintained. "Maybe that background helped me. [The Indians] sure were missing that fastball."[11] Spahn was referring to a large section of green-painted bleachers in center field. They were kept vacant to provide a backdrop for the hitters free from white shirts where the ball can seem invisible. "Spahn's sidearm pitches did not come to the plate from that direction. He appeared to bring the ball out of the thousands of standees on the sloping ramp in front of the bleachers,"[12] wrote Hugh Fullerton in his syndicated World Series column.

On the special overnight trains that took the two teams to Boston, the main subject of conversation was the enormous, record-setting crowd at Game Five. When he learned that about 12,000 of those fans had occupied the standing-room area behind the portable, inner fence of the stadium, Boston husky first baseman Earl Torgeson was impressed. "Imagine that! Twelve thousand!" he exclaimed. "Why, that's six times the number of people in my hometown of Snohomish, Washington."[13]

Boston manager Billy Southworth quickly affirmed Bill Voiselle as his Game Six starter. For what it was worth, the 29-year-old righthander had never lost to any AL club in the nine times during his career when he had faced them in spring-training games. It was merely a confirmation of what Southworth had earlier told reporters when he assured them the World Series would be returning to Boston.

Bob Elliott had been derided as "the bust of the World Series" among some baseball scribes for his poor offensive numbers before Game Five. After Game Four, his former roommate on road trips, the ailing Jim Russell, asked Elliott when he was going to display his batting prowess. According to Russell, the prescient Elliott purportedly said, "I'll hit two [homers] for you tomorrow."

Hugh Fullerton believed that Boston's Game Five win would be just a slight inconvenience to the Indians in the long run; the favorites from Cleveland would still surely prevail in the World Series in one of the two games at Braves Field. He wrote assuredly, "Despite this Boston hitting, long overdue, the Indians are still very much in the driver's seat. Boudreau has Lemon, with one win under his belt, poised for [Game Six] and Bearden is ready to work tomorrow if Game Seven in necessary at Braves Field."[14]

Harold Kaese of the *Boston Globe*, showing his allegiance to his hometown, took an altogether different view of things. "Are the Indians doomed to be the Red Sox of 1946? On the threshold of baseball supremacy, will they lose the next two games to the Braves in Boston?" he asked. "Let these Braves be the first team since the 1925 Pirates to win a World Series after trailing by the hopeless 3–1 margin."[15]

Frank B. Ward, the sports editor of the *Youngstown Vindicator*, saw something in Game Five that was overlooked by most of his colleagues in the press box: He was thoroughly impressed by the sportsmanlike reaction of the Cleveland fans to Warren Spahn's fine relief outing for Boston. He admiringly wrote in his October 12 column,

16. World Series Game Five

When Spahn took over the pitching, [he] turned in a high-class performance. Slowly but surely, it was apparent that the Braves were going to win. There was one other duty the fans had to [perform], and that was to pay proper tribute....

After each inning, the applause for the Boston pitcher became louder and louder. Finally, when it was self-evident that Spahn had turned in a great job of hurling, the applause became a stentorian thunder.

Game Five Box Score
Boston Braves 11, Cleveland Indians 5
Game played on Sunday, October 10, 1948, at Cleveland Stadium

Boston Braves	ab	r	h	rbi	Cleveland Indians	ab	r	h	rbi
Holmes rf	5	2	2	0	Mitchell lf	3	1	1	1
Dark ss	4	1	1	0	Doby cf	4	0	0	0
Torgeson 1b	5	1	2	1	Boudreau ss	4	0	2	0
Elliott 3b	4	3	2	4	Gordon 2b	3	1	1	0
Rickert lf	5	1	1	1	Keltner 3b	3	1	0	0
Salkeld c	4	2	1	1	Judnich rf	3	1	1	1
McCormick cf	5	1	1	1	Boone ph	1	0	0	0
Stanky 2b	3	0	1	1	Peck rf	0	0	0	0
Potter p	2	0	1	0	Robinson 1b	4	0	0	0
Spahn p	2	0	0	1	Hegan c	4	1	1	3
Totals	39	11	12	10	Feller p	2	0	0	0
					Klieman p	0	0	0	0
					Christopher p	0	0	0	0
					Paige p	0	0	0	0
					Rosen ph	1	0	0	0
					Muncrief p	0	0	0	0
					Tipton ph	1	0	0	0
					Totals	33	5	6	5

Boston	3	0	1	0	0	1	6	0	0	--	11	12	0
Cleveland	1	0	0	4	0	0	0	0	0	--	5	6	2

Boston Braves	IP	H	R	ER	BB	SO
Potter	3.1	5	5	5	2	0
Spahn W (1–1)	5.2	1	0	0	1	7
Totals	9.0	6	5	5	3	7

Cleveland Indians	IP	H	R	ER	BB	SO
Feller L (0–2)	6.1	8	7	7	2	5
Klieman	0.0	1	3	3	2	0
Christopher	0.0	2	1	1	0	0

Cleveland Indians	IP	H	R	ER	BB	SO
Paige	0.2	0	0	0	0	0
Muncrief	2.0	1	0	0	0	0
Totals	9.0	12	11	11	4	5

E—Doby (1), Keltner (1). **2B**—Cleveland Boudreau (3, off Spahn). **HR**—Boston Elliott 2 (2, 1st inning off Feller 2 on, 1 out, 3rd inning off Feller 0 on, 2 out); Salkeld (1, 6th inning off Feller 0 on, 1 out), Cleveland Mitchell (1, 1st inning off Potter 0 on, 0 out); Hegan (1, 4th inning off Potter 2 on, 1 out). **SH**—Dark (1, off Feller). **Team LOB**—6. **Team**—4. **BK**—Paige (1). **U**—George Barr (NL), Bill Summers (AL), Bill Stewart (NL), Bill Grieve (AL), Babe Pinelli (NL), Joe Paparella (AL). **T**—2:39. **A**—86,288.

— 17 —

Game Six Scuttlebutt

Feller's Second Failure,
Veeck Eyeing Chisox,
Railroad Woes

The major talking points after Game Five were split between Boston surprisingly extending the World Series to a sixth game and Bob Feller's second failure to win a Fall Classic contest.

The latter packed more of an emotional punch for the average baseball follower because many sensed that Feller may never have another opportunity for another World Series starting assignment. When Feller trudged off the mound in a quiet Municipal Stadium, defeated, a United Press article poetically noted, "A star had fallen, and not many among those 86,288 fans believed that fireballer Bobby Feller could ever glow as brightly again."[1]

A surprise and unsubstantiated report out of Cleveland stated that Indians owner Bill Veeck was suddenly interested in buying the Chicago White Sox! This would, of course, mean that Veeck would have to give up his interest in the Indians as it was a violation of MLB rules for a person to have financial stakes in more than one team. A United Press article, largely based on speculation, explained,

> Looking for new worlds to conquer, Bill Veeck ... was ready today to pick up his tomahawk and look for new scalps. Veeck simply hasn't much left to accomplish in Cleveland. He gave the town its first American League pennant winner in 28 years.
>
> The big topic of conversation was that Veeck would leave Cleveland, pick up some downtrodden ball club and rebuild it in the same manner as he did the Indians. The best guess is that it would be Chicago where his father ran the Cubs, and he has plenty of friends.[2]

Many sportswriters applauded the Braves for valiantly staving off elimination in Game Five. Still, more than a few grumpy scribes, who were convinced that their chances of returning to Boston were slim, bemoaned the tightness of the 1948 World Series schedule—one that did not allow for days off despite the considerable distance between Cleveland and the Hub and insisted on 1 p.m. starting times. All sorts of travel arrangements had to be hastily arranged or rearranged. Vince Johnson of the Associated Press wrote that Tommy Holmes' single that gave the visitors a 6–5 lead that they never relinquished "changed the destinations of thousands of fans and caused a flurry of action in the dispatcher's office of the New York Central Railroad." He continued, "Special trains carrying both clubs, the 789 newspapermen, and 187 photographers assigned to follow them, had to be readied within a couple of hours. The trains that brought newspapermen from Boston to Cleveland [after Game Two] had been late and many [journalists] missed the first game [at Municipal Stadium] entirely."[3]

The sudden offensive spurt by the Braves came as a pleasant and overdue surprise to Al Abrams of the *Pittsburgh Post-Gazette*. He wrote in his October 11 sports column,

> Up to the time when they snapped out of it on Sunday when they won their second game, the Braves' defeatist bearing was a sickly thing to watch. They won the first game because of Johnny Sain's shutout pitching, but [they] fought like baby kittens ... in the next three.
>
> They got so far behind and were hammered so unmercifully by the press and radio that they were goaded into doing something about it. They did on Sunday when they pounded Feller off the mound....[4]

Much of the postgame chatter dwelt on whether or not Bob Feller was left in the game too long. Chester L. Smith of the *Pittsburgh Press* believed Lou Boudreau may have been blinded by emotion and loyalty to his star hurler in his reluctance to pull Feller from the game much earlier than he did. Smith wrote, "All over Ohio last night [fans] were asking whether Boudreau let sentiment get away with him because he kept Feller in there even when the vendors with their soft drinks, their peanuts, their popcorn and their pennants could see that the ex-resident of Van Meter, Iowa, was selling himself at par."

Smith conceded that by Boudreau letting Feller continue as long as he did, he at least spared the Indians from having to dip into their starting pitching if a sixth or seventh game was needed. "The Indians now have Bob Lemon and Gene Bearden to throw at the Braves," he accurately stated. "No one expects both to fold."[5]

— 18 —

World Series Game Six
Indian Summer Concludes

Date: Monday, October 11, 1948
Site: Braves Field, Boston, Massachusetts

> "Needing a victory to tie [the World Series] at three games apiece, manager Bill Southworth of the Braves nominated Bill Voiselle to face the chastened Indian clubbers in Braves Field, which a prevailing east wind off the Charles River converts into a pitchers' paradise."[1]—Gayle Talbot, Associated Press

> "No recent Series ... has seen so many former infielders and outfielders rack up mound victories. Bob Lemon was both an infielder and an outfielder at one time. Steve Gromek played the infield. John Sain once roamed the outfield. It may get to be a habit, this switching around."[2]—Jim Britt, Mutual Broadcasting System, from his Game Six pregame show

The city of Boston seemed especially upbeat when the World Series returned for Game Six. The banner headline of the October 11 morning edition of the *Boston Herald* proclaimed "Welcome home, Braves! Everyone salutes you!" Fire engines and a huge throng of fans had gathered at Trinity Place Railroad Station to warmly greet the never-say-die NL champions when their train arrived on Monday morning at about 8:30.

Brave fans were eager to scoop up whatever seats could be had for Game Six. In fact, when the Braves jumped out to a 3–0 lead in the first inning of Game Five, the ticket office at Braves Field began receiving visitors and premature telephone inquiries about ducats for the sixth World

A scorecard vendor is well stocked for his duties at Braves Field. For just a dime you got not only a scorecard for the game but a sharpened pencil too (courtesy Boston Public Library, Leslie Jones Collection)!

Series contest. Once the result of Game Five became final, sales of the remaining available tickets for Game Six at Braves Field did begin, but they were suspended by the police in the interest of public safety when the crowds at the ticket office became dangerously large.

Cleveland tinkered with their starting lineup and came up with a slightly different version for Game Six. Larry Doby was still batting second for the Tribe, but he had been shifted to right field. Thurman Tucker was the new center fielder for the Indians. He was acquired from the Chicago White Sox in a January 1948 trade as the Cleveland front office regarded him as one of baseball's best defensive outfielders. Tucker batted lefthanded, threw right, and wore eyeglasses. He batted .260 in the 83 games he played for Cleveland during the 1948 regular season. In Game Six he would bat sixth.

Boston made no changes in their usual starting eight. Bill Salkeld continued his catching duties for the Braves despite being at less than 100 percent health.

As reported by Mel Allen after Game Five, a reporter from *Time* magazine asked Boudreau who would be his starting pitcher for Monday's

18. World Series Game Six 173

Game Six. When Boudreau replied it would be Bob Lemon, the reporter had a daring follow-up question for him. "What about Tuesday?"

"There will be no game on Tuesday,"[3] Boudreau tersely replied.

Taking a predictably contrary stance, Boston manager Billy Southworth confidently announced that Johnny Sain would be the Braves starting pitcher in Game Seven.

Bill Voiselle, a 6'3" righthander with a 13–13 regular-season record, was Boston's Game Six starter. Voiselle had experienced success pitching in meaningless spring-training games versus the Indians, but Monday's World Series encounter would be the most meaningful game of 1948.

After a local military band played the national anthem, Dale Mitchell led off Game Six for Cleveland. He hit a sinking line drive off Voiselle, but it was successfully run down and caught by center fielder Mike McCormick for the first out. Larry Doby was next up. Continuing with his hot bat, Doby lined a shot over shortstop Alvin Dark for a base hit. It was his sixth hit of the World Series. Lou Boudreau batted next and was smacked in the back by a Voiselle toss, just above his hips, making him the first batter to be hit by a pitch in the 1948 World Series. Doby moved to second base. Second baseman Joe Gordon followed Boudreau. He launched a line drive to deep left field that caused the home team's fans to groan, but Marv Rickert was there to grab it for the second out of the frame. Ken Keltner, who was just 1-for-17 in the World Series thus far, batted next. He grounded to Alvin Dark who threw across the diamond to Earl Torgeson for the inning's final out. The Indians failed to score in their first turn at bat in Game Six and stranded two baserunners.

Tommy Holmes led off for the Braves in the bottom of the first inning. He hit a slow bouncer to pitcher Bob Lemon who tossed the ball to first baseman Eddie Robinson for the first out. (It was a familiar scene as Holmes had grounded out to Lemon three times in Game Two.) Alvin Dark followed Holmes. Dark skillfully bunted for a base hit down the third-base line. Lemon nicely made an accurate off-balance throw to first base, but Dark still was safe by a step. Earl Torgeson hit a fading fly ball that looked like it was going to drop into a hit in front of Larry Doby in right field. Dark certainly thought so; he sprinted recklessly toward second base. However, center fielder Thurman Tucker speedily made a running catch. Alvin Dark was easily doubled off first base to complete the inning as the home crowd let out a collective groan. After one inning, the score of Game Six was 0–0.

Cleveland's first two batters in the top of the second were retired quickly. Thurman Tucker popped up to third baseman Bob Elliott in foul territory. Eddie Robinson lined out to second baseman Eddie Stanky. Jim Hegan got the second Cleveland hit of the game off Bill Voiselle, a single that dropped untouched into left field. Hegan was stranded at first base, however, as pitcher Bob Lemon flied out to left field for the third out of the inning.

Bob Elliott, the first Boston batter of the second inning, caught a break when his bounding ball to Cleveland third baseman Ken Keltner turned into an adventure. It took an odd hop and veered away from him. Keltner never truly got a handle on it, and his throw to first base pulled Eddie Robinson off the bag. It was ruled an infield hit by the trio of official scorers. Shortly thereafter, Bob Lemon committed a careless balk when he decided to throw to Robinson to keep Elliott close to the bag—only to discover his first baseman was playing off the bag. Lemon stopped his throw. (Since Lemon was still on the rubber, the move was, by rule, a balk and properly called as such by the umpires. Elliott was duly awarded second base.) Marv Rickert batted next. His fly ball to deep center field was caught by Thurman Tucker, but it was deep enough to advance Elliott to third base with just one out. Bill Salkeld's at-bat was a wasted one as he hit a sharp ground ball to first baseman Robinson. Robinson fielded it without difficulty, looked at Elliott for a moment, and made the unassisted putout at the bag. Elliott stayed put at third base. Now there were two men out. Mike McCormick grounded out to Keltner at third base. The Indians had escaped a minor jam unscathed. The crucial game remained scoreless. For the sixth consecutive game, neither the Indians nor the Braves scored a run in the second inning.

Dale Mitchell, the first Cleveland batter in the top of the third inning, hit a stand-up double into the left field corner. Larry Doby followed Mitchell to the plate. The first pitch Doby saw from Bill Voiselle, he launched to deep left field. It was caught about five feet from the fence for an out. Mitchell bluffed that he was going to third and was nearly caught sleeping when the throw went behind him to first baseman Earl Torgeson who had sneakily moved close to second base. There was no double play, but the Brave fans vigorously applauded their team's creative defensive effort. The next Cleveland batter was Lou Boudreau. His sinking line drive into right field was nearly caught waist high by Tommy Holmes. It only ticked his glove, however, as it fell to the ground. Holmes probably thought he should have had it, but it was scored a two-base hit for Boudreau. Mitchell scored from second base to give the AL Tribe an important 1–0 lead. Boudreau ended up at second base. Cleveland got no further runs in the frame as Joe Gordon popped out in foul territory to Bob Elliott and the still-struggling Ken Keltner struck out. Keltner, who batted .297 during the regular season, had not gotten a hit since his first at-bat of Game One. Nevertheless, Cleveland had surged in front of the Braves by a 1–0 score.

Second baseman Eddie Stanky led off the bottom of the third inning

18. World Series Game Six

for Boston. Stanky quarreled slightly with plate umpire Bill Grieve about a called strike before drawing a walk off Bob Lemon. (It was the fifth base on balls that Stanky had received in the Series.) This presented Bill Voiselle, the number-nine hitter in the Boston batting order, with an opportunity to lay down a sacrifice bunt. Voiselle was a poor hitter, but his bunt was a success. Jim Hegan fielded it along the first-base line. He threw to Joe Gordon who was covering the bag, making extra sure the toss was not going to strike Voiselle as he ran to first base. Stanky advanced on the sacrifice to second base with one out. The next Boston batter, Tommy Holmes, lined a base hit into left field that moved Stanky only to third base. With the large crowd becoming excited, Alvin Dark had a chance to be a Boston hero, but he hit into an inning-ending double play on a 3–1 pitch. The ground ball was fielded by Bob Lemon. He threw to shortstop Lou Boudreau at second base to retire Holmes. Boudreau relayed the ball to Eddie Robinson in plenty of time to complete the twin-killing. It was the seventh double play the AL Tribe had turned in the World Series. Thanks to it, Cleveland retained its shaky 1–0 edge three innings into Game Six.

The first batter of the top of the fourth inning for the Indians was Thurman Tucker. He grounded out to Boston second baseman Eddie Stanky for the first out. Eddie Robinson batted next. He lined out to Tommy Holmes in right field who made a tough running catch look easy. Cleveland's catcher Jim Hegan followed Robinson to the plate. He was struck out by Bill Voiselle to complete a quick one-two-three inning. With three and a half innings in the books in Game Six, the visitors still held a narrow 1–0 edge.

Earl Torgeson, on a 2–2 pitch from Bob Lemon, flied out to Dale Mitchell in left field to start the bottom of the fourth. Bob Elliott was the next Brave to bat. Lemon fell behind him 3–0 in the count, then got two strikes to get the count to 3–2. On the sixth pitch he saw, Elliott dribbled a ball down the third-base line. Ken Keltner, playing deep, had absolutely no play on the ball. Bob Lemon hustled from the mound to try to make the play, but he never really had a chance to retire Elliott at first base. It was the fourth Boston hit of Game Six. Remarkably, three of them had been infield hits. Rickert, a lefthanded hitter, smacked a long drive to left field. It was caught about eight feet from the fence by Dale Mitchell for a loud out. Elliott did not advance on the play. The next Brave batter, catcher Bill Salkeld, worked Lemon for a walk on five pitches as action began in the Cleveland bullpen. Salkeld now had five walks in the World Series. Elliott advanced to second base. Next up was Mike McCormick. He drove a base hit through the middle of the infield. Elliott scored on the play and Salkeld moved to second base. It was the first earned run Lemon had given up in the World Series. The score was now level at 1–1 as the Boston crowd cheered the dramatic change in the game's momentum. Eddie Stanky was up next. While the Boston second baseman batted, the Indians twice tried their feared pickoff play at second base without success. Stanky eventually drew a walk—his specialty—to load the bases with two outs. The light-hitting Bill Voiselle was the next Boston batter. Voiselle made contact on a 2-2 pitch, but it was a simple ground ball to second baseman Joe Gordon. Gordon made the throw to Eddie Robinson for the third out. Lemon had escaped a serious jam.

To start the Cleveland fifth inning, Bob Lemon led off and flied out in foul territory to first baseman Earl Torgeson on the first pitch he saw from Bill Voiselle. Dale Mitchell fouled out too. His popup was caught by third baseman Bob Elliott in the vast stretch of foul territory in Braves Field. Larry Doby was more patient at the plate—and it paid off: He walked on four pitches. It was the first base on balls issued by Bill Voiselle in Game Six. Lou Boudreau followed Doby. He hit a routine fly ball to Marv Rickert in left field to end the inning, stranding his teammate.

Tommy Holmes led off the bottom of the fifth inning for Boston. He was 4-for-23 in the World Series thus far. He knocked a 300-foot fly ball to left fielder Dale Mitchell who had no difficulty making the catch for the first out. Shortstop Alvin Dark slapped a ground ball back to Lemon. The pitcher recorded his third assist of the day by tossing Dark out at first base for the second out. Earl Torgeson popped out to Cleveland second baseman Joe Gordon in shallow right field to conclude the frame. The score remained deadlocked, 1-1. It was the first time in Game Six in which Lemon had retired the Braves without a Boston man reaching base safely.

The top of the sixth inning was led off by Joe Gordon in spectacular fashion. Gordon drove a high home run to left field. It was his fourth hit of the 1948 World Series—and his first home run. The 33-year-old Gordon had homered in three previous Series (in 1938, 1941 and 1943) when he played for the New York Yankees. Suddenly the visitors from Cleveland were leading the crucial sixth game by a 2-1 score. Ken Keltner followed Gordon to the plate, but his severe batting slump continued as he swiftly fouled out to Boston third baseman Bob Elliott. Thurman Tucker drew a base on balls—the second free pass given up by Bill Voiselle. (Radio announcer Jim Britt noted that Tucker bore a remarkable resemblance to comedian Joe E. Brown.) On a hit-and-run play, Eddie Robinson singled into right field. Tucker, moving on the pitch, advanced to third base easily. Jim Hegan batted next. He looked to have batted into an inning-ending double play to Bob Elliott at third base. Robinson was forced out at second base, but Eddie Stanky's throw to first base was a poor one. It was high. First baseman Earl Torgeson was only able to knock it down, but he could not catch it. Hegan was safe at first base. More importantly, Tucker scored on the play, adding another run to Cleveland's total. Pitcher Bob Lemon batted next. On the first pitch he saw from Voiselle, he grounded out to Earl Torgeson at first base. The inning was over, but Cleveland had extended its lead to 3–1. With a two-run edge and Lemon doing well on the mound, the AL Tribe could smell the World Series title.

In the bottom of the sixth inning, Bob Elliott, the first Boston batter, drove a single into center field. The Boston crowd became excited, but their joy was short-lived. Elliott was quickly erased from the basepath when Marv Rickert grounded into a 4–6–3 double play. The next Brave batter, catcher Bill Salkeld, grounded out to second baseman Joe Gordon to end the inning. With two-thirds of Game Six complete, Cleveland still led, 3–1.

In the top of the seventh inning, Dale Mitchell flied out to center fielder Mike McCormick, but Larry Doby followed and got his third base hit off Bill Voiselle, a single to center field. Lou Boudreau concluded the inning by hitting into a 5–4–3 double play. The crowd at Braves Field cheered the twin-killing mightily, but their team was still trailing. Boston had nine outs left to salvage Game Six and extend the World Series.

During the top of the seventh inning, Jim Britt announced the official paid attendance for Game Six to his radio listeners: 40,103. He commented that the sellout crowd, and even the players themselves, seemed far more subdued than they had been in Game Five at Municipal Stadium in Cleveland.

The bottom of the seventh inning began with Braves center fielder Mike McCormick striking out swinging on a Bob Lemon fastball as ominous clouds began to gather overhead in the afternoon Boston sky. Eddie Stanky, who had walked twice, followed McCormick to the plate. This time Stanky put the ball in play. He hit a ground ball to Ken Keltner. The Indians third baseman bobbled the slow roller briefly, but he still had time to throw out the hobbling Stanky at first base. Buck McCormick pinch hit for Bill Voiselle. He too grounded out to Keltner to end the inning. The score of Game Six stood at 3–1 in favor of Cleveland as time appeared to be winding down on the Braves' 1948 season.

With Bill Voiselle now out of the game, Warren Spahn was brought in by Billy Southworth as the new Braves pitcher. He got a tremendous round of applause from the Brave fans who recalled his excellent relief work in Game Five in Cleveland. Joe Gordon started the top of eighth inning by smashing Spahn's first pitch to left field. Marv Rickert made a terrific sprawling catch which ended in something akin to a somersault just in front of umpire Babe Pinelli. Jim Britt commented, "There, incidentally, is another reason why having those umpires stationed on the outfield lines is an excellent idea because Pinelli was only about ten feet away from Rickert ... so he was in perfect position to see if Rickert had held onto the ball."[4]

Rickert's acrobatic putout was his 20th of the 1948 World Series, equaling a record for an outfielder in a six-game tilt.

The next Cleveland batter, Ken Keltner, finally got an overdue hit, but he needed it to ricochet off Spahn for it to happen. Nevertheless, Keltner stood on first base with one out thanks to his infield single. Center fielder Thurman Tucker got his first look at Spahn and promptly slapped a hit into right field, advancing Keltner to second base. "Spahn is not the puzzle to the Indians that he was yesterday,"[5] Jim Britt astutely observed. Eddie Robinson got the third consecutive hit off Warren Spahn. It dropped into right field. Keltner scored from second base and Tucker moved to third base. Cleveland now led 4–1. Robinson's hit was Cleveland's tenth of the game. Jim Hegan struck out swinging against the reeling Spahn for the second out.

Bob Lemon came to bat next and got a smattering of applause from the sportsmanlike Brave supporters who appreciated good pitching regardless of who did it. Lemon did not see a pitch, though. The Indians gambled trying to put the game out of reach with some daring baserunning. Robinson took a huge lead off first base and basically challenged Spahn to pick him off. Indeed, Spahn did make a throw to first baseman Earl Torgeson. Robinson was caught in a pickle, so Thurman Tucker broke for the plate. Tucker was tagged rather roughly on his face by catch Bill Salkeld for the third out—which broke his eyeglasses! The unusual play went 1-3-2-5-2. Robinson was not given credit for a stolen base even though he was standing at second base when the putout on Tucker was made by the Boston catcher to end the frame. Despite the out, Cleveland now led Game Six, 4–1.

The bottom of the eighth had to be delayed because the nearsighted Thurman Tucker needed a replacement pair of spectacles from the Indians' clubhouse before he could take his position in center field. The impatient Boston crowd booed the delay as Cleveland's batboy completed the errand. A slight cut could be seen on Tucker's face from his collision with Salkeld.

The first Brave to face Bob Lemon was Tommy Holmes in the home half of the eighth inning. On the first pitch that Holmes saw, he smacked a single into center field. Alvin Dark followed with a fly ball to right field that was caught by Larry Doby. Earl Torgeson batted next. He drilled a hit down the right field line for extra bases. He safely slid into second base with a double. Holmes advanced to third base. Suddenly, the Braves had the tying run in the batter's box. Three pitchers began warming up furiously in the Cleveland bullpen—including Bob Feller. Bob Elliott was the next batter. He drew a walk to load the bases with one out. Lou Boudreau asked for time and took the ball from Lemon. Lefthander Gene Bearden

18. World Series Game Six

was his replacement. Bearden had pitched a shutout in Game Three. Clint Conatser was sent in by Billy Southworth to bat for Marv Rickert. Tension was thick at Braves Field.

Conatser only saw one pitch from Bearden. He hit a promising line drive to center field that Thurman Tucker caught for the second out of the inning. Holmes tagged up and scored easily to reduce Cleveland's lead to 4–2. Phil Masi, batting for Salkeld, drilled a Bearden pitch off the left-field wall for a double. It missed being a home run by about five feet. Torgeson scored to whittle the Indians' advantage to just 4–3 as the crowd went into a frenzy. Lou Boudreau opted to change left fielders, putting in the strong-armed Bob Kennedy to replace Dale Mitchell. Mike McCormick came up next. Bearden got a strike on a fastball. On Bearden's second pitch, McCormick hit a sharp grounder back to the mound. Bearden cleanly fielded it—more by reflex action than anything else—and threw out McCormick at first base. Years later, McCormick biographer C. Paul Rogers speculatively wrote, "If Bearden had been a righty instead of a southpaw, McCormick's comebacker may have instead been a two-run single up the middle which likely would have evened the Series and forced a seventh game." Cleveland retained its lead, but it was now just a tenuous 4–3 advantage.

As Game Six moved into the ninth inning, Masi stayed in the game as the Braves catcher. Mike McCormick moved over to left field. Clint Conatser moved into center field but batted in the spot vacated by Marv Rickert. Pitcher Gene Bearden, sporting a remarkable .667 batting average for the World Series, batted for the visitors against Warren Spahn. Spahn got Bearden to strike out swinging. Bob Kennedy, who was batting 1.000 from one at-bat in the Fall Classic, came up next for Cleveland. He struck out swinging too. Larry Doby, who had seven hits in the Series, was the next man to face Spahn. Doby whiffed to make it four straight strikeouts for Warren Spahn. The Braves pitcher was given a huge ovation as he walked to the Braves' dugout, but Boston was down to their final three outs and trailed the Indians, 4–3.

Eddie Stanky led off the last half of the ninth inning as the sky became decidedly overcast and gloomy. Perhaps it was symbolic for the home team. The Boston fans were now cheering on every pitch that Gene Bearden threw to the Braves to encourage their team to make one last effort to tie the score. Stanky watched two Bearden offerings sail in for balls. The next two pitches were strikes. Stanky eventually drew a seven-pitch walk. It was his third base on balls of Game Six and, remarkably, his seventh of the World Series. With clamor building at Braves Field. Tommy Ryan came in to run for Stanky. Billy Southworth inserted Sibby Sisti into the Boston lineup to bat for Warren Spahn. It was Sisti's first plate appearance of the World Series. Batting righthanded, Sisti bunted, but it was not a good one. The ball was caught by the secure hands of Jim Hegan just in front of home plate. Ryan, running on the play, was two-thirds of the way to second base when the catch was made. He was easily doubled up with Hegan's careful throw to second baseman Joe Gordon who was covering first base on the play. It was the fourth double play Cleveland had turned in the game—and it took the remaining life out of the Boston Braves and their supporters. Gayle Talbot wrote, "One moment the crowd of 40,103 was sitting on the edge of their seats, expectant of a rally that would square the Series at three games apiece and carry the playoff right down to a seventh game tomorrow. The next moment it was all over for the Boston players and the fans."[6]

Boston manager Billy Southworth later told reporters, "Sibby has done a marvelous job bunting this year. I suppose the lad is entitled to one pop-up every so often."[7]

With two Braves out and the bases suddenly empty, Braves Field became ominously quiet. Discouraged fans, anticipating defeat, began leaving the ballpark. Tommy Holmes assumed his place in the batter's box. He took a strike from Bearden. He then fouled a pitch off which sailed into the press box. With the count 0–2, Holmes hit a fly ball to left field where Bob Kennedy retreated slightly and made the routine catch for the third out. Jim Britt described the scene unfolding in front of him for his Mutual radio audience: "The Cleveland Indians are the world's champions of 1948! They are leaping joyously as they go off the field. Bearden is being mobbed as is Lou Boudreau. Out in center field Tucker and Kennedy come running in arm in arm. Camera flashbulbs are exploding all over the premises as the Braves Billy Southworth congratulates Lou Boudreau."[8]

The usual clamor descended upon Cleveland when the last out was made at Braves Field. The Associated Press reported, "Horn tooting, pennant waving, and paper showers from office buildings followed the word yesterday that the team had beaten Boston for the title. Euclid Avenue was crammed with automobiles bearing noisy celebrants."[9]

Boston manager Billy Southworth sportingly ventured into the joyous Indians clubhouse to congratulate Lou Boudreau a second time—this time it was orchestrated for the benefit of the newsreels and still photographers. He then glumly walked back to where the home team was conducting interviews. It was the fourth World Series Southworth had managed. His record was now level at 2–2. He had won Fall Classics in 1942 and 1944 with the St. Louis Cardinals, but also lost with them in 1943. Seeing that Southworth was sulking, Boston owner Lou Perini approached his manager and gave him the old refrain, "Don't worry, Billy. We'll get them next year." Corny as the remark was, it seemed to cheer up

18. World Series Game Six

Southworth and his mood became noticeably brighter. Southworth told reporters it was the cleanest World Series he had ever seen. He noted, "It's been a real pleasure for all of us to play against such true sportsmen as Lou and his players."[10]

Jerry Nason of the *Boston Globe* figured the home team's defeat came down to a ten-foot deficit in the bottom of the seventh inning. He explained, "That was the distance by which Phil Masi's tremendous pinch-hit blow, with two on and as many out, missed clearing the wall in dead left field."

In the victorious Cleveland clubhouse, Bob Kennedy made sure that Gene Bearden got the last ball used in the 1948 World Series as a souvenir. (Kennedy had purposely not relinquished the ball Tommy Holmes had hit to him for the final out.) Among the happy Indians was Bearden's father, Henry, who told reporters that his son had become a pitcher after he had spent $50 to send him to a baseball school in Little Rock, Arkansas, after his high school graduation. Reporter Roger Birtwell wrote, "Quietly, with just a suspicion of tears in his eyes, he shook hands with his son."[11]

It was reported that Bearden had possessed a good-luck talisman for the past month—an old, cloth fishing hat that had certainly seen better days. Ken Keltner had given it to Bearden at a team golf event in September. Bearden had not lost a game since he started wearing it. Bearden was alarmed when he could not find it in his cubicle after Game Six. When he was about to depart Braves Field without it, Bob Feller revealed he had hidden it as a prank and returned it to him with a smile. "I really ought to swipe that thing," Feller said. "I could use a little luck myself."[12]

In the visitors' clubhouse, Lou Boudreau took the opportunity to address his happy players while he could still command their attention. He said, "I want to tell you fellows something, something that's deep in my heart. I want to tell you how grateful I am for your loyalty. You have conducted yourselves like gentlemen on and off the field. You have been absolutely magnificent."[13]

Rookie Al Rosen, who had played a combined dozen games for the Indians in 1947 and 1948, and had gotten just one at-bat in the World Series, declared that Cleveland was the greatest place in the world to play baseball and he hoped he could spend his entire professional career there. Rosen, as an Indian, would be unanimously chosen as the AL MVP in 1953. True to his wish, Rosen would never play for another MLB club.

Shortly after the Indians departed Braves Field, a victory party was quickly organized by Bill Veeck at the team's hotel. The impromptu, happy gathering had been going on for several minutes when it was noticed that neither Larry Doby nor Satchel Paige was present. (Nobody thought much about it at the time, but Cleveland's victory in Game Six made them the first black ballplayers to play on a World Series winner; Jackie Robinson had played on the losing side in 1947.) The other Indians quickly went looking for the missing twosome. They were found relaxing at *their* hotel—Boston still had largely segregated lodgings in 1948—and they were swiftly brought to the team party to join the fun and camaraderie. In June, President Harry Truman had formally desegregated America's armed forces, but the steadily growing number of black MLB players still routinely dealt with racially divided restaurants and inns when they were away from home.

A baseball insider who was particularly thrilled by Larry Doby's excellent World Series stats and all-around performance was Effa Manley, the female general-manager of the Newark Eagles of the Negro National League. Doby had played for her club before signing with the AL's Cleveland Indians in 1947. Referring to Doby as "the hero of the World Series," the 51-year-old Manley told J.G. Taylor Spink of *The Sporting News*, "In the American League for little more than one season, and he took charge. Just watch him for the next two years. Got seven hits. One of those catches of his, in the last game, saved the title for the Indians. Yes, we around here are quite excited about Doby."

A more-than-boisterous party occurred on the Indians' return trip to Cleveland. Veeck—who had received a touching standing ovation from his players and their wives when he boarded the train—was likely the wildest celebrant of the bunch. He gleefully poured anything liquid over everyone assembled. Author Paul Dickson noted in his biography of Veeck, "Bottles of sparkling burgundy were shaken, opened, and aimed like guns. The entire dining car was a shambles and a worried conductor demanded payment for damages. Traveling secretary Spud Goldstein told him to send a bill, which came to $3,000."[14]

Cleveland feted its baseball champions with a 10-mile parade covering 107 blocks through its city streets on Tuesday, October 12—the day after Game Six. Twenty open cars were assigned to carry the victors along the route. There was an impromptu aspect to it. The starting time for the procession was not long after the Indians arrived back in Cleveland at 8:30 a.m. The Associated Press reported that Cleveland's schools were open, as usual, but children would be excused from class if they could provide a note from a parent stating they had attended the festivities honoring the Indians. The story noted, "A big turnout of Catholic pupils was anticipated since their schools were closed in observance of Columbus Day."[15] According to the *Cleveland Press*, a minimum of 200,000 giddy fans turned out on short notice on a weekday morning to witness the procession. The Police Department's estimate was 50 percent greater, putting the attendance at approximately 300,000 persons.

Few of the smiling witnesses to that day's parade could have foreseen

18. World Series Game Six

that, as of October 2022, there has not been another Cleveland World Series triumph to celebrate. At 74 years it is presently the longest such drought for any MLB team.

For reasons not stated, three Indians—Ken Keltner, Satchel Paige and Gene Bearden—opted to fly back to Cleveland rather than take the team train. They met their teammates at the railroad station. It was reported that Paige consumed three large dinners during the flight without much difficulty. When the stewardess asked him if he wanted yet another tray brought to him, Paige promptly and politely replied, "No, ma'am. That's all. It's not that I'm full, I'm just tired of eating."[16]

When the official, city-wide celebrations ended and the players were about to disperse for the winter, Veeck told them they were welcome to keep their uniforms and team jackets as mementos of their championship season. New ones would be provided for 1949. Author Dickson mentioned this type of generosity was "a far cry from the [club's] pre–Veeck days, when balls hit into the stands were considered property of the club and collected from the fans."[17]

The heroes of the World Series for Cleveland were certainly named Boudreau and Bearden, Doby and Lemon, but Ed McAuley wrote in his report for *The Sporting News*, "The 1948 world championship is Bill Veeck's world championship. In all the history of baseball there probably never has been another case in which a club president contributed so much to the success of a team." *TSN* also reported that Veeck—always an entertaining public speaker—was booked solid for personal appearances through March 1, 1949. Such demands on his time were an absolute pleasure, Veeck insisted.

In summarizing the six games of the Fall Classic, Grantland Rice wrote, "The 1948 World Series was one that ran strictly to advance form. The Indians were rated above the Braves in just about every department. The margin wasn't too wide, but it was big enough to leave Billy Southworth's squad with a two-game deficit. The better team won and by the correct margin."[18] Rice concluded his report by quoting an indisputable truism borrowed from William Shakespeare's *Much Ado About Nothing*: "When two men ride a horse, one must ride behind."[19]

On the day the 1948 World Series concluded, Lou Boudreau picked up an honor utterly unrelated to baseball: He was named one of the "five most virile men in America" by the International Artists Committee. The other four honorees were singer Jack Smith; actors Clark Gable and Victor Mature; and California governor/presidential candidate Earl Warren. Committee chairman Reno Biondi explained, "Ever since the advent of the new look, artists have needed more virile men as models. An extreme [sic] feminine woman needs a very manly opposite to bring out the best points in both. These five are about as virile as you can get."[20]

Even though his team was not a World Series participant, Dominic DiMaggio of the Boston Red Sox made news on the day of Game Six by getting married at 11 a.m. The center fielder's bride was Emily Frederick of Wellesley Hills, Massachusetts, age 24. The nuptial mass took place at St. Paul's Church in Emily's hometown. According to Mary Cremmen of the *Boston Globe*, the couple would be honeymooning in Montreal before heading to San Francisco where Dom owned a restaurant/cocktail lounge. Along with many other DiMaggio family members, older brother Joe of the New York Yankees was present for the ceremony. (He too was absent from the 1948 Fall Classic.) The 31-year-old groom declined to discuss the World Series on his wedding day, but he did issue one terse sports-related statement: "I'd just like to set that reporter straight who said that baseball came before my marriage."[21]

With the 1948 baseball season over, Bob Feller traveled home to tiny Van Meter, Iowa, to relax and tend to his growing peripheral business interests. Despite Feller posting a horribly disappointing 0–2 record in the World Series, the tight-knit rural community surprised its MLB hero with a grand civic reception. There he was presented with more than $1,000 worth of gifts. The theme of the day was appropriately "When a Feller Needs a Friend."

Game Six Box Score
Cleveland Indians 4, Boston Braves 3
Game played on Monday, October 11, 1948, at Braves Field

Cleveland Indians	ab	r	h	rbi	Boston Braves	ab	r	h	rbi
Mitchell lf	4	1	1	0	Holmes rf	5	1	2	0
Kennedy lf	1	0	0	0	Dark ss	4	0	1	0
Doby rf	4	0	2	0	Torgeson 1b	4	1	1	0
Boudreau ss	3	0	1	1	Elliott 3b	3	1	3	0
Gordon 2b	4	1	1	1	Rickert lf	3	0	0	0
Keltner 3b	4	1	1	0	Conatser ph,cf	1	0	0	1
Tucker cf	3	1	1	0	Salkeld c	2	0	0	0
Robinson 1b	4	0	2	1	Masi ph,c	1	0	1	1
Hegan c	4	0	1	1	McCormick M. cf,lf	4	0	1	1
Lemon p	3	0	0	0	Stanky 2b	1	0	0	0
Bearden p	1	0	0	0	Ryan pr	0	0	0	0
Totals	35	4	10	4	Voiselle p	1	0	0	0
					McCormick F. ph	1	0	0	0
					Spahn p	0	0	0	0
					Sisti ph	1	0	0	0
					Totals	31	3	9	3

18. World Series Game Six

Cleveland	0	0	1	0	0	2	0	1	0	--	4	10	0
Boston	0	0	0	1	0	0	0	2	0	--	3	9	0

Cleveland Indians	IP	H	R	ER	BB	SO
Lemon W (2-0)	7.1	8	3	3	4	1
Bearden SV (1)	1.2	1	0	0	1	0
Totals	9.0	9	3	3	5	1

Boston Braves	IP	H	R	ER	BB	SO
Voiselle L (0-1)	7.0	7	3	3	2	2
Spahn	2.0	3	1	1	0	4
Totals	9.0	10	4	4	2	6

E—None. **DP**—Cleveland 4, Boston 1. **2B**—Cleveland Mitchell (1, off Voiselle); Boudreau (4, off Voiselle), Boston Torgeson (3, off Lemon); Masi (1, off Bearden). **HR**—Cleveland Gordon (1, 6th inning off Voiselle 0 on, 0 out). **HBP**—Boudreau (1, by Voiselle). **Team LOB**—7. **SH**—Voiselle (1, off Lemon). **Team**—7. **BK**—Lemon (1). HBP–Voiselle (1, Boudreau). **U**—Bill Summers (AL), Bill Stewart (NL), Bill Grieve (AL), George Barr (NL), Joe Paparella (AL), Babe Pinelli (NL). **T**—2:16. **A**—40,103.

— 19 —

Why Cleveland Won

"As always, victory finds a hundred fathers, but defeat is an orphan."[1]—Count Galeazzo Ciano

"Baseball statistics are like a girl in a bikini. They show a lot, but not everything."—Toby Harrah

In winning the 1948 World Series, the Cleveland Indians defeated the Boston Braves four games to two. So how did they do it?

In many cases, when one conducts a postmortem of a Fall Classic, the reason for one team's victory is often obvious. It might be a case of superior pitching, offensive dominance, outstanding defense, speed on the basepaths, or any combination of those factors. When one looks at the raw team statistics from the 1948 World Series, however, the most striking feature is how similar they are for both Boston and Cleveland. The numbers do not present a picture of a clear winner.

During the course of those six games, newspaper reporters frequently pointed out that the numbers the Braves were putting up were not a whole lot different than those accrued by the victorious Indians. In fact, by the time the Series concluded, Boston held a slight edge in many key statistical departments. Nevertheless, when one listens to the Mutual radio broadcasts of the 1948 World Series three-quarters of a century later, Cleveland seemed to be the team in control of the World Series from early in Game Two onward.

Over the course of the six games of the Fall Classic, each team scored exactly 17 runs. (The trouble for the Braves was that they scored 11 of them in Game Five and another three in Game Six. In the other four World Series games, runs were exceedingly scarce commodities for the NL champions to find.) The Braves actually outhit Cleveland by a 43:38 ratio, had a better team batting average (.230 to .199) and recorded a superior slugging percentage (.291 to .250). To date, Cleveland's tepid team average is the fourth worst among all World Series-winning teams. Both teams hit exactly four home runs and accrued 16 RBIs. Each team's leader in the latter category had five: Jim Hegan and Bob Elliott. Cleveland had seven doubles to Boston's six. Neither team hit a triple. Stolen bases were almost irrelevant in the Series, but the Indians held a 2:1 edge.

As for pitching, the Indians' team ERA was 2.72 while Boston's was 2.60—not much difference there. The only Boston pitcher with poor numbers was Nels Potter who had a glaringly bad ERA of 8.44. Four Boston hurlers saw no action whatsoever in the Series while only one Cleveland pitcher sat out the entire Fall Classic. Indian pitchers walked 16 Braves over the six games with Eddie Stanky getting seven of them. Boston pitchers walked 12 Indians. However, one stat that stands out in the Indians' favor is this: The first four starting pitchers used by Cleveland all tossed complete games.

One category in which Cleveland had a noticeable advantage over the Braves was in team fielding. Boston made six errors to the Indians' three. More importantly, Cleveland also was excellent in turning rally-squelching double plays. The Indians had two in Gene Bearden's shutout victory in Game Three. The four twin-killings that Cleveland's defense made in Game Six were especially timely and deflating to the NL champions.

In baseball, bunching hits, walks and opponents' errors together is the key to winning games where home runs are not flying out of the park regularly. The Braves scored more than 82 percent of their runs in the last two games—and only won one of them. It is remarkable that they managed a victory in even one of the first four games. In those contests, Boston seldom put together back-to-back hits. (Rogers Hornsby made of point of mentioning this Braves' failure in his column about Game Three.) Accordingly, Cleveland's pitchers usually managed to extricate themselves from "jams" that often consisted of just one Boston baserunner.

There were not many big offensive innings for either team during the six games. Only three times in the World Series did the Indians score more than one run in an inning. That was the same frequency as Boston. Cleveland simply did a better job of manufacturing runs, scoring just enough times to edge the Braves in the games they won. (Interestingly, the highest run output the Indians had in any game was in Game Five; they lost that one, 11–5.)

From an offensive standpoint, the key difference in the Indians winning the 1948 World Series came down to two basic intangibles that seemed to elude the Braves: Timing and luck. Although the squad from Cleveland managed fewer hits than Boston, the timing of their hits proved to be the eventual difference. When they needed a hit, they were able to manufacture one, and when then needed a ball to find a hole, it did just that. When assessing his pitching prowess, Yankee hurler Lefty Gomez once famously said, "I'd rather be lucky than good."[2] If timeliness is akin to luck, Cleveland just had more of it than Boston did. The Indians' anemic offensive numbers were far from good in the Series, but their hits were just timely enough to be all they needed to win games one run at a time.

On paper, the experts overwhelmingly believed that Cleveland was the stronger team going into the World Series. That perceived edge did not really manifest itself over the six games, at least statistically, as the 1948 Fall Classic was remarkably close. In the end, the Indians were better able to win more closely fought contests than the Braves were. That characteristic—which separates champions from also-rans in every team sport—ended up being the difference in determining the victors in the 1948 World Series.

— 20 —

Postscripts

Official MLB attendance figures for 1948 showed the game had reached new levels of popularity. The combined regular-season attendance for both major leagues was 20,849,524, with the American League drawing the lion's share of paying customers with 11,236,652. The turnstile count surpassed the old record, set the previous year, of just under 20 million MLB ticket-buyers. Baseball was the national pastime. It was undeniable.

Because of the issue with late-departing trains from Boston after Game Two that caused numerous reporters and fans to either miss Game Three or arrive late for it, MLB Commissioner Happy Chandler announced a common-sense solution: All future World Series that involved a significant distance between the two teams' ballparks would feature built-in days off where travel could be done on a less hectic schedule.

Three participants in the 1948 World Series won individual honors for their play during the regular season. Lou Boudreau was named the AL MVP. (Stan Musial took the honors in the NL; Johnny Sain finished second in the voting.) Boston's Alvin Dark won the Rookie of the Year Award, the last time there would be just one single trophy for both major leagues in that category. (Gene Bearden finished second in the voting.) The Cy Young Award did not exist in 1948, but Cleveland's Bob Lemon won the equivalent: He was named the American League's Outstanding Pitcher by *The Sporting News* for his terrific year in which he threw 10 shutouts.

Umpire Bill Stewart received a lot of flak in the World Series, but he got a surprising amount of support too. Telegrams addressed to him started arriving in the umpires' room at Braves Field not long after Game One concluded. Many were very positive. One lengthy wire that Stewart kept for his scrapbook was sent by a sympathetic Chicago banker whom he did not know. "Right or wrong," it said in part, "you've got the guts to call 'em as you see 'em. I have to make decisions in my business just like you have to do in yours. We have second-guessers in our league too. But the man who makes big business go is the man who calls 'em as he sees 'em."

According to newspaper reports, umpire George Barr, who had a controversy-free World Series, was confined to his home in Tulsa, Oklahoma, under the orders of his physician about a week after the Fall Classic ended. The NL arbiter's family members declined to publicly state what was ailing the 56-year-old arbiter, but Barr was known to have had a history of cardiac issues.

Boston's Eddie Stanky, who had played hurt during the World Series, finally had his right ankle operated on once the season concluded. Doctors removed two bone fragments from Stanky's damaged ankle joint. The tough-as-nails Stanky played in all Six World Series games for Boston in which he compiled a .524 on-base percentage, drew seven walks, and had four hits in his team's losing effort. Stanky told Roger Birtwell of *The Sporting News* that he intended to golf frequently in Alabama during the off-season to strengthen his injured leg—even though he had never before set foot on a golf course in his life.

Denny Galehouse, the surprise starter (and loser) for the Boston Red Sox in their one-game playoff versus Cleveland to decide the 1948 AL pennant, only played in two games for the Red Sox in 1949. Galehouse's last appearance was a brief relief stint versus Detroit on May 3 in which he faced two batters. The first Tiger hit a bases-loaded triple. The second batter drew a walk, after which Galehouse was yanked from the game by Joe McCarthy. His name never appeared again in an MLB box score. Galehouse eventually became a scout. Among the many teams who employed him were the Red Sox and the Indians.

After the one-game playoff in 1948, there would not be another such game in the AL until October 2, 1978, when the Red Sox hosted the New York Yankees in another winner-take-all clash at Fenway Park. This one would decide the American League East divisional title. Despite being the home team again after winning a coin toss, the Red Sox lost again—thanks to the batting heroics of Reggie Jackson and Bucky Dent. The winning manager that day for New York was Bob Lemon.

Boston relief pitcher Red Barrett was eager to resume his offseason singing engagements. He brashly told the *New York Times*,

> As usual I will resume my musical career as soon as possible. That means as soon as anybody offers me money to sing. I'll admit I'm not one of the world's topflight vocalists. But I do sing loud and I've been able to make more money with my voice during the cold winter months than I could driving a truck. I'll let you know as soon as one of the more astute Boston night club owners comes through with a professional engagement. Be sure to come up and see me and bring all your friends. But be prepared to pick up the check.[1]

Boston pitcher Johnny Sain and Braves manager Billy Southworth seldom spoke to each other after the 1948 World Series. Sain took umbrage

20. Postscripts

at a few particularly self-aggrandizing postseason comments of Southworth's in which he said the Braves' 1948 pennant was largely attributable to his managing rather than the obvious contributions of the team's fine pitching staff.

Decades after the fact, it was revealed that the Indians had created a special home field advantage at Municipal Stadium in 1948: a telescope to help them steal signs from the opposing catcher. The telescope belonged to Bob Feller. He had often handled it on the USS *Alabama* during his navy days and he had kept it as a souvenir at the end of the war. "I used it to pick up enemy aircraft coming in on us,"[2] the great pitcher recalled. Perhaps 30 inches long, the telescope was mounted on a tripod placed in the stadium's scoreboard and aimed directly toward home plate. It was manned by either Feller or Bob Lemon. What it lacked in size, it made up for in brilliant clarity. (Lemon said it was so powerful that he could see if the catcher had dirty fingernails.) Whoever was looking through the scope would relay what the next pitch would be to the club's groundskeepers, who then passed along that information to the Cleveland batter by a changing system of signals, also on the scoreboard. The devious system was apparently flawless as no opponent suspected anything was amiss.

Phil Masi, the Boston pinch runner who was controversially called safe at second base in the critical pickoff play in Game One of the World Series, died on March 29, 1990, at age 74. In his will, Masi bequeathed a long overdue nugget of truth to baseball fans: He admitted that umpire Bill Stewart blew the important call and he should have been ruled out on the play. (When one of the authors of this book spoke to Bob Feller in Cooperstown in 1993 about that famous incident, the retired pitcher was quick to reference Masi's posthumous confession.) Previously, Masi had generally given vague or inconclusive responses to anyone who asked him about the famous play—even longtime teammates. Sometimes he only admitted to the play being close, sometimes he indicated that he might have been safe. Stewart died in 1964. In October 2003, Stewart's grandson, Paul, a National Hockey League referee, spoke at a meeting of the Boston Braves Historical Association. He had obviously not been invited to chat about hockey officiating but rather to discuss his late grandfather's contentious call in the World Series 55 years earlier. He told the gathering of fans and ex-Braves with a smile, "I led two professional hockey leagues in penalty minutes, then I went on to officiate. One thing I learned from making the transition is something none of you players will know: Phil Masi may have thought he was out, but he wasn't out. You know why? Because the umpire is always right—and so is the referee!"[3]

When the official MLB film of the 1948 World Series was debuted to a select group of baseball reporters on November 30, many of the scribes were less than impressed that Bill Stewart's contentious safe call on the Game One pickoff play had been minimized even though it was the major talking point of the entire Fall Classic. It was shown quickly from a camera angle that made it unclear if the umpire had erred. Some reporters outright questioned whether MLB had deliberately edited the film *to not show* that Stewart had missed the important call. New York baseball scribe Joe Williams was among them. He cynically wrote the following day in the *New York World-Telegram*, "[The cameras] captured in full detail every other key play. Time after time the film is stopped to show by what a narrow margin a runner is thrown out, or beats the ball, or breaks up a double play. How they managed to catch every play but this one will continue to be a mystery as baffling as any the FBI ever grappled with."[4]

Ironically, the director credited for creating the documentary was Lew Fonseca, a former MLB infielder whose best years were spent playing with the Indians from 1927 to 1931.

There was no official World Series MVP award in 1948, but that did not stop baseball historian Shane Tourtellotte from naming one retroactively in 2020. His choice was Gene Bearden—and it is difficult to argue with the selection. Tourtellotte explained his selection of Bearden on the website *The Hardball Times*:

> Another rookie pitcher made good in the [1948] World Series, though Bearden's tale had a rockier ending. In Game Three Bearden allowed five baserunners, erasing two on double plays, in a shutout effort. At bat, he doubled and singled, scoring Cleveland's first run in a 2–0 win. Three days later, he entered Game Six with Cleveland up three and five outs from the title, but with the bases loaded. Gene let two inherited runners score before getting the third out, then escaped the ninth with the help of a pop-bunt 2-4 double play. It still got him the save, and it still left him the most effective player of the series.

The unusual case of Marv Rickert presented a problem when the World Series shares were divvied up. He had been added to the Boston roster as a replacement for Jeff Heath after the Braves' paperwork had already been submitted to the Commissioner's office, so technically he was entitled to nothing for his efforts in the five games in which he appeared. (Rickert went 4-for-19 at the plate with a home run and two RBIs. He also made a record 20 putouts in the Boston outfield with no errors.) The good-natured Rickert joked with Arthur Daley of the *New York Times* that he was just playing "for fun" in the Fall Classic. Daley duly reported Rickert's situation to his readers, declaring he was "the first amateur in World Series history."[5] No fair-minded person thought Rickert should go uncompensated for his fine work for the vanquished Braves. Accordingly, by special order of Commissioner Happy Chandler, the 27-year-old Rickert was paid a one-third share of what each Brave got as being a member of the losing team in the Fall Classic. This amounted to $1,523.58.

Steve Gromek, the almost forgotten Cleveland pitcher who pitched an impressive complete-game victory in Game Four, was given a surprise $5,000 bonus by Bill Veeck. Prior to the season, the Indians had reduced Gromek's pay by $2,500. "I told [Veeck] he was a real Santa Claus," the grateful Gromek recalled.

The Indians used 23 of their 25 players who were eligible for the World Series. The Braves used 20 of theirs. One of the two Indians who saw no action in the six games was Johnny Berardino, a strikingly handsome 31-year-old utility player who could easily be slotted into infield or outfield positions whenever necessary. Berardino was acknowledged as Cleveland's best bench-jockey because of his sharp wit. He also brought laughter to the Indians' clubhouse with his terrific impersonations of celebrities. (His Charles Laughton impression was said to be superb.) After his baseball career ended in 1952, Berardino got the acting bug. He tweaked the spelling of his last name slightly (dropping the second R) and enjoyed a substantial career in movies and television. He is best remembered for portraying Dr. Steve Hardy for 33 years on the long-running ABC soap opera *General Hospital* from the show's inception in 1963 until his death from pancreatic cancer in 1996. Eagle-eyed fans of the program noticed that Berardino often wore his 1948 World Series ring while playing the physician. Berardino has the quirky distinction of being the only person with a star on the Hollywood Walk of Fame who also played on a World Series winner.

Speaking of acting, 31 members of the World Series champions—including Bell Veeck, Hank Greenberg and Tris Speaker—made appearances in a 1949 Hollywood flick titled *The Kid from Cleveland*. Berardino was the only one who had a major role in the film, playing a sleazy character called Mac the Fence. All the other Indians played themselves. The plot of the drama has Cleveland's baseball team helping a teenage fan, Johnny Burrows (played by Russ Tamblyn), who is trying to escape a troubled home life. Actual game footage from the 1948 World Series is used in the movie. Apparently none of the Indians received a salary for their thespian efforts—only a share of the film's profits. They probably did not amount to much. *The Kid from Cleveland* received mixed reviews and did not fare especially well at the box office.

In 2020, ESPN ranked all 116 World Series from the modern era (since 1903) and determined the 1948 Fall Classic to be only the 77th best of the bunch. Considering that five of the six games between the Indians and the Braves ended in close scores—and the one outlier was tied after six innings—that ranking might be a little bit harsh.

— 21 —

The Decline and Relocation of the Boston Braves

"You would never know it from the gate receipts that so many people wanted the Braves to stay in Boston."[1]
—unnamed associate of Boston Braves owner Lou Perini after the club announced it was relocating to Milwaukee

"Sadly, it did not last. The Braves could almost equal the Red Sox attendance when they were winning the pennant, but could not really compete otherwise. Internal conflicts and dissention contributed to their fall."[2]—Mark Armour, baseball historian

The Braves' freefall from popular NL champions to utter irrelevance in Boston was staggeringly swift.

As the 1950s began, attendance at Braves Field dangerously declined by about 50 percent each year. In 1950, the Braves had finished a respectable fourth in the NL standings and had drawn more than 944,000 spectators. It was still a reduced number from the previous season, though. As was the customary excuse at the time, team executives blamed the drop from more than one million fans in 1949 on excessive television coverage of Braves home games.

The following year, the fourth-place Braves of 1951 could not attract even 500,000 fans to The Wigwam. By 1952, the dismal Braves finished seventh in the NL with just 64 wins, 32 games out of first place. They drew just 281,278 paying customers all season, the lowest total in the major leagues. By comparison, the Boston Red Sox—who had long supplanted the Braves in popularity in the Hub—drew more than 1.1 million fans to Fenway Park in 1952. (By this time Lou Boudreau was managing the Red Sox.) With the NL club hemorrhaging money, things could not continue as they were for much longer.

21. The Decline and Relocation of the Boston Braves

As the 1952 season wound down, the Braves 49-year-old owner Lou Perini anticipated his club would absorb an enormous loss of approximately $500,000 for the season. Still, in an article in the September 6 edition of the *Boston Globe*, Perini insisted the club would be in the Hub in 1953. Nevertheless, good times were becoming a distant memory for Perini and everyone else associated with the historic NL baseball club. As a Bostonian and a baseball traditionalist, Perini publicly stated he wished to keep the Braves where they were because of the team's long history in the city, but he insisted he was "not going to be stubborn about it. We are going to [experience] the greatest financial loss in the history of baseball [in 1952], and if it becomes necessary at a future time and the proper opportunity arose [to transfer the franchise elsewhere], we'd be silly if we didn't consider it."[3] On October 8, *The Sporting News* hinted at the inevitable in an editorial about the struggling Boston Braves (and Pittsburgh Pirates) which said, in part, "No businessman in his right mind, regardless of his wealth, would continue for any length of time to swim against such a flood-tide of red ink."

There were 8,822 spectators who sat scattered around Braves Field on Sunday, September 21, 1952; remarkably, it was the club's largest crowd for a day game that season. The *New York Times* reported that visiting Brooklyn Dodger fans made up a significant percentage of the paying patrons that day. The Dodgers won the game, 8–2. The throng had absolutely no idea they were attending the final Boston Braves home game ever to be played. Two members of the 1948 Braves played in what turned out to be a historic game: Earl Torgeson and Warren Spahn. (Spahn's appearance was as a pinch hitter!) Tommy Holmes, who began the 1952 season as the Braves player-manager before being axed, was in uniform too. He was sitting in the Brooklyn dugout, playing out the final few games of his MLB career as an occasional pinch hitter for the NL champion Dodgers. In the September 22 edition of the *Boston Globe*, baseball scribe Bob Holbrook penned, "[Owner] Perini is going to stick with Boston. He hasn't quit and he has no immediate intention of quitting, but let another season like this nightmare transpire and this city could be a one-team town."

The Boston Braves finished their 1952 schedule at Ebbets Field in Brooklyn. The team's final game, played on Sunday, September 28, finished in a 12-inning, 5–5 deadlock. Righthander Lew Burdette—who would go on to great feats for the franchise—threw the final four innings for Boston without surrendering a hit to the Dodgers. Johnny Logan scored the Braves' final run to tie the game in the top of the ninth inning. He was driven home by Eddie Mathews whose double resulted in the club's final RBI. Both sides mutually agreed to call the game after Brooklyn failed to break the tie in the 12th frame. Roger Birtwell of the *Boston Globe* reported, "As the skies were still bright, the game was apparently called for the convenience of the players and umpires. Umpire-in-chief Al Barlick had left the game at the end of the tenth [inning] to catch a train. He apparently wanted to get a quick start for spring training."

In truth, neither team desired to prolong the meaningless affair any further. The Dodgers wanted to be well rested and focused for their upcoming World Series games versus the New York Yankees. Conversely, the Braves were preparing for a winter plagued with ever-increasing uncertainty.

The time to cease being stubborn and the opportunity to move to the more promising locale that Lou Perini had alluded to came faster than almost anyone had anticipated. In November 1952, Perini bought out the other members of team's ownership group. Four months later the players arrived at their spring training facilities to find the familiar letter "B" on their caps and "Boston Braves" stenciled on the team's equipment crates as usual. However, with lackluster advance ticket sales showing no promise of better attendance at Braves Field for the 1953 season, on Friday, March 13—just a month before the new season was to begin—Perini made a startling announcement from Florida: Pending the formal approval of the other seven NL owners, the Braves would be moving their operations to Milwaukee—the city where their top farm club operated. A headline on that day's *Boston Globe*'s front page screamed in huge capital letters, "Braves Leave Hub." The news came both as a shock and a major inconvenience to many players. Several had to cancel housing arrangements in Boston. Instead, they scrambled to secure new lodgings in Wisconsin. Warren Spahn had intended to open a restaurant in the vicinity of Braves Field. That enterprise was swiftly scuttled.

Perini was well liked among his fellow NL magnates. Therefore, it was no surprise that five days later permission was officially granted by the Senior Circuit for the team's relocation following a 3½-hour meeting with the club owners. (The franchise's top minor league team—also owned by Perini—was subsequently shifted from Milwaukee to Toledo.) The decision was officially recorded as a unanimous one, although Brooklyn Dodgers owner Walter O'Malley unofficially objected to it. O'Malley told reporters that he was opposed to the NL leaving New England. He also sympathized with the longtime Boston Braves fans who had just lost their beloved team.

Tom Fitzgerald of the *Boston Globe* reported that March 18, 1953, was strangely just another day at Braves Field. The club's publicity department was preparing statistical summaries from the team's Grapefruit League game against the Yankees the previous day, along with reports about the Braves' minor league prospects as if nothing noteworthy had happened in

21. The Decline and Relocation of the Boston Braves

Florida. Fitzgerald found that comments about the team's imminent move to Wisconsin were difficult to elicit from employees. Longtime secretary Raynhild Stenberg was somewhat talkative. On the Braves' payroll for a quarter century, Stenberg was non-committal about whether she would move with the team to Milwaukee. Blake J. Romeo, the club's ticket manager with seven years' service on his résumé, admitted he now had little to do. Without receiving specific instructions from Perini, Romeo had independently ceased telephoning the 1952 Braves season-ticket holders about renewals on March 13. He stated the obvious: "There isn't much point in contacting perspective customers in a situation like this."

The following day the *Boston Globe* reported that only 420 Braves season tickets for 1953 had been sold. Of course, all buyers had their money returned. The refunds came with a personal letter from Lou Perini. The *Globe* printed one. It said, in part,

> Dear sir,
> I am returning to you with this letter the money which you sent us for your 1953 season tickets at Braves Field.
> I can't begin to express my thanks for your loyalty to the Braves, nor can I begin to express my regret that it is necessary to move the franchise from Boston.
> Though well aware of the fine interest and faithfulness of people like yourself, I have slowly come to painful realization that, in spite of all our efforts, the large majority of Boston and New England fans do not feel as you and I do.

One city's loss was another city's windfall, of course. A celebratory headline dominating the front page of the *Milwaukee Sentinel* on March 18 boasted, "We're the Home of the Braves!" There was one other complication that had to be ironed out: In 1953, Braves Field was supposed to host the All-Star Game for the second time in its history. MLB quickly shifted the July 14 event to Crosley Field in Cincinnati. Remarkably, the annual preseason Braves–Red Sox "City Series" games would still be played. There would be two contests at Fenway Park in April—after the first two had been played in Milwaukee.

"The Braves may have left, but Boston's apathy for them remained," opined Joseph F. Dinneen, Jr., in the March 19 edition of the *Boston Globe*. "Few fans became emotional over the loss of the franchise, and it was generally accepted that fandom would be satisfied to follow the Red Sox, as had been [the case] in recent years anyway, to the chagrin of Lou Perini." Dinneen said the sincerest mourners were not necessarily baseball fans, but folks who had personal financial interests in the Braves remaining in the Hub, such as hoteliers, cab drivers, and merchandise vendors.

In that same newspaper, the *Globe* published on its front page a creative, eight-stanza poem about the death of the Boston Braves penned by

Paul Benzaquin. It was titled "Money Ha-Ha"—a parody of the 1855 Henry Wadsworth Longfellow epic poem "The Song of Hiawatha" and its female character Minnehaha. It featured references to the club's glory days of 1914 and 1948 and sadly ended by noting that the Great Chieftain Perini was now in search of wampum elsewhere.

The end of the Boston Braves floored many baseball fans who scarcely thought the uprooting of an MLB club was possible. (The last time it had occurred was in 1903.) Sports journalist Dan Daniel called the stunning move "an abrupt break with tradition."[4] It was indeed, but from a business standpoint, it was a necessary one. An Associated Press correspondent accurately declared, "Boston's Braves can point to a glorious baseball past, but, at the same time, they have to point to a steady and harmful decline in attendance in the last few years."[5] The club had to dispose of nearly 1.3 million tickets that had already been optimistically printed for admission for 1953 home games. The suddenly useless ducats—calculated to have a face value of about $2.5 million—were set ablaze in a bonfire. Nobody thought of keeping them as curiosities.

The Boston Braves truly were a historic sports franchise. A Boston club had continually operated in the NL since its inaugural season, winning the first NL game ever played on April 22, 1876. They captured 10 pennants, eight of them coming before 1900. Prior to joining the NL, they had also been the dominant force of the old National Association from 1871 to 1875. All told, the Boston NL franchise—the team of King Kelly, Hugh Duffy, Rabbit Maranville, Tommy Holmes, Warren Spahn and Johnny Sain—had compiled an overall sub-.500 record of 5,118 wins and 5,598 losses. They had famously won the 1914 World Series over the invincible Philadelphia Athletics in what was arguably MLB's greatest upset. The longest game in MLB history—a titanic 26-inning, 1–1 tie between Boston and Brooklyn on May 1, 1920—had been played at Braves Field. By relocating to Wisconsin, the Braves became the first NL club to switch cities since the 19th century.

In the March 25, 1953, edition of *The Sporting News*—which featured a large cartoon of a native American with five foaming mugs of beer assembled before him—Boston correspondent Lester Smith succinctly explained why the surprise move had occurred:

> There is room for only one major league team in the Hub. That's the simple reason for the removal of the Braves to Milwaukee.
>
> For a long time, Lou Perini and his associates refused to recognize this fact. Even after last year's disastrous results, the Braves' boss was not willing to concede that Boston had become an American League city. He magnanimously assumed the blame for the poor showing "because the owners failed to field a team justifying the support of the Boston fans."[6]

21. The Decline and Relocation of the Boston Braves

Was the team's departure out of the Hub an inevitability? Not necessarily. One Boston historian suspects the history of baseball in that city would have changed drastically if the Braves had won the 1948 World Series instead of the Indians. In a 2012 interview, Tom Whalen opined,

> It makes you wonder, if the Braves had been able to hang on and become World Series champions, would they have stayed? People forget Hank Aaron was signed to a Boston Braves contract. Eddie Mathews and Johnny Logan had already been brought up. The core of the great [Milwaukee] Braves teams of the 1950s was already there. [Meanwhile], the Red Sox in the '50s were on this downward slope toward mediocrity. They became kind of a laughingstock. You've got to figure the Red Sox would have been the candidate to move—not the Braves.[7]

When the newly christened Milwaukee Braves began drawing enormous crowds in 1953, two struggling AL clubs—the St. Louis Browns and Philadelphia Athletics—could not help but take notice. Within two years, both would mimic the mobile Braves, leaving their ancestral homes and famous names to the pages of history. Those teams transferred to Baltimore and Kansas City respectively. The New York Giants and Brooklyn Dodgers—arguably the two most storied franchises in NL history—were both enticed to relocate to California after the 1957 season with the promises of fabulous attendance and other perquisites. The original Washington Senators, poorly supported for years, threw in the towel after the 1960 season and moved their operations to Minnesota where they became the Twins.

Lou Perini would be the primary owner of the Milwaukee Braves for ten seasons. Over that time the talented Braves won two NL pennants and the 1957 World Series. He sold all but 10 percent of the club in 1962 to a Chicago-based corporation after the Braves posted a deficit for the first time in Wisconsin that year. Previously, the team had accrued about $7.5 million in combined profits over its first nine seasons there, but the novelty of MLB had waned. Perini succumbed to cancer at the age of 68 on April 16, 1972, after a four-month battle with the disease. Although he died in West Palm Beach, Florida, Perini had maintained a home in Boston for many years after the Braves had left town. In the years following 1952, Perini reputedly received very little flak from the locals for moving their NL club 967 miles westward.

By the end of 2021, there were no living ex–Boston Braves. The last surviving player to have participated in an MLB game for them was Del Crandall. (He had no connection to the 1948 World Series club, however, as he was on the team's roster only in 1949 and 1950, appearing in 146 games.) Crandall then served two years in the military. By the time his stint had ended in March 1953 and he rejoined the team, the Braves had relocated to Milwaukee. Crandall passed away on May 5, 2021, at the age of 91 years and two months.

The last surviving person to have worn a Braves uniform during their 1948 championship season was Frank McNulty. As a 17-year-old, he served as one of three batboys employed by the Braves. Everlasting fame came to McNulty as he was the inspiration for the central character in Norman Rockwell's marvelous baseball-themed cover "The Dugout." It appeared on the September 4 issue of *The Saturday Evening Post*. (Curiously, the artist chose to portray McNulty as a forlorn figure clad in a Chicago Cubs uniform.) McNulty had a full and varied life. A Korean War veteran, he served two terms as the mayor of Seabrook Island, South Carolina. McNulty was also the president of *Parade* magazine—the popular Sunday newspaper insert that once boasted a weekly readership of 32 million people. It was a position he held for a decade. McNulty died in January 2020 at age 88, about five months after Clint Conatser—the last remaining Braves player from the 1948 Fall Classic—had passed away.

Even though Boston's once-famous NL club vanished from the Hub after the 1952 season, and a wrecking ball did its work in 1955, portions of Braves Field still exist today. Boston University bought the ballpark and its property from Perini for $430,000. The gaudy old Braves' ticket office underwent major renovations and was converted into the headquarters for the BU campus police. Commencement ceremonies for the school were sometimes held on the infield that Eddie Stanky and Alvin Dark so ably patrolled during the memorable 1948 season. Parts of Braves Field's bleachers and entry gate were incorporated into the design of Nickerson Field where the university's lacrosse and soccer teams now play. (It was also the home of BU football until the gridiron program was discontinued after the 1997 season. The AFL's Boston Patriots—now the NFL's New England Patriots—played home games at the venue from 1960 to 1962.)

Those old remnants have now benefited the university far longer than they served Boston's NL club and its fans for the 38 seasons that The Wigwam existed as the home field of an MLB club. A plaque marks the spot where the ballpark's home plate had been located. Of course, those fans who can remember the joy and excitement the 1948 Braves brought to the city of Boston in that now-abandoned baseball locale become fewer and fewer with each passing summer.

The team's fandom lives on today via the Boston Braves Historical Association and its approximately 300 members. "We have a few, a very few, members who actually attended the 1948 World Series," BBHA president Bob Brady noted in an October 2021 interview when MLB's first Red Sox–Braves World Series clash very nearly became a reality. Of course, the Braves were nearly 70 years removed from Boston—and the NL team now calls Atlanta its home. Despite that one rather important detail, Brady believes such a Fall Classic, had it occurred, would have sparked a wave of welcome curiosity in Boston's old NL club. He ruefully said,

> It would have provided a level of interest going back in the Braves' history, and the Boston version of it. We would have had more of an opportunity to expose the baseball world to the days of the Boston Braves. That interest is pretty much dissipating [as the years go by], so we've lost that opportunity with our primary objective, which is preserving the memory and the history of the Boston Braves and exposing others to it.[8]

When a record-breaking crowd in excess of 47,000 fans turned out for the first NL contest at Braves Field in 1915, *The Sporting News* gushed that the professional game's newest cathedral was "a great monument of concrete and steel" and an appropriate answer to all foolish naysayers

When the money-losing Braves franchise shifted to Milwaukee following the 1952 season, Braves Field was eventually acquired by Boston University. A wrecking crew demolished most of the NL ballpark in 1955. A few segments exist today as part of Nickerson Field (courtesy Boston Public Library, Leslie Jones Collection).

who dared to ask, "What's wrong with baseball?"[9] However, not even four decades later, that question could have been posed more seriously as one of the sport's iconic franchises abandoned its roots and headed westward toward greener pastures. Three-quarters of a century later, the famous Boston Braves have receded into the realm of nostalgia.

— 22 —

Whatever Became Of…

"Boast not thyself of to-morrow, for thou knowest not what a day may bring forth."—Proverbs 27:1

Here are mostly brief synopses of what happened to the key participants (and some peripheral figures) of the 1948 World Series once that Fall Classic had entered into history. Sadly, a great many of them did not enjoy long lives.

Mel Allen became a household voice to baseball fans. When NBC owned the rights to both radio and TV coverage of the World Series, the network instituted a policy whereby at least one broadcaster from each of the two participating teams would call the games. With the Yankees almost always winning the AL pennant in the first two decades after the war, Allen seemed to be permanently linked to the Fall Classic. Some fans thought that Allen called postseason games with a biased eye toward *his* Yankees. He never really denied the accusation. Once, in 1947, when the almighty Yankees were on a small losing streak, Allen refused to get a haircut until they won a game. (Allen liked to tell an amusing story about a World Series game in which he received a telegram from a fan during its early innings. It read, "Shut up you Yankee homer and let me enjoy the game!" Allen, taken aback, tried his best not to come across as rooting for New York for a little while. Then he noticed the time stamp on the telegram: It had been sent well before the game's first pitch had even been thrown!) His last World Series, the Yankees-Dodgers clash in 1963, featured a sad ending for Allen. During the fourth game, Allen lost his voice. Los Angeles Dodger announcer Vin Scully professionally picked up the slack and continued to call the portion of the game that had been earmarked for Allen. (Some cynical fans cackled that Allen just could not bear to broadcast his beloved Yankees losing the Fall Classic in a four-game sweep.) The Yankees also won the AL pennant in 1964. Midway through the season, the club announced that Allen's contract would not be renewed for 1965. The surprising decision was never adequately explained to the public. Former shortstop Phil Rizzuto, who would take over from Allen, worked the 1964 World Series for NBC. Nevertheless, Allen maintained a seemingly positive relationship with his old employers, regularly showing up to broadcast Yankee old-timers' games and emcee various on-field ceremonies whenever he was asked. He stayed prominent in the sport that made him famous by narrating the popular syndicated *This Week in Baseball* program until his death in 1996 at age 83. His memorial plaque at Yankee Stadium refers to Allen, quite properly, as "The Voice of the Yankees."

Following the World Series, as he had done for years, NL umpire **George Barr** ran an umpires' school during the offseason. It was a spartan regimen for the enrollees, according to a story that appeared in the January 22, 1949, edition of the *Toledo Blade*. "We will tolerate no drinking, gambling, or whistling at girls," Barr dutifully warned his students. "If you do not believe we mean this, just try it. You will be expelled from class. You cannot be a good umpire if you have these bad habits." On August 21, 1949, in the second game of a Giants-Phillies doubleheader at Shibe Park, Barr was working at first base in a three-man umpiring crew when things got a little bit out of hand. In the top of the ninth inning, Barr ruled that Philadelphia center fielder Richie Ashburn had trapped—not caught—a fly ball hit by New York's Joe Lafata. The call turned an apparent out into an RBI double for the visitors to extend their lead to 4–2. The home team's supporters showed their displeasure by littering the diamond with bottles and other debris, forcing the umpires to flee to their dressing room and abandon the game. (It was ruled a forfeit win for New York.) The ugly incident prompted the sale of bottled refreshments to be banned at Shibe Park and, not long afterwards, everywhere else in MLB. Barr retired shortly after that season. He stayed connected to baseball with his school and as the president of two minor pro circuits: the Western Association and the Kansas-Oklahoma-Missouri League. Barr died from cardiac issues in 1974, a week past his 82nd birthday, after enduring several years of poor health.

Red Barrett pitched one more season for Boston before ending his MLB career. It was not an especially good year. The 34-year-old Barrett finished 1949 with a 1–1 record and a 5.68 ERA in 23 relief appearances and then vanished from the majors forever. However, Barrett remained in organized baseball for four more seasons as a minor leaguer on clubs in Los Angeles, Nashville, Buffalo, Toronto, and Tampa. He finished his pro baseball odyssey in 1953 in Texas with the Paris Indians of the Big State League at the age of 38. That season Barrett compiled a record of 6–4 in 15 appearances. After baseball, he settled in North Carolina and worked for Sealtest Ice Cream as a plant manager. In 1988, Barrett appeared at a

40th anniversary gathering of the 1948 Braves in Boston where he was persuaded to demonstrate his vocal talents as well as answer fans' questions. He died of cancer on July 28, 1990, at age 75 in Wilson, North Carolina.

In the seasons that followed 1948, the victorious pitcher in the playoff game at Fenway Park, **Gene Bearden**, never had another campaign anywhere close to what he achieved that terrific year when he won 20 games for Cleveland and had the second-best winning percentage in the AL. Bearden pitched until 1953 without ever recording another winning record. His best win total after 1948 was a mere eight—and he did that in 1949. A hedonistic lifestyle and a hip injury were both certainly factors in Bearden's decline, but it was more likely that Bearden's career went into an irreversible tailspin once AL hitters began to realize his knuckleball seldom hit the strike zone. Batters laid off it—and Bearden's ERA rose dramatically when he constantly fell behind in the count and had to throw strikes with a less than overpowering fastball. Bearden was shipped off to the Washington Senators, Detroit Tigers, St. Louis Browns and Chicago White Sox in quick succession before his career ended in 1953. Following the 1948 season, Ted Williams predicted that Bearden would not win another 20 games over the rest of his MLB career. Williams' estimate was not too far off: Bearden accrued just 25 more victories. Bearden achieved a small degree of fame away from baseball in moviedom when he played himself in *The Stratton Story*—a hugely popular 1949 Hollywood biopic about Chicago White Sox pitcher Monty Stratton, starring Jimmy Stewart and June Allyson. (Like most of the other 1948 champs, he appeared as himself in another 1949 flick: *The Kid from Cleveland*.) Bearden died at age 83 on March 18, 2004, in Alexander City, Alabama.

Vern Bickford, the 27-year-old rookie who pitched well for the Braves in a losing effort in Game Three, continued to improve his mound performances over the next two years. Bickford's record in 1949 was 16–11. He appeared in that season's All-Star Game at Ebbets Field. In 1950, according to one biographer, "Bickford went from a reliable number-three pitcher to one of the finest righthanders in the [National] League."[1] Bickford was noted for both his fiery, no-nonsense approach to pitching, but also for his extreme politeness and amiability as soon as a game ended. Bickford pitched a no-hitter versus the Brooklyn Dodgers on August 11, 1950. He ended that season with a 19–14 record, failing six times to notch a 20th victory. Bickford won 11 games in 1951 and seven in 1952. For a time, he became a local TV star in Boston, making regular appearances on a program called *Braves' Baseball in Your Living Room* in which he and other members of Boston's NL club offered playing tips to youngsters. Bickford went with the Braves when they moved to Milwaukee in 1953, but his MLB career was approaching its end. He was traded to the Baltimore Orioles in

1954 and had little impact there. The following year Bickford was trying to salvage an existence in the minors. He won one game for the Richmond Virginians of the International League before retiring. With baseball out of the picture, Bickford sold cars and worked as a carpenter and as a traveling salesman in the short time he had left to live. Bickford died of lung cancer on May 6, 1960. It was not long after he gave an interview from his hospital bed in which he said he was hoping to return to baseball in some capacity once he got well. Sadly, Bickford was just 39 years old.

Don Black, the Indians pitcher who collapsed with a cerebral hemorrhage during a game at Cleveland Municipal Stadium on September 13, 1948, lived for six and a half more years. When he left baseball behind, he also left his hard-won sobriety behind on a couple of publicized occasions. He died in his home while watching an Indians game on television on April 21, 1959. He was only 42.

Cleveland's **Ray Boone** had a hugely productive career after his one unproductive at-bat in the World Series. Primarily playing shortstop and third base, Boone played 13 seasons in the majors but he never got back to the Fall Classic. After being traded to Detroit in 1953, he twice appeared in the annual MLB All-Star Game (in 1954 and 1956). Boone was traded to the White Sox in June 1958 and spent the remainder of his career in short-term stints with Chicago, Kansas City, Milwaukee and Boston. A back injury finally terminated the 37-year-old Boone's playing days in 1960. Recognizing Boone's baseball smarts, Red Sox owner Tom Yawkey hired him to be the club's scout for the southwest region of the country—a position Boone held for nearly 33 years. Boone—a descendant of Daniel Boone—was the first of three generations in his family to make it to the majors. Son Bob and grandsons Bret and Aaron all played for MLB teams. When Boone died on October 17, 2004, at age 81 after a lengthy hospitalization, a moment of silence was held before Game Four of the ALCS at Fenway Park.

After leading his team to the World Series championship and winning the AL MVP award, **Lou Boudreau** got a raise in pay to $62,000 for 1949. When the Indians failed to repeat as AL pennant winners in 1949, Boudreau sensed his time was approaching an end in Cleveland. He felt that Hank Greenberg, Bill Veeck's assistant, was impeding him as manager. Veeck had been aloof with Boudreau in 1948; he was even more so in 1949. That season Boudreau proved his versatility by playing all four infield positions. He batted .284, while hitting four homers and driving in 60 runs. Boudreau's last season in Cleveland was 1950. Playing in only half his team's games, Boudreau batted .269 and hit just one homer. Ellis Ryan took over as principal owner from Bill Veeck that season and put Greenberg in charge of the team. Thus, it did not come as a shock to Boudreau

22. Whatever Became Of... 207

on November 10 when he was given his release by the Indians after 12 years of devoted service as a player, nine of which were as Cleveland's player-manager. Boudreau was acquired by the Boston Red Sox in 1951 and eventually managed that AL team from 1952 to 1954. After being fired in Boston, Boudreau managed the Kansas City Athletics from 1955 through 1957. When that job terminated, he was quickly hired to do television work for the Chicago Cubs. Two years later the stumbling Cubs signed him to be the club's manager. By 1961 he was back as the team's broadcaster, however, and stayed there through the 1987 season. In the interim, Boudreau was elected to the Hall of Fame in 1970. At the induction ceremony, Commissioner Bowie Kuhn glowingly introduced Boudreau by saying, "There are hitters in the Hall of Fame with higher batting averages, but I do not believe there is in the Hall of Fame a baseball man who brought more use of intellect and advocation of mind to the game than Lou Boudreau." Boudreau died on August 10, 2001, at age 84, in Olympia Fields, Illinois.

Largely forgotten today, **Jim Britt** continued to call both Red Sox and Braves home games in Boston through 1950. Beginning in 1951, the Red Sox decided to broadcast both home and away games, which made Britt's arrangement with the two teams no longer possible. He chose to stick with the Braves. (Curt Gowdy replaced Britt as the Red Sox announcer and held the job for the next 15 seasons.) When the Braves left Boston for Milwaukee after the 1952 season, Britt did not go with them. He was eventually hired to broadcast Cleveland Indian games on TV from 1954 to 1957. Alcoholism and an eye injury combined to end Britt's announcing career. Not especially popular with his peers — one called him "a Felix Unger type" — Britt died in late 1980 (the exact date varies by source) at about age 70. Police found him dead in his Monterey, California, apartment. He had no next of kin. In Britt's *Boston Globe* obituary, sportswriter Ray Fitzgerald sadly noted that "life had turned its back on him a long time ago."

Commissioner **Happy Chandler** held his lofty post only until the middle of the 1951 season. He resigned effective July 15 of that year because he knew he was not going to be offered a contract renewal by the 16 MLB club owners. Chandler had displeased them with his decisions on several issues. Among other things, Chandler had directed all the monies from World Series broadcast rights to the players' pension fund. Ford Frick became MLB's new boss. Chandler returned to Kentucky politics and won another term as governor. He died on June 15, 1991, at age 92.

Cleveland relief pitcher **Russ Christopher**, who failed to retire either of the two Boston batters he faced in Game Five, also died young — at age 37 — on December 5, 1954. It was remarkable that Christopher was a professional baseball player at all, let alone an MLB pitcher, having been afflicted with a badly damaged heart after a boyhood bout with rheumatic fever. He had leaky heart valves and was seemingly always out of breath. Sometimes his face would suddenly turn blue, understandably alarming his teammates. "The doctors know what's wrong," he once told a reporter. "They say it doesn't matter what I'm doing. I'm a pitcher. If I'm going to die, I might as well die pitching."[2] Christopher's brief appearance in a mop-up role in Game Five was the last time he pitched in the majors. His ERA for the World Series was the dreaded sideways eight: infinity. Nevertheless, he was a valuable member of the Indians bullpen in 1948. In an October 1992 interview for the Baseball Hall of Fame's oral history project, manager Lou Boudreau recalled Christopher's extreme submarine delivery giving opponents trouble. "Christopher was the type of pitcher who would relieve and do a good job," recalled Boudreau. "He had a good sinker, good control. I used him quite a bit. It was difficult for a hitter to pick up his delivery from the knees."

Outfielder **Allie Clark** played parts of three more seasons with Cleveland but he never became a regular starter for the Indians—or any other MLB team. During the offseason he frequently worked in the steel industry in Perth Amboy, New Jersey. Clark ended up having stints with the Philadelphia Athletics from 1951 to 1953 and briefly with the Chicago White Sox until he was released in June 1953. Clark then signed a minor league contract with the St. Louis Cardinals and spent the better part of five productive seasons with their affiliate in Rochester. (He was inducted into the Rochester Red Wings Hall of Fame in 1998.) Clark finished his pro baseball career in 1958 by shuttling between clubs in New Orleans, San Antonio and Indianapolis. He worked steadily in the iron industry in his post-baseball life. Clark died at age 88 in Morgan, New Jersey, on April 2, 2012.

Clint Conatser of the Boston Braves had a brief MLB career. The 1948 season was the outfielder's rookie campaign; the 1949 season was his swansong. Conatser was batting .263 in 1949 when he was demoted to the Braves' top minor league team in Milwaukee in July. He was never able to work his way back to the parent club. He suddenly retired from pro baseball partway through the 1952 season at age 30 despite doing well with the Portland Beavers in the Pacific Coast League. "There was just no financial incentive," Conatser recalled. "I gave it my best shot, but I had to go make some money. It's wonderful to be a ballplayer, but you've got to make a living." Conatser spent the rest of his working days in the air-conditioning business that was burgeoning throughout America—especially on the west coast—during the 1950s. He lived to be 98 years old, dying on August 23, 2019, in Laguna Hills, California. Conatser had been the last surviving player from the Braves' 1948 pennant-winning team.

After winning Rookie of the Year laurels in 1948, **Alvin Dark** had a

22. Whatever Became Of...

slightly disappointing 1949 campaign—a season when the Braves dropped from first to fourth place. Dark batted just .276. At the end of the year the Braves dealt both Dark and Eddie Stanky to the Giants—a move that benefited both men. Dark, to his surprise, was appointed the team's captain in 1951 by manager Leo Durocher who admired his insightful new shortstop. Dark fared well in New York and regularly attained solid offensive numbers. He was with the Giants in 1954 when they upset the heavily favored Cleveland Indians in an unlikely four-game World Series sweep. Injuries hurt Dark's performance in 1955, however. By 1956 Dark was part of a multi-player deal that sent him to the St. Louis Cardinals. Now playing mostly third base, Dark was traded to Chicago, Philadelphia, Milwaukee and San Francisco before calling it quits as a player. However, in 1961, he was hired to be the manager of the San Francisco Giants. In 1962, his club won the NL pennant and only narrowly lost the seven-game World Series to the New York Yankees. In 1964, Dark came under fire after criticizing his players for making mental mistakes. He mentioned no players specifically, but because most of the Giants were black or Latino, Dark was accused of racism. Notable baseball figures, such as Jackie Robinson, came to Dark's defense, but he was fired anyway at season's end. Dark got a job as a coach with the Chicago Cubs and then as a manager of the Kansas City Athletics. He lasted less than a year under mercurial owner Charlie Finley. Dark managed the Cleveland Indians from 1969 to 1971. In 1974, Dark was rehired by Finley to manage his Oakland A's where he won the World Series. (The following July, Dark became the first man to manage the AL team and NL team in All-Star Games.) The A's again won the AL West in 1975, but were swept out of the ALCS by the Boston Red Sox. Dark's contract was not renewed for 1976. Dark managed the San Diego Padres for most of 1977 but he was fired during spring training of 1978. Dark lived to be 92 years old. He died on November 13, 2014, in Easley, South Carolina.

The Indians **Larry Doby** followed his superb 1948 World Series with an excellent 1949 season in which he clouted 24 home runs and accrued 85 RBI. In 1950, Doby particularly stood out among his peers when he was ranked the best center fielder in all of MLB by *The Sporting News*. He batted a career best .326 and got 164 hits—also a lifetime high. In the voting for the AL MVP, Doby finished eighth. Cleveland's sports journalists named Doby their Baseball Man of the Year. From 1951 through 1955, Doby's numbers dipped as injuries began to take a toll on him. Still, Doby played in seven All-Star Games and on the Indians' 1954 AL pennant winner. Once the 1955 season concluded, Doby was traded to the Chicago White Sox. It was the start of short stays on many clubs for Doby. Doby led his new team in both home runs and batting average in 1956. After the 1957 season, Doby was dealt by the White Sox to the Baltimore Orioles.

Before the 1958 season began, he was traded back to Cleveland. The following March he was traded to Detroit. Two months later, Doby's contract was sold to the Chicago White Sox. He played 21 games in Chicago before being demoted to the minor leagues. Doby never again played at the MLB level. He retired in 1960 after failing to earn a roster spot on the minor league Toronto Maple Leafs. Doby later returned to the sport to play professionally in Japan. Doby managed a liquor store for a time. He then worked in the Montreal Expos organization as a coach and batting instructor. Doby became the second black MLB manager in 1977 when Bill Veeck hired him as a midseason replacement for old teammate Bob Lemon. Doby finished the 1977 season but was not offered a contract by the White Sox for 1978. Doby was elected to the Hall of Fame by the Veterans Committee in 1998. He died of cancer on June 18, 2003, at the age of 79 in Montclair, New Jersey. Doby's image appeared on a U.S. postage stamp in 2012. As for being the only black starting player on the 1948 Indians and in that year's World Series, Doby told an interviewer in 1979, "I never thought about it. I just went out and played. I ran. I hit. I threw just like the rest of them."

Bob Elliott had productive years for Boston in both 1949 and 1950. One highlight was a three-homer game versus Philadelphia on September 4, 1949. Elliott's 76 RBIs that season gave him 903 for the decade—the highest total for any MLB player in the 1940s. His offensive numbers started to tail off in 1951, however, and he got into a bitter contract dispute with the Braves in 1952 at a time when the team was suffering badly at the gate. Before the season began, Elliott was traded to the New York Giants where he played in 98 games. No longer a full-time player, Elliott asked for his release at the end of the season—and got it. Having done well in a tryout and exhibition games with the St. Louis Browns in 1953, Elliott was signed by Bill Veeck who, by then, was the Browns owner. Elliott attained his 2,000th MLB hit while playing for the Browns, but midway through the season he was traded to the Chicago White Sox. A leg injury curtailed Elliott's playing time and ended his career. Elliott managed one season with the San Diego club in the Pacific Coast League and one season in the AL—1960—with the Kansas City Athletics. (At season's end, Elliott was fired for no particular reason by mercurial owner Charles O. Finley, who made a habit of going through managers at a dizzying rate.) With his baseball days over, Elliott settled in San Diego and worked as a beer distributor for a time. He died young. In 1966, Elliott suffered a ruptured windpipe and passed away on May 4 at age 49.

Bob Feller never did win a World Series game. In fact, he never even appeared in another Fall Classic. Thus, his 1948 World Series stats are his only postseason numbers: He was 0–2 with an unflattering 5.02 ERA. (Feller did make one further All-Star game appearance. In 1950 he faced three batters in mop-up duties in a 4–3, 12-inning NL victory.) The next time the Indians won the AL pennant, in 1954, Feller, approaching age 36, was still a member of the Indians' pitching staff, but he was perceived to be past his prime despite posting an excellent 13–3 record with a 3.09 ERA in a season in which his workload was reduced to about one start per week to preserve his aging arm. He was not used by Cleveland manager Al Lopez in any of the World Series contests that autumn, making him the only Indians hurler eligible for the Fall Classic who saw no action. (In retrospect, perhaps Feller should have gotten a start. Cleveland won an AL record 111 games in 1954, but they were shockingly swept by the underdog New York Giants in the World Series.) In a lengthy 2009 interview for MLB-TV conducted by Bob Costas, Feller insisted that the 1948 Indians were actually a better team than the 1954 version! Feller's performance dipped dramatically in 1955. (He had a 4–4 record and only completed two of 11 starts.) Then Feller failed to win even one game in the 1956 season, after which he retired. In that same 2009 interview, Feller confirmed the rumors that in 1948 his arm was not what it once had been. He said he had injured it in a game at Philadelphia's Shibe Park prior to the 1947 All-Star Game where he tried to break his single-game strikeout record of 18 after whiffing eight Athletics in the first three innings. [Authors' note: It had to be the game played on June 13, 1947.] Feller recalled slipping on the mound during a pitch—and, at age 28, he could never again throw with the same authority. He was elected to the Hall of Fame in 1962 in his first year of eligibility, his name appearing on 150 of 160 voters' ballots. For exercise, Feller enjoyed playing catch every day of his long retirement. (He thus laid claim to the unprovable title of having thrown more baseballs than anyone who ever lived.) One of MLB's great ambassadors, Feller reported in his 1990 autobiography that he still received an average of 25 fan letters per week. Seventeen months before he died, Feller pitched to three batters as part of an exhibition game in Cooperstown in 2009—at age 90. Feller died of leukemia-related causes in Cleveland on December 15, 2010, at age 91.

Decades removed from the pennant-winning season, Eddie Robinson declared **Joe Gordon** to be the on-field leader among the 1948 Indians. (Lou Boudreau, as the team's player-manager, was disqualified from Robinson's consideration.) Following the World Series, the Cleveland second baseman played just two more MLB seasons. In 1949, Gordon's offensive numbers dipped noticeably: He batted .251 while driving in 81 runs. In 1950 his performance declined further. Gordon played in 119 games, batted .236 and drove in just 57 runs. It was a transition year where promising newcomer Bobby Avila would slowly become the Tribe's regular second baseman. The 35-year-old Gordon was released by Cleveland following the 1950 season. In 1951 he became the player-manager for the Sacramento

Solos of the Pacific Coast League, a position he held for two seasons. Gordon scouted for the Detroit Tigers for a few years before moving away from baseball. That was only temporary. Gordon sold insurance for a while until he was summoned back to Cleveland midway through the 1958 season to pilot the Indians. It was the beginning of a wild odyssey of MLB managing jobs for the ex-second baseman. Gordon lasted in Cleveland until September 1959 when he announced he could no longer get along with Indians general manager Frank Lane and had no intention of returning as manager for 1960. Lane gave Gordon the ax before the 1959 season ended. A few days later, Lane reconsidered his move and rehired Gordon. Lane amusingly told the press, "I've decided the best man to replace Joe Gordon is Joe Gordon."[3] Gordon did return in 1960, but on August 3 he was a figure in one of the oddest trades in sports history as the Tigers and Indians swapped managers! Gordon relocated to Detroit and Jimmy Dykes went to Cleveland. Gordon finished the season with the Tigers, resigned, and then signed to manage the Kansas City Athletics in 1961. Gordon was fired after just 59 games, having won 23 of them. Gordon had one more stint as an MLB manager with the expansion Kansas City Royals in 1969, leading them to a fourth-place finish in the AL West. A heavy smoker for most of his life, Gordon died of a heart attack at age 63 on April 14, 1978. He was posthumously enshrined in the Hall of Fame in 2009.

Umpire **Bill Grieve** drew practically no attention during the 1948 Fall Classic—exactly the goal of an MLB arbiter. He worked one more World Series (1953) and one more All-Star Game (1949) before settling into retirement after an 18-year career as an AL ump. He died of cancer on August 15, 1979, at a hospital in Yonkers, New York. There remains some dispute about Grieve's true age; some sources claim a 1900 birth year for him while others list 1896 as being correct.

Despite Bill Veeck's optimistic public prediction that **Steve Gromek** might be the ace of the Indians' staff in 1949, the righthander continued his role as something akin to a fifth wheel among Cleveland pitchers. Gene Bearden turned out to be just a one-season star, but the Indians acquired Early Wynn from Washington. Rookie Mike Garcia joined the Cleveland staff too, relegating Gromek to the status of occasional starter. "Steve didn't start enough to work up a good sweat,"[4] wrote Cleveland baseball scribe Ed McAuley. It was only a slight exaggeration as Gromek got just a dozen starts and pitched only 92 innings in 1949. The same pattern continued through 1952 even though Gromek put up decent yearly statistics. Gromek was, in effect, languishing in Cleveland. One biographer wrote, "Gromek's name was seldom mentioned in trade rumors. Other teams may have accepted Cleveland's judgment that he was second-rate. He was not good enough to crack the Indians' rotation, but too good to trade away for nothing."[5] On June 15, 1953, Gromek was happy to be dealt to the Detroit Tigers, a struggling club with a weak pitching staff. It also meant he would be playing near his hometown. Gromek joyfully told the *Detroit Free Press*, "It's like starting over. I'm a rookie again." The 34-year-old Gromek threw a shutout for Detroit on Opening Day 1954 versus the newly christened Baltimore Orioles. The ace of a poor team, Gromek compiled an 18–16 record and pitched 252⅔ innings—a personal seasonal high—but he also allowed the most home runs among AL pitchers: 26. Gromek gave up another 26 home runs in 1955. He was also suffering back pain which reduced his workload to 181 innings. After only appearing in 15 games in 1956, and with his aching back not getting any better, Gromek retired before the season ended. Gromek managed a Class D club in Erie, Pennsylvania, for a season and served as a scout for a time. He spent the rest of his working life selling insurance. Gromek died in Clinton Township, Michigan, at age 82 on March 12, 2002.

Jeff Heath, the Boston outfielder who missed the World Series because of a late-season severe ankle fracture, only played one more MLB campaign. He played in 36 games in 1949 and batted a respectable .306. However, at age 34 and with a loss of mobility, Heath's playing days were numbered. The Braves released him at the end of the 1949 season. Heath played one year in the Pacific Coast League for the Seattle Rainiers and then did radio broadcasts for the club for several seasons. The hotheaded Heath mellowed with age. (One interviewer in 1964 described him as affable and talkative.) However, his old feistiness surfaced every once in a while. During one broadcast he became annoyed about some technical difficulties and cussed, not realizing his microphone was live. When the station manager confronted him about it, Heath lost his temper and threw the man down a flight of stairs. At age 42, Heath suffered a serious heart attack while participating in a parade. He survived that one. On December 9, 1975, he was not so lucky. That day Heath was stricken with a fatal heart attack in Seattle. He was 60 years old.

Cleveland catcher **Jim Hegan** played another nine years with the Indians following the 1948 World Series in a career that eventually spanned 17 seasons. Never a great batsman, Hegan's best seasonal average after 1948 was the .238 mark he attained in 1951. But Hegan was not in the Indians' lineup for offense; he was there because he was an excellent catcher. Casey Stengel once commented that if he could have his pick of any of Cleveland's ace pitchers from the early 1950s, he would prefer to have Hegan because, "He's what makes 'em."[6] Hegan's teammates concurred. Pitcher Herb Score said, "[Hegan] was so good that if you crossed him up, nobody knew it. He had the best hands I ever saw. If I crossed him up, he might not tell me for a week."[7] Another Cleveland pitcher, Mike

Garcia, once said of Hegan, "If a foul ball went in the air and stayed in the ballpark, it was an automatic out. [Hegan] didn't stagger around under it. He went right to the spot of the ball."[8] Hegan became a coach for the New York Yankees after his playing days ended. (Hegan's son, Mike, a first baseman, was on the New York roster at the time. After going to Oakland, Mike played in the 1972 Fall Classic with the A's, thus making the Hegans the first father-and-son combination to each win a World Series.) Hegan died at the age of 63 on June 17, 1984, after suffering a heart attack.

Tommy Holmes, perhaps the most popular player on the 1948 Braves, played two more seasons with Boston before stepping into a managerial role. When the 1950 season concluded, the 33-year-old Holmes was appointed player-manager of the Braves' Class A affiliate in Hartford. The 34-year-old was batting .319 there when Billy Southworth experienced health problems and the Braves began an irreversible decline. The 58-year-old Southworth suddenly resigned on June 19, some 60 games into the season. Holmes was quickly promoted to the parent club as his replacement. He pinch-hit occasionally, too. The team improved marginally with the managerial switch, playing just above .500 ball for the rest of that season. However, when the Braves began the 1952 season with a disappointing 13–22 mark, Holmes was fired. He told the press that the Braves management were "wonderful people. They probably hated twice as much telling me I was fired as I disliked hearing it."[9] Years later Holmes was more truthful. In a 1986 interview with the *Boston Herald*, Holmes admitted, "It broke my heart when they let me go. I was ready to have a home built up there. I don't think I ever got over that, even yet."[10] Holmes latched on with the Brooklyn Dodgers for the remainder of 1952 as an occasional player where, that October, he concluded his playing career in the World Series. (He appeared in three games and was hitless in his lone at-bat.) Holmes stayed active in baseball by returning to the minors to manage teams affiliated with the Dodgers and Braves. Later Holmes was hired by the New York Mets as "director of amateur baseball relations"—a post he held for 30 years. He retired at age 86. On April 14, 2008, Holmes died in Boca Raton, Florida, 16 days after his 91st birthday.

He did not know it, but **Wally Judnich** only had ten games left in his MLB career after the 1948 World Series ended. In February 1949, the Pittsburgh Pirates purchased Judnich's contract from the Indians with the intent of making him a full-time first baseman. The experiment did not last halfway through May. The Pirates sold Judnich's contract to the San Francisco Seals—and Judnich never again played in the majors. Judnich was shuffled amongst various clubs in the Pacific Coast League through the 1953 season. He decided to retire rather than report to the Louisville Colonels for 1954. A very private person, Judnich refused to even talk about his interests outside of baseball. He died in Glendale, California, at age 55 on July 10, 1971.

Popular Cleveland third baseman **Ken Keltner** had a dismal World Series at the plate (batting .095), but that did not stop him from being pictured with his family on a Wheaties box at the end of 1948 in honor of his superb regular season. (His compensation was a year's supply of the cereal.) Keltner's production dropped off dramatically at age 32 in 1949, however. After receiving a bad spike wound in the lower leg, Keltner appeared in just 69 of the Tribe's games at third base that season. Furthermore, his batting average when he did play was a poor .232. Al Rosen, who had been languishing on Indian minor league teams for years because of how good Keltner was, finally got his chance and became Cleveland's new regular third sacker. He ascended to stardom. The Indians released Keltner at the end of 1949. The Boston Red Sox picked up Keltner for the 1950 season. He played in just 13 games with Boston to ingloriously end his MLB career, although he did play for Sacramento in the Pacific Coast League in 1951. After his retirement from baseball, Keltner returned to Wisconsin (where he had grown up) and worked in sales for a bicycle wholesaler and a chemical company. For a short time, he ran a restaurant in Bay View, Wisconsin, called Keltner's Hob Nob. In 1969, Cleveland fans voted Kelter their all-time third baseman. He suffered a fatal heart attack on December 12, 1991, at the assisted-living facility in New Berlin, Wisconsin, where he resided. He was 75 years old.

Bob Kennedy, the man who caught the fly ball to end the 1948 World Series, remained as an Indian outfielder through 1953. From 1949 through 1951 Kennedy experienced the most productive years in his 16-season MLB playing career. Early in the 1952 season, he was one of four Second World War veterans in the majors who were recalled to active duty to serve in the Korean War, thus Kennedy only played in 22 games for Cleveland that year. He returned to the Indians during the 1953 season. In 1954, Kennedy was traded to Baltimore and then to the Chicago White Sox. He then ended up with the Detroit Tigers, then went back to the White Sox, and then was grabbed on waivers by the Brooklyn Dodgers in 1957. While there, Kennedy became the answer to a trivia question. At Philadelphia's Shibe Park, on September 29, 1957—the final day of the season—Kennedy was the last man to bat for Brooklyn before the storied team relocated to Los Angeles in 1958. (He flied out to Phillies center fielder Don Landrum in a 2–1 loss.) It also turned out to be Kennedy's last MLB at-bat. He was released by the Dodgers on October 15. Kennedy stayed involved in the game as a coach and scout. Eventually he managed both the Chicago Cubs and Oakland A's. Kennedy also served in front-office positions with the St. Louis Cardinals and San Francisco Giants, finally retiring in 1992 after a lifetime of service to the sport. He settled in Mesa, Arizona. That is where Kennedy died on April 7, 2005, at the age of 84.

Pitcher **Ed Klieman** did not stay long on the Cleveland roster after the team's World Series win. Before the end of 1948, he was part of the Indians' huge trade with the Washington Senators that sent both Mickey Vernon and Early Wynn to the Tribe. Klieman's impact on the Senators was a small one. He pitched in just two games for Washington before his contract was sold to the Chicago White Sox. Klieman won two decisions as a reliever for Chicago in 1949. During the offseason, he was traded to the Philadelphia Athletics. He fared poorly for the A's in five relief appearances in 1950, posting a 9.53 ERA. He was soon demoted to the minor leagues and never got back to the majors. Klieman retired from baseball after the 1951 season. Klieman died at the age of 61 in Homosassa, Florida, on November 15, 1979.

Pitcher **Bob Lemon**, who had a breakout year as a Cleveland starter in 1948, had another excellent season in 1949. He clearly became the ace of the Indians' staff as Bob Feller's effectiveness began to wane. Lemon was 22–10 with a 2.99 ERA. (He had a good year at the plate too, hitting seven home runs.) Lemon was 23–11 the following year. After winning just 17 games in 1951, Lemon rebounded with 22 victories in 1952 and 21 wins in 1953. Lemon, who by then had mastered a baffling slider to add to his pitching arsenal, had a spectacular 1954 season for an Indians team that won an AL record 111 games. Lemon was 23–7 with a 2.72 ERA. Bob Broeg wrote in *The Sporting News* that December, "No statistic, though, could capture the man's competitive fire, his bulldog nature that made him the Indians' most-feared pitcher."[11] That same year, in a poll of Cleveland sportswriters, Lemon was voted the wittiest *and* the most conceited of the Indians. In 1955, Lemon suffered two leg injuries and still won 18 games. He recorded his last 20-win season in 1956 at age 36. Further injuries hastened the end of Lemon's playing career in 1957 when he won just six games while losing 11. Early in the 1958 season, Lemon was pulled from a game in the second inning and never made another MLB start. He began a second career in baseball managing in the minor leagues with great success. In 1971 he was hired by the Kansas City Royals to be their new manager. He was fired after the 1972 campaign by owner Ewing Kaufman for making a facetious remark to a reporter that he would like to retire from baseball and live on a remote island. Lemon went back to managing in the minors. He returned to the majors in 1977 when his old boss, Bill Veeck, hired him to pilot the Chicago White Sox. Lemon was named Manager of the Year for leading Chicago to a surprising 90-win season. Lemon was fired early in the 1978 season when the team started slowly. However, Lemon was quickly hired by George Steinbrenner to replace Billy Martin in the circus atmosphere that pervaded the New York Yankees. Apparently, the easygoing Lemon was precisely what the Yankees needed at the time. Outfielder Jay Johnston commented, "Lem's sort of like an Andy Griffith character. You know, 'Take it easy, don't panic, we'll think of something.'"[12] New York won the World Series that year. Sixty-five games into the 1979 season, however, Lemon was fired by Steinbrenner. He was rehired by New York in 1981 and led his club to the World Series which they lost to the Los Angeles Dodgers in six games. Lemon was fired 14 games into the 1982 season and returned to California for good. He did not have to find other employment because he was reputedly under a lifetime contract to the Yankees as a reward for managing the 1978 World Series champions. After a lengthy period of failing health, Lemon died in a nursing home in Long Beach, California, at age 79 on January 11, 2000.

Boston catcher **Phil Masi**—who will forever be remembered as the man who was controversially called safe on the infamous Game One pick-off play—lasted on the Braves' roster just halfway through June 1949. Young Del Crandall was the Boston catcher of the future so, struggling with a poor .210 batting average, the 33-year-old Masi was shipped to Pittsburgh where he would be that club's third-string catcher for the rest of the season. On February 9, 1950, the Chicago White Sox purchased Masi's contract from the Pirates after he had passed through waivers in the NL. The move seemed to rejuvenate Masi, who batted .279 and earned high praise for his savvy handling of Chicago's young pitchers. He batted almost as well for the White Sox in 1951, but Masi's playing time was reduced significantly that season. In 1952, Masi's role with the White Sox was cut even further when the club acquired a much younger catcher, Sherm Lollar, in a trade with the St. Louis Browns. The White Sox released Masi at the end of the season, but he did have one final hurrah in professional baseball. In 1953, Masi agreed to play for the minor league Dallas Eagles. Masi proudly recalled years later in a *Baseball Digest* article, "The owner of the Dallas Eagles, Dick Burnett, called Paul Richards, the White Sox manager. He said he wanted a catcher who could win the Texas League division championship, the playoffs, and the Little Dixie World Series. Richards recommended me, so Burnett signed me up for the next season—and we won all three."[13] Masi died of cancer on March 29, 1990, at age 74, at his home in Mount Prospect, Illinois, admitting in his will that he was out at second base.

Frank McCormick, the 1940 NL MVP, retired as a player after the 1948 World Series. Beginning in 1949, McCormick managed in the minor leagues for two years and later did some television broadcasting for the Cincinnati Reds, the team with whom he was most associated as a player. Towards the end of his life, he was in charge of season-ticket and group-ticket sales for the New York Yankees. McCormick died of cancer, at age 71, on November 21, 1982, in Manhasset, New York.

Mike McCormick's last game for the Boston Braves was Game Six of the 1948 World Series. His MLB career lasted three more seasons with four more teams: Brooklyn and New York (briefly) in the NL and Chicago and Washington in the AL. (McCormick was sent to the Dodgers as the key part of Boston's trade for Pete Reiser in December 1948.) He finished with a lifetime .275 batting average. While attending the Los Angeles Dodgers' home opener on April 13, 1976, McCormick was stricken by a massive heart attack and died while on his way to Queen of Angels Hospital. He was about three weeks shy of his 59th birthday.

Cleveland's **Dale Mitchell**—who finished third in the 1948 AL batting race behind Ted Williams and Lou Boudreau—continued to be a fine offensive and defensive asset to the Indians into the 1956 season. In 1949, Mitchell led the AL in three offensive categories (hits, singles and triples) while striking out only 11 times all season. By the end of July 1956, Mitchell was far off his typical form, batting just .133. He was acquired by the Brooklyn Dodgers on waivers. Despite posting a .312 career batting average and a .985 lifetime fielding percentage, Mitchell is probably best known for being the final out in Don Larsen's perfect game in the 1956 World Series. (Mitchell was rung up on strikes by umpire Babe Pinelli on a pitch he thought was out of the strike zone. Mitchell refused an offer to appear on *Good Morning, America* with Larsen and New York catcher Yogi Berra because he was unenthusiastic about going on television solely to discuss striking out.) Mitchell retired after the 1956 season. After baseball, Mitchell worked in the oil business and then in the cement business where he did quite well. He stopped attending MLB old-timers' events when he learned how destitute some of his former teammates and diamond adversaries had become. Mitchell had a history of cardiac problems. He died of a heart attack at age 65 in Tulsa, Oklahoma, on January 5, 1987. The baseball facility at the University of Oklahoma—where Mitchell had been a star collegiate athlete—is named after him.

Bob Muncrief's 1948 season, when he pitched for a World Series winner, was his only year as a Cleveland Indian. A month after the Fall Classic ended, Cleveland sold Muncrief's contract to the Pittsburgh Pirates. Partway through the 1949 season, the Pirates put Muncrief on waivers. He was acquired by the Chicago Cubs. Between the Pirates and Cubs, Muncrief compiled a 6–11 record with an unimpressive 5.12 ERA. He spent all of 1950 in the minor leagues before returning briefly to the majors as a New York Yankee in 1951. Muncrief spent five further seasons in the minors before calling it a career. Muncrief died nine days after his 80th birthday in 1996 in Duncanville, Texas.

22. Whatever Became Of... 219

Pitcher **Satchel Paige** remained on the Cleveland roster in 1949, but his record was not an impressive one. He was 4–7 with an ERA of 3.04. Paige pitched mostly as a reliever, starting five games and coming out of the bullpen in 26 others. Paige was released by the Indians when the season ended. Apparently in dire financial straits, Paige returned to his barnstorming roots playing wherever anyone would pay him to show up. Bill Veeck purchased the majority interest in the St. Louis Browns in 1951 and signed Paige as a drawing card. He was 3–4 that season and sported an ERA of 4.79. Paige continued with the Browns for two more years. He was chosen by Casey Stengel as one of his staff for the All-Star Games in both those years. The second selection was based more on nostalgia than merit as Paige finished 1953 with a 3–9 record and was released after Veeck sold the Browns to an ownership group who would move it to Baltimore. Paige bounced around the minor Leagues for a while. He made a onetime stunt return to the majors for the Kansas City Athletics in 1965. Owner Charles O. Finley hired him to pitch one game against the Boston Red Sox on September 25. Paige, who was seated in a rocking chair in the A's bullpen prior to the game, pitched three innings, faced 10 Red Sox batters, and only surrendered one hit: Carl Yastrzemski lined a double off him. When he was removed from the game, the relatively small crowd of 9,289 gave Paige a standing ovation and sang "The Old Gray Mare." He died on June 8, 1982, of a heart attack at his Kansas City home. Paige was (perhaps) a month short of his 76th birthday.

Umpire **Joe Paparella** worked three more World Series (1951, 1957, and 1963) before retiring from baseball in 1965 after 20 seasons of service in the AL. In 1962 he set an MLB record that still stands: He worked 176 games that season! Sixty of those games were in the form of 30 doubleheaders. The National Baseball Hall of Fame has in its archives an undated audio interview of Paparella conducted by author Larry R. Gerlach for his book *The Men in Blue*. As soon as Gerlach mentioned the 1948 World Series, Paparella, without being prompted, said he had a great look at the famous pickoff play in Game One. Then he laughed and said, "I'm not going to make any comments on it here." Paparella, stationed along the left field line, said he knew the pickoff attempt was forthcoming because, as an AL ump, he was quite familiar with Cleveland's timing play involving signals flashed between Lou Boudreau, Joe Gordon and (usually) Bob Feller. Paparella also emphasized to Gerlach that the Indians' excellent pickoff play had been discussed among the six men in blue prior to the game, largely to give the three NL officials a bit of advance warning. Without specifically saying in so many words that NL umpire Bill Stewart had blown the important call at second base, Paparella merely admitted, "Bill was caught flat-footed." In that same interview, Paparella insisted that working in the majors was far easier than in the minors because minor league ballplayers typically reacted much more angrily and sometimes violently to questionable calls than the MLB players did. He also recalled the commonly substandard facilities for the sport's arbiters, especially in the low minors. (On one occasion he had to dress for a game in the ballpark's toolshed.) Paparella died in Sebastian, Florida, on October 17, 1994, at age 85.

Hal Peck—the man whose promising baseball career was derailed for a time by an odd, self-inflicted firearms mishap—was retained by Cleveland for the 1949 season, but he did not play much. When the Indians acquired Bob Kennedy in 1948, it meant that Peck's role was basically reduced to pinch-hitting. That trend continued in 1949, too. A knee injury that season reduced Peck's playing time further. He was removed from Cleveland's active roster in May but he was reinstated in July. Peck played just 33 games in 1949, but he did bat .310 in 29 official at-bats that season. Peck refused demotion to the Portland Beavers of the Pacific Coast League in 1950, opting to retire instead. He died in Milwaukee on April 13, 1995, at age 77.

Before retiring, NL umpire **Babe Pinelli** worked two more World Series: 1952 and 1956. Both times he served as the crew chief. His last plate assignment ever was a noteworthy one: Game Five of the 1956 Fall Classic—which happened to be Don Larsen's perfect game for the New York Yankees. The last Brooklyn Dodger batter that game was a familiar face from the 1948 Fall Classic: Dale Mitchell. When Pinelli returned to the umpires' room afterward, the drama of the game, its historic impact, and the realization that he would never again work another MLB contest behind the plate suddenly overwhelmed the 22-year veteran arbiter—causing him to weep uncontrollably. Pinelli died in Daly City, California, four days after his 89th birthday in 1984. He was posthumously inducted into the National Italian Sports Hall of Fame in 2000.

Veteran pitcher **Nels Potter** had a mediocre World Series—and it was a sign of what was ahead for him in 1949. The Braves hurler, in what would be his last season in the majors, went 6–11, mostly in relief tasks. It dropped his career won-lost total to a sub-.500 mark of 92–97. The Braves finished a disappointing fourth in 1949 and parted ways with many of the veterans from their 1948 pennant winners. Nelson was one of them. He was put on waivers and claimed by Cincinnati. However, the 38-year-old Potter had decided to walk away from the sport. He explained, "I didn't want to stay in baseball. I'd traveled for so many years. In a hotel on a road trip, you'd hang up your clothes for three days, so I was happy to hang my clothes in a closet at home."[14] He returned to his hometown of Mount Morris, Illinois, where he worked as a pressman and became active in local politics. He later built and managed a bowling center. Potter died on September 30,

1990, at the age of 79. He was watching a Mets-Cubs game on television when he passed away.

After having a very good World Series as a late addition to the Boston lineup, **Marv Rickert** was offered a contract by the Braves for the 1949 season. The Braves were later embarrassed to learn that Rickert's contract was actually a $1,500 pay cut from what he had been earning with the minor-league Milwaukee Brewers in 1948. Rickert said he would not play in the majors for less than he was making in the minors and eventually attained a satisfactory deal with Boston. Rickert appeared in 100 games for the Braves in 1949, often playing first base while Earl Torgeson was injured. He batted .292 in 1949—his best MLB average ever. Prior to the 1950 season, Rickert was traded to Pittsburgh. He played just 17 games with the Pirates, batted .150, and ended up finishing the year—and his MLB career—with the Chicago White Sox. After baseball ended for Rickert, he worked in parks and recreation in Pierce County in his home state of Washington and died from a heart attack at the young age of 57 on June 3, 1978.

After the 1948 World Series ended, Cleveland first baseman **Eddie Robinson** never played another game for the Indians. He was traded before the 1949 season to the Washington Senators. (Robinson reputedly did not get along with Indians player-manager Lou Boudreau.) Robinson would eventually play for seven of the eight AL clubs of the era, missing only the Boston Red Sox. His post–Cleveland playing career featured both highs and lows. As a member of the 1951 White Sox, he became the first Chicago hitter to smash a home run over Comiskey Park's right-field grandstand, but as a member of the 1955 New York Yankees, he tied a dubious MLB record by hitting into three double plays in a game (a mark since broken). After his playing days ended, Robinson eventually became the general manager of the Texas Rangers, a position he held from 1977 to 1982. One man Robinson hired to be the club's manager lasted just a single game—which he won—before he resigned, citing homesickness. That man was Eddie Stanky, one of his World Series opponents from 1948. Robinson replaced Stanky with Connie Ryan—another member of the 1948 Braves! When the Cleveland Indians reached the World Series in 2016, Robinson publicly expressed disappointment that, as the only living member of the 1948 Indians, he had not been approached to represent the club in any manner. (The adverse publicity prompted an apology from the Indians—and an invitation for Robinson and his wife to attend Game Six at Progressive Field.) In 2019, the 99-year-old Robinson became the oldest living ex-MLB player. In 2020, Robinson had a remarkable streak of 74 years attending at least one MLB game come to an unfortunate end because of the coronavirus pandemic. Prior to that trying year, the last season in which Robinson did not see an MLB game in person in any capacity was 1945 when he was in the navy. He celebrated his hundredth birthday on December 15, 2020. Two months earlier, Robinson began a new venture: starring in a semi-regular podcast in which he discussed his long career in the sport and the times in which he played. It was called *The Golden Years of Baseball*. Displaying a sharp mind an accurate memory, Robinson made 25 broadcasts over the final year of his life with the podcasts' revenues going to the Alzheimer's Foundation. Robinson died on October 5, 2021— two days after the Cleveland AL team played its final game as the Indians. One obituary noted that Robinson had been born about two months after Cleveland's first World Series triumph.

Cleveland's **Al Rosen**, who had one unsuccessful at-bat as a pinch-hitter in the World Series, went on to have a marvelous career with the Indians. Rosen eventually replaced the very popular Ken Keltner as the Tribe's third baseman. He played for eight more seasons for Cleveland, compiled a lifetime batting average of .285, and hit 192 home runs. A four-time All-Star, Rosen won the AL MVP Award in 1953. Chronic injuries persuaded Rosen to retire at the end of the 1956 season. After baseball, Rosen spent 17 years as a stockbroker in Cleveland. In 1978 he returned to baseball and spent 18 tumultuous months as "president and chief operating officer" of the New York Yankees under George Steinbrenner during the height of the owner's plentiful feuds with manager Billy Martin. Rosen reigned in utter frustration in July 1979. Rosen later worked for both the Houston Astros and San Francisco Giants in executive capacities. Rosen left baseball for good after the Giants were swept by the Oakland A's in the 1989 World Series. Rosen died at age 91, on March 13, 2015, in Rancho Mirage, California.

Jim Russell, who missed the World Series because of serious health issues, played one more season with the Braves, but his cardiac problems sapped much of his vigor. He batted .231 in 1949 for Boston. After the season Russell was claimed on waivers by the Brooklyn Dodgers where he spent the next two seasons shuttling between the parent club and Brooklyn's top farm team in Montreal. After 1951, Russell played two seasons for Portland in the Pacific Coast League before retiring as a player. He worked as a scout for a time for the Dodgers and Senators before going into a beer distributor business with his brother. Russell was later employed as a salesman for Smith-Corona. He became active in local politics, serving on the school board that encompassed his hometown of Fayette City, Pennsylvania. Russell died of a heart attack on November 24, 1987, shortly after boarding an airplane for a hunting trip. He was 69 years old.

Connie Ryan of the Braves enjoyed a steady but unspectacular 12-year MLB career, most of it spent as an infielder with NL clubs. He is best remembered in Braves' lore for an amusing incident in the second game of a meaningless Ladies Day home doubleheader versus Brooklyn on September 29, 1949. With his team having dropped the first game, trailing 8–0 in the second game, and enthusiasm for the battle waning, Ryan donned a long, black raincoat in the Boston on-deck circle to emphasize that the umpires ought to terminate the game. Ryan was promptly ejected for his creative temerity by umpire George Barr who did not appreciate being "shown up." Ryan was frequently asked what prompted him to put on the slicker that memorable day at Braves Field. He replied, "They [the umpires] wouldn't listen to us when we hollered from the bench that it was raining too hard to play. They wouldn't even take a hint when we built a little fire out of programs and newspapers in front of the dugout. I just thought I'd try to convince them some other way, that's all."[15] [Authors' note: The contest was called on rain not long after Ryan was ejected—and five full innings had been completed to make it a legal game.] Ryan was traded in May 1950 to the Cincinnati Reds. He later played for the Philadelphia Phillies and Chicago White Sox before returning to the Reds to conclude his MLB career. Known mostly for his defensive play, Ryan was a lifetime .248 hitter who fell 12 hits short of attaining 1,000. Ryan was a keen student of the sport. His baseball smarts got him coaching and then managing jobs for various minor league outfits and two clubs in MLB: the Atlanta Braves and Texas Rangers for one season apiece. After baseball, Ryan kept active within his community with various civic and charitable projects through his connections to Catholic churches and local service clubs. Ryan died of a heart attack at age 75 on January 3, 1996, in Metairie, Louisiana.

Johnny Sain had been one of the top NL pitchers from 1946 to 1948—recording 65 wins over those three seasons. The following year Sain suffered through a disastrous 1949 campaign by his standards, posting a 10–17 record, which he blamed on a sore shoulder from overwork during the Braves' 1948 push to the pennant. Sain rebounded with a 20–13 mark in 1950, but he was a miserable 5–13 in 1951 when the Braves sold him to the New York Yankees. Sain was mostly used as a relief pitcher by the Yankees until 1955 when he was sold to the Kansas City Athletics. He pitched his last MLB game in July 15 of that year and was released by the A's the following day. Jan Finkel, Sain's SABR biographer, wrote, "For someone who toiled in the minors for six years, lost three more years to the war, and got started at an age when most players are entering their peak, Sain had a fine career: 139 wins against 116 losses."[16] Sain operated a successful car dealership in Arkansas for a time. Later Sain returned to baseball as a pitching coach for several teams, constantly instilling the importance of throwing strikes low in the zone. Sain's charges generally thought highly of their mentor, who strongly encouraged them to get as much money as possible—even if it meant attempting to renegotiate their salaries in midseason. Not surprisingly, owners often frowned upon Sain offering such advice. Sain's last coaching gig was with the 1986 Atlanta Braves. He died in a nursing home at age 89 on November 7, 2006, in Downers Grove, Illinois.

The highlight of Boston catcher **Bill Salkeld**'s short MLB career was his home run off Bob Feller in Game Five of the 1948 World Series. Salkeld had been a highly scouted prospect as a teenager who never lived up to inflated expectations. In 1949, there were three catchers vying for the Braves' first-string job (Salkeld, Phil Masi and 19-year-old rookie Del Crandall). The 32-year-old Salkeld was considered by the Braves to be expendable even though he was Warren Spahn's favorite backstop. Boston sold Salkeld on waivers to the Chicago White Sox before the season ended. He was the Opening Day catcher for the White Sox in 1950, but Chicago was also well stocked with catchers, so Salkeld's contract was sold to the Seattle Rainiers of the Pacific Coast League after playing just one game. His career sputtered to an inglorious conclusion a year later with the Portland Beavers in 1951. Salkeld did, however, have a brief comeback as the player-manager of the Stockton Ports of the Class C California League in 1953 where he only batted .227. After his professional baseball days wound to an end, Salkeld worked for U.S. Steel. Salkeld died from inoperable cancer at the young age of 50 on April 22, 1967.

Boston's **Ray Sanders**—who saw exactly one pitch in his one pinch-hit at-bat the World Series—did not see many more pitches in his MLB career. After breaking his wrist during spring training, he played in just nine games for the Braves in 1949 and batted .143. In his seven-year career in the majors, Sanders hit 42 home runs and batted a respectable .274. Sanders played the 1950 season for the minor league Milwaukee Brewers before retiring. Along with playing on a pennant winner in Boston, Sanders had played on St. Louis Cardinals squads that won the World Series in both 1942 and 1944. After his playing days ended, Sanders scouted for the Cleveland Indians. Sanders was killed in an automobile accident in Washington, Missouri, on October 28, 1983. He was 66 years old.

Starting in 1949, manager **Billy Southworth** began to fall out of favor quickly in Boston. Partway through that season, with the team possessing a record just slightly above .500 and discontent fomenting in the ranks, Southworth temporarily stepped down as the Braves manager for what were euphemistically called "health reasons" in the Boston media. Columnist Bill Cunningham called him "the first major casualty of the new superpowered, high speed, postwar, extravagantly bonused, high salaried, and heavily box office pressured baseball."[17] Owner Lou Perini did feel that Southworth was on the verge of a serious mental breakdown, but

Southworth, who had past issues with alcohol, was likely imbibing heavily, too. *Boston Globe* sportswriter Harold Kaese wrote,

> The Braves were an old club, crabby, bitter, set in their ways. Players who could no longer deliver blamed their ineptness on Southworth. Victory, which sugar-coated the bitterness underneath last season, eluded the crippled Braves and left bare the acrid taste of defeat, futility and animosity. Southworth, one of the great managers, could not cope with the situation. Perhaps he was too aloof, too domineering, too cocky, and while he did not need the friendship of his players, even he could not afford to lose their respect.[18]

Johnny Cooney took over the reins of the Braves on an interim basis. Southworth returned to the club in 1950—a move that was not especially popular with the club's veterans—but he resigned about one-third of the way through the 1951 season. He was 58 at the time. Some rumors had him taking over the managerial post in Pittsburgh or perhaps with the St. Louis Browns, but no such offers were forthcoming. Southworth later worked as a Braves scout. In that capacity he was the man responsible for signing future home-run king Hank Aaron to a contract. Southworth had quit smoking in the 1940s, but he was felled by emphysema more than two decades later, dying on November 15, 1969, in Columbus, Ohio, at the age of 76. He was elected to the Hall of Fame by the Veterans Committee in 2007.

Despite growing up in abject poverty and having his pro baseball ambitions sidetracked by his lengthy and distinguished service in the Second World War, **Warren Spahn** went on to become one of the greatest pitchers in MLB history. He compiled 363 career wins (against 245 losses) and is generally regarded to be the best left-hander ever to take the mound in the NL. Spahn's famed high kick in his throwing motion disguised that his delivery was exceedingly smooth which put little pressure on his arm, undoubtedly contributing to his longevity in the sport. While the Braves faltered after their 1948 pennant year, Spahn still thrived, winning a total of 64 games over the following three seasons. One day at the Polo Grounds in 1951, Spahn gave up a home run to a New York Giants rookie named Willie Mays who had been hitless in his previous 12 MLB at-bats before facing the Boston ace. When reminded of this tidbit of trivia, Spahn, who had a wonderful sense of humor, liked to joke, "I'll never forgive myself. We might have gotten rid of Willie forever if I had only struck him out."[19] After the Braves relocated to Milwaukee, Spahn won his only Cy Young Award in 1957 at age 36. He threw two no-hitters in his terrific career—both of which occurred after his 39th birthday. Upon concluding his MLB career with the 1965 New York Mets, Spahn became a pitching coach in Japan and later worked in the California Angels' minor-league system. He retired after the 1981 season because he disliked flying. Staunchly conservative in his beliefs, Spahn disliked the appearance of modern long-haired, unkempt players. He especially loathed the designated hitter rule, opining it was depriving pitchers of being true athletes. Outside of baseball, Spahn and his wife became rich from cattle ranching in Oklahoma and some cagy real estate investments in Florida. Spahn was elected to the Hall of Fame in 1973. A statue of him was erected in front of Turner Field in Atlanta in August 2003. By then the ex-pitcher was suffering from a number of age-related ailments and confined to a wheelchair; it was obvious that Spahn did not have much time left. He died on November 24, 2003, in Broken Arrow, Oklahoma, at the age of 82.

Feisty **Eddie Stanky** returned to the Braves in 1949 with his damaged ankle healed, but it was not a happy year for "The Brat" (as his friends and enemies often called him). Stanky disapproved of manager Billy Southworth's overworking of players in spring training and was vocal about it. When the team stumbled and Southworth was rumored to be heading out the door, Stanky was similarly rumored to be the new Boston manager. Stanky already had the authority to make managerial decisions while batting, such as calling specific plays. This created some controversy on July 23 when he was accused of running pitcher Warren Spahn too hard on a pair of hit-and-run plays on an especially hot day. (Spahn blew a three-run lead in the ninth inning in a game the Braves lost to Pittsburgh, 12–9.) When a few teammates grumbled to the press that Stanky was developing a "takeover" personality, Stanky furiously responded in kind by saying he was only interested in playing winning baseball and those who complained about him were "second-guessing bushers."[20] Stanky was traded to the New York Giants at the end of the 1949 season. Stanky thrived in New York in the two seasons he was there as manager Leo Durocher basically let Stanky do whatever he wanted on the diamond. At the end of the 1951 season, Stanky was traded to the St. Louis Cardinals where he was the player-manager for a time. Stanky was named *The Sporting News* Manager of the Year in 1952. Nevertheless, he was eventually fired early in the 1955 season when his headstrong philosophies about how to play the game did not resonate with his players. Stanky managed in the minors for a time and then had a successful run as a third-base coach in Cleveland. Stanky did not manage in the majors again until 1966 when he was handed the reins of the Chicago White Sox. In 1967, it looked as if his club was going to win the AL pennant, but the White Sox faltered badly on the last weekend of the season and finished in fourth place. Still, Stanky was given a four-year contract extension, but he was fired partway through the 1968 season—a campaign in which Chicago finished a disappointing eighth. In 1969, Stanky became the baseball coach at the University of Southern

22. Whatever Became Of... 227

Alabama where he startlingly adopted a much more easygoing leadership style with his young players. He kept his job there for 14 years and turned the team into a national powerhouse. (Stanky briefly left the school at the end of the 1977 season after being hired to manage the Texas Rangers. Citing "homesickness," Stanky quit after just one game because he missed the collegiate ranks. He happily returned to the Southern Alabama baseball program.) On June 6, 1999, Stanky died in a hospital in Fairhope, Alabama, after suffering a heart attack. He was 83 years old.

Bill Stewart, the most prominent umpire from the 1948 World Series, worked one more Fall Classic, in 1953. He resigned from the National League's staff of umpires after the 1955 season when he was not promoted to a new "league supervisor" position by new NL president Warren Giles. (Stewart claimed that the previous NL prexy, Ford Frick, had promised him the job. The post was never filled.) After walking away from umpiring, Stewart stayed connected with baseball as a scout for both Washington and Cleveland. Stewart remained heavily involved in hockey too. He was the head coach of the U.S. national amateur team that was supposed to play at the IIHF World Championship tournament in Moscow in 1957. They never got there. The State Department banned the squad from travelling to the Soviet Union after that country's invasion of Hungary in 1956. Stewart suffered a stroke in early 1964 and died in a veterans' hospital in a Boston suburb about two weeks later on February 18. He was 68. Stewart was posthumously inducted into the U.S. Hockey Hall of Fame in 1982.

Bill Summers once modestly summed up his career by saying, "I wasn't much of an umpire, at first; but I could keep the peace, and that's an umpire's most important job."[21] After the 1948 World Series, Summers worked three more World Series and four more All-Star Games. He was the plate umpire in Game One of the 1955 World Series when Brooklyn's Jackie Robinson stole home—and New York Yankee catcher Yogi Berra nearly went berserk disputing Summers' safe call. (Opinions still vary about the accuracy of it.) A passionate scholar regarding the sport's rules, Summers served many years on MLB's Rules Committee. During his tenure, baseball's rule book was greatly overhauled and improved to make it more user-friendly. Summers retired following the 1959 World Series after 26 years in the AL, but he kept himself busy for the remainder of his life by giving rules clinics and lectures on umpiring all over North America and at U.S. military bases around the world. Summers died at his Upton, Massachusetts, home at age 70 on September 12, 1966.

Joe Tipton, who had one pinch-hit at-bat in the World Series for Cleveland—a strikeout—did not have much of a future with the Indians. Tipton was the backup catcher to the very reliable Jim Hegan, so his playing time with the Tribe would be minimal. Tipton was traded to the

Chicago White Sox before the 1949 season began. Things did not go especially well there. At one point Tipton got into a fight with Chicago manager Jack Onslow who accused him of tipping pitches to an opponent. It was a harbinger of future integrity problems for Tipton. In October 1949, Tipton was traded to the Philadelphia Athletics for future Hall of Fame second baseman Nellie Fox—one of baseball history's most lopsided deals. Tipton eventually returned to Cleveland in 1952 and resumed his old role as Jim Hegan's backup. His final MLB stop was with the Washington Senators in 1954. Tipton did make occasional forays in the minor league both as a player and as a manager. He was eventually banned from minor league baseball for life for his peripheral involvement in a game-fixing scandal centering on a former MLB player named Jesse Levan who was in cahoots with gamblers. (The bizarre scheme focused on players deliberately fouling off pitches for the benefit of gamblers in the ballpark who bet on the frequency of this common occurrence!) Removed from baseball under a dark cloud, Tipton ran a service station and then an automobile dealership in Birmingham, Alabama. He died there on March 1, 1994, at age 72.

Boston first baseman **Earl Torgeson** had a dismal 1949 season. In a May 14 game versus the Brooklyn Dodgers, Torgeson slid awkwardly at second base trying to upend Jackie Robinson on a double-play grounder. He suffered a separated shoulder which kept him out of the Braves' lineup for three months. Upon returning to the team in August, Torgeson almost immediately broke his thumb in a fight away from the ballpark that involved teammate Jim Russell and three soldiers. (The details of what prompted the scuffle were never made public; Torgeson always refused to comment. The incident hastened the temporary departure of Braves manager Billy Southworth who was perceived as having lost control of his players.) The two injuries combined to limit Torgeson's 1949 action to just 25 games. In 1950, Torgeson rebounded spectacularly. Playing in all 156 of Boston's games, he batted .290 with 23 home runs and 87 RBIs. He also led the NL in runs scored with 120. Torgeson's offensive stats for 1951 were almost identical. The 1952 season, however, was a poor one for Torgeson, in which he batted an uncharacteristically low .230. He was traded to the Philadelphia Phillies in 1953 and rebounded with a .274 batting average. However, in a freak accident in January 1954, Torgeson stumbled over his dog in a dark bedroom and dislocated his right shoulder. He kept quiet about the injury, telling only the team trainer—and his performance suffered. Torgeson batted a respectable .271, but he only hit five home runs because the shoulder injury sapped much of his power. Over the next few seasons, Torgeson drifted among three AL clubs: Detroit, the Chicago White Sox and New York Yankees before ending his career in 1961. (Torgeson had two plate appearances for Chicago in the 1959 World

Series.) After nearly a decade away from pro baseball, Torgeson worked in the short-lived Seattle Pilots organization as a minor league manager. On November 8, 1990, Torgeson died of leukemia, at age 66, only about six weeks after first being diagnosed with the disease. He passed away at his home in Everett, Washington. Shortly before Torgeson's death, a baseball field in Snohomish, Washington, was named in honor of him.

Outfielder **Thurman Tucker** spent the rest of his MLB career as a member of the Cleveland Indians with dwindling results. Tucker batted .244 in 80 games in 1949 and .178 in 57 games in 1950 when he experimented with switch-hitting for a time. He got into one game in 1951 for the Tribe before being sent to the minors. He stayed in the lower ranks of professional baseball through 1956, serving as a player-manager for some teams. Tucker was one of the first scouts hired by the expansion Houston Colts in 1962. After his baseball days concluded, Tucker was employed in the insurance industry. He died on May 7, 1993, in Oklahoma City at age 75.

Bill Veeck's glorious reign as the owner of the fabulous Cleveland Indians did not last very long. In 1949, Veeck's wife, Eleanor, divorced him. It was not a very amicable parting. According to Ohio civil law, she was entitled to 50 percent of his assets. This, of course, included his baseball team. With most of his money tied up in the Indians, Veeck had no choice but to sell the Indians to pay his divorce debt. Veeck had owned the Indians for just three and a half MLB seasons—but they were memorable ones. The new owners were a syndicate headed by an insurance magnate named Ellis Ryan. The sale netted Veeck $2.5 million. After a short hiatus from baseball, Veeck moved on to own the lowly St. Louis Browns and then the struggling Chicago White Sox. His enduring publicity masterpiece was using stunt midget Eddie Gaedel as a pinch hitter in the second game of a Browns' home doubleheader versus Detroit on August 19, 1951. Such a stunt was true to Veeck's credo about MLB ownership: He once stated, "A losing team plus bread and circuses [is] better than a losing team and a long, still silence."[22] By the early 1980s, escalating player salaries had driven him out of MLB ownership. A longtime smoker, Veeck died of lung cancer in a Chicago medical center on January 2, 1986, at the age of 71.

Bill Voiselle was back in Boston's four-man starting rotation in 1949, but the 30-year-old ran afoul of Braves manager Billy Southworth for reasons seemingly unknown to anyone else but the Boston pilot. Twice Southworth went extended periods without giving Voiselle a start, despite him having generally positive results when he did pitch. In August, Voiselle had a 6–3 record with four shutouts. Southworth temporarily stepped down (or was ousted) later that month. Voiselle was put back into the Braves' rotation by interim manager Johnny Cooney—but he failed to take advantage of the opportunity, going a poor 1–5 over the remainder of 1949. Traded to the Chicago Cubs after the season concluded, Voiselle had a short and disastrous stay with his new team in 1950, going 0–4 before being sent to the minors. Biographer Saul Wisnia wrote, "Less than two years after starting the biggest Braves game in 30 years, [Voiselle] had been unable to hold his job with the NL's seventh-place outfit."[23] Voiselle pitched in the minors on and off until 1957. After his baseball career concluded, Voiselle returned to his small, beloved hometown of Ninety-Six, South Carolina, where he often organized charity ballgames. Late in his life, in 2001, Voiselle was formally honored by South Carolina's House of Representatives for bringing "honor and glory to the state of South Carolina through his athletic and charitable endeavors." Voiselle was modest about his fame. "Everything I got, I owe to baseball," he said in an interview. "I'm a little old cotton mill boy."[24] Voiselle died two days past his 86th birthday in 2005. In one newspaper story about Voiselle's passing, a mournful neighbor stated, "He was just a wonderful guy, and everybody loved him to death."[25]

— 23 —

Has Anyone Seen the 1948 World Series Pennant Recently?

After a painful and unacceptable one-year absence from the World Series, the New York Yankees rebounded to win another American League pennant in 1949 under the leadership of new manager Casey Stengel, thus making the Cleveland's Indians' reign as AL kingpins a brief one. Some Cleveland rooters took their third-place finish in 1949 very hard.

Never one to miss an opportunity to organize an offbeat publicity stunt, Cleveland owner Bill Veeck capitalized on the profound civic grief and had his 1949 Indians bury their 1948 World Series pennant in center field at Municipal Stadium! The 14-by-20-foot banner featured a backwards image of Chief Wahoo, the Indians mascot, looking proudly at a crown resting upon his head. It bore the words "1948 World Champion Cleveland Indians" in large letters. "It wasn't fancy," wrote Anthony Castrovince in a 2016 article for MLB.com, "but it was seemingly finite."[1]

The oddball "funeral" occurred as a pregame ceremony on Saturday, September 24—one day after the Indians had been mathematically eliminated from the 1949 AL pennant race. Veeck had given the team's fans some vague advance notice of what would transpire that evening by placing an enticing advertisement in that day's edition of the *Cleveland Plain Dealer*. It read, "Unusual ceremonies will precede the Indians' game with the Detroit Tigers tonight at the stadium and fans are urged to be in their seats by 8 and ready to take part in the fun."

Veeck's idea of "fun" was to dress as a mortician and preside over the weird ceremony which featured a 19th-century horse-drawn hearse and a marching band playing dirges. Veeck (of course) sat atop the vehicle, trying his best to look somber. In lieu of a traditional Bible, Veeck clutched a copy of *The Sporting News*—the publication that billed itself as "The Bible of Baseball." The flag was respectfully placed inside a pine box and laid to rest beyond the outfield wall in Municipal Stadium. Photos show that a cheap cardboard headstone with the inscription "Here Lies the 1948 Champs" once marked the location. The ceremony garnered mixed reviews in Cleveland. "That stunt outraged some of his players and fans,"[2] wrote one Veeck biographer.

Presently, the fate of the Indians' hard-won 1948 World Series pennant is unknown. Perhaps it was quietly disinterred sometime; no one has ever claimed to have possessed it or even seen it since the night of the faux funeral. "It's bizarre," the club's curator Jeremy Feador said. "After that, you [didn't] hear anything about it. Did someone dig it up after the game? Did it stay there? No one really knows. The legend is just quiet after that."[3]

During the 2016 Cubs-Indians World Series when there was renewed interest in the 1948 AL champs, Feador told an ABC News reporter that the forgotten burial site may have been accidentally dug up in the early 1990s when Municipal Stadium was torn down and its retro-style replacement—then called Jacobs Field—was being erected in its place. If that was the case, Feador fears the 1948 World Series pennant may be lost forever in a landfill site somewhere. There is also the possibility it might presently reside in Lake Erie, as chunks of the old ballpark were dumped there to become part of a fish habitat. The optimist in Feador, however, is hopeful that some Cleveland fan or baseball memorabilia collector somewhere quietly has it in his possession and is just waiting for an opportune time to unveil it.

Because of the planning that went into Veeck's mock funeral, Feador clings to the happy idea that the flag may have been salvaged by someone connected with the team. "It wasn't like this big flag got thrown in the dumpster and now it's gone," he noted. "No, there was this elaborate event, and clearly there was symbolism attached to it. To be able to find that [pennant], I think, would be neat, because it's one of those cool, tangible reminders of the past."[4]

— 24 —

1948 World Series Composite Statistics

Composite Line Score

Team	1	2	3	4	5	6	7	8	9	R	H	E
Cleveland Indians (AL)	2	0	3	7	1	2	0	1	1	17	38	3
Boston Braves (NL)	4	0	1	1	0	1	7	3	0	17	43	6

Average game time: 120 minutes; **Total attendance:** 358,362; **Average attendance:** 59,727; **Winning player's share:** $6,772; **Losing player's share:** $4,571.

Composite Batting Statistics: Cleveland Indians

Player	AB	R	H	AVG	RBI	2B	3B	HR
Bearden	4	1	2	.500	0	1	0	0
Boone	1	0	0	.000	0	0	0	0
Boudreau	22	1	6	.333	3	4	0	0
Christopher	0	0	0	.000	0	0	0	0
Clark	3	0	0	.000	0	0	0	0
Doby	22	1	7	.318	2	1	0	1
Feller	4	0	0	.000	0	0	0	0
Gordon	22	3	4	.182	2	0	0	1
Gromek	3	0	0	.000	0	0	0	0
Hegan	19	2	4	.211	5	0	0	1
Judnich	13	1	1	.077	1	0	0	0
Keltner	21	3	2	.095	0	0	0	0
Kennedy	2	0	1	.500	1	0	0	0
Klieman	0	0	0	.000	0	0	0	0
Lemon	7	0	0	.000	0	0	0	0
Mitchell	23	4	4	.174	1	1	0	1
Muncrief	0	0	0	.000	0	0	0	0

Player	AB	R	H	AVG	RBI	2B	3B	HR
Paige	0	0	0	.000	0	0	0	0
Peck	0	0	0	.000	0	0	0	0
Robinson	20	0	6	.300	1	0	0	0
Rosen	1	0	0	.000	0	0	0	0
Tipton	1	0	0	.000	0	0	0	0
Tucker	3	1	1	.333	0	0	0	0
Totals	**191**	**17**	**38**	**.199**	**16**	**7**	**0**	**4**

Stolen Base: *Gordon, Hegan*

Composite Batting Statistics: Boston Braves

Player	AB	R	H	AVG	RBI	2B	3B	HR
Barrett	0	0	0	.000	0	0	0	0
Bickford	0	0	0	.000	0	0	0	0
Conatser*	4	0	0	.000	1	0	0	0
Dark	24	2	4	.167	0	1	0	0
Elliott	21	4	7	.333	5	0	0	2
Holmes	26	3	5	.192	1	0	0	0
Masi	8	1	1	.125	1	1	0	0
McCormick, F.	5	0	1	.200	0	0	0	0
McCormick, M.	23	1	6	.261	2	0	0	0
Potter	2	0	1	.500	0	0	0	0
Rickert	19	2	4	.211	2	0	0	1
Ryan	1	0	0	.000	0	0	0	0
Sain	5	0	1	.200	0	0	0	0
Salkeld	9	2	2	.222	1	0	0	1
Sanders	1	0	0	.000	0	0	0	0
Sisti	1	0	0	.000	0	0	0	0
Spahn*	4	0	0	.000	1	0	0	0
Stanky	14	0	4	.286	1	1	0	0
Torgeson	18	2	7	.389	1	3	0	0
Voiselle	2	0	0	.000	0	0	0	0
Totals	**187**	**17**	**43**	**.230**	**16**	**6**	**0**	**4**

Stolen Base: *Torgeson*

*Note: Sacrifice flies were not an official MLB statistic in 1948. Under modern scoring rules, Spahn would have been credited with a sacrifice fly in Game Five as would Conatser in Game Six.

24. 1948 World Series Composite Statistics

Composite Pitching Statistics: Cleveland Indians

Pitcher	W	L	G	GS	CG	IP	ERA
Bearden*	1	0	2	1	1	10.2	0.00
Christopher	0	0	1	0	0	0.0	
Feller	0	2	2	2	1	14.1	5.02
Gromek	1	0	1	1	1	9.0	1.00
Klieman	0	0	1	0	0	0.0	
Lemon	2	0	2	2	1	16.1	1.65
Muncrief	0	0	1	0	0	2.0	0.00
Paige	0	0	1	0	0	0.2	0.00
Totals	**4**	**2**	**6**	**6**	**4**	**53.0**	**2.72**

Balk: Lemon, Paige

*****Note:** Saves were not an official MLB statistic in 1948. Under modern scoring rules, Bearden would have earned a save in Game Six.

Composite Pitching Statistics: Boston Braves

Pitcher	W	L	G	GS	CG	IP	ERA
Barrett	0	0	2	0	0	3.2	0.00
Bickford	0	1	1	1	0	3.1	2.70
Potter	0	0	2	1	0	5.1	8.44
Sain	1	1	2	2	2	17.0	1.06
Spahn	1	1	3	1	0	12.0	3.00
Voiselle	0	1	2	1	0	10.2	2.53
Totals	**2**	**4**	**6**	**6**	**2**	**52.0**	**2.60**

Composite Fielding

Double Plays Made by Cleveland: 8

Double Plays Made by Boston: 4

Cleveland Errors: Doby, Gordon, Keltner

Boston Errors: Dark (3), Elliott (3)

Cleveland had two players on its 25-man roster who did not play in the 1948 World Series: Johnny Berardino (infielder) and Sam Zoldak (pitcher).

Boston had five players on its 25-man roster who did not play in the 1948 World Series: Bobby Hogue (pitcher), Al Lyons (pitcher), Clyde Shoun (pitcher), Bobby Sturgeon (infielder) and Ernie White (pitcher).

Chapter Notes

Introduction

1. *New York Tribune*, June 14, 1914.

Chapter 1

1. T.H. Murnane, "Tim Thinks Macks Will Pull Through," *The Sporting News*, October 8, 1914, 1.
2. Bill Nowlin (editor), *Spahn, Sain and Teddy Ballgame: Boston's (Almost) Perfect Baseball Summer of 1948* (Burlington, MA: Rounder Books, 2008), 333.
3. "Braves Win NL Flag," *Meriden Record*, September 27, 1948, 4.
4. Carl Lundquist, "Southworth Favors Hustling Players," *Meriden Record*, September 27, 1948, 4.
5. "Braves Win NL Flag," *Meriden Record*, September 27, 1948, 4.
6. "'Happiest Day of My Life' Says Perini After Clincher," *The Sporting News*, October 6, 1948, 2.
7. Jack Barry, "Jeff Heath Won't Play in Series," *Boston Globe*, September 30, 1948, 1.
8. Paul Harvey III, "As Jeff Heath Sees It, You Always Slide," *Eugene Register-Guard*, June 11, 1964, 1D.
9. Bill Nowlin (editor), *Spahn, Sain and Teddy Ballgame: Boston's (Almost) Perfect Baseball Summer of 1948* (Burlington, MA: Rounder Books, 2008), 338.
10. "Heath Visited by 1914 Brave," *Meriden Record*, October 5, 1948, 8.

Chapter 2

1. "Bill Veeck Quotes," Brainyquote.com.
2. Gerald Eskenazi, *Bill Veeck: A Baseball Legend* (New York: McGraw-Hill, 1988), 105.
3. *Cleveland Times*, October 11, 1920.
4. Oscar K. Ruhl, "Veeck Predicts Scramble for Colored Stars," *The Sporting News*, July 17, 1947, 3.
5. C. Paul Rogers III, "Bob Feller," SABR Biography Project.
6. *Ibid.*
7. Paul Dickson, *Bill Veeck: Baseball's Greatest Maverick* (New York: Walker, 2012), 158.
8. *Ibid.*
9. Ed McAuley, "Fan's Right to Have Fun in Own Way," *The Sporting News*, July 14, 1948, 1.
10. Ed McAuley, "Portrait of a Man Who Came Back—Don Black," *The Sporting News*, July 23, 1947, 11.
11. *Ibid.*

Chapter 3

1. "George Vecsey Quotes," Brainyquote.com.
2. Warren Corbett, "Steve Gromek," SABR Biography Project.
3. Art Morrow, "A's Seek Speed, Power in Swaps," *The Sporting News*, September 29, 1948, 10.
4. "Tradition Battling for the Yankees," *The Sporting News*, September 29, 1948, 6.
5. "Bronx Bombers Dumped 4–2 by Tail-End Chicago Club," *Saskatoon-Star Phoenix*, September 24, 1948, 16.
6. "Red Sox Drop Yankees into Second Place," *Pittsburgh Press*, September 26, 1948, 29.

7. "Tribe, Bosox, Yankees Enter Crucial Week," *Pittsburgh Press*, September 27, 1948, 18.
8. "Defeats Today Would Bounce Red Sox, Yanks," *Pittsburgh Press*, September 30, 1948, 40.
9. "Feller Wins 19th; Tribe Nears Flag," *Pittsburgh Post-Gazette*, September 30, 1948, 20.
10. James Doyle, "Only the Church Bells," *Cleveland Plain Dealer*, October 4, 1948, 20.
11. Bob Feller with Bill Gilbert, *Now Pitching, Bob Feller: A Baseball Memoir* (New York: Sports Publishing, 1990), 145.

Chapter 4

1. Ben Bradlee, Jr., *The Kid: The Immortal Life of Ted Williams* (New York: Little, Brown, 2013), 298.
2. *Ibid.*
3. Ralph Berger, "Gene Bearden," SABR Biography Project.
4. Hugh Fullerton, Jr., "Gene Protects Tattered Shirt," *Cleveland Plain Dealer*, October 5, 1948, 23.
5. Ralph Berger, "Lou Boudreau," SABR Biography Project.
6. Bill Nowlin (editor), *Spahn, Sain and Teddy Ballgame: Boston's (Almost) Perfect Baseball Summer of 1948* (Burlington, MA: Rounder Books, 2008), 338.
7. Rick Malwitz, "Allie Clark," SABR Biography Project.
8. *Ibid.*
9. J.G. Taylor Spink, "Looping the Loops," *The Sporting News*, October 6, 1948, 4.
10. Franklin Lewis, "Cleveland Celebrates Great Pennant Victory," *Calgary Herald*, October 5, 1948, 19.
11. Ed McAuley, "Indians Prove 'Best Team Won' in AL Race," *The Sporting News*, October 6, 1948, 5.
12. Joseph Wancho, "October 4, 1948: Rookie Bearden wins 20th, Boudreau homers twice as Indians win pennant in AL tiebreaker," SABR games project.
13. Arthur Sampson, "Bearden Earns Sox Admiration," *Boston Herald*, October 5, 1948, 20.
14. Gayle Talbot, "War Hero Twirls Five-Hitter in 8–3 Victory Over Boston," *Youngstown Vindicator*, October 5, 1948, 16.
15. *Ibid.*
16. Ralph Berger, "Gene Bearden," SABR Biography Project.
17. Laurie Brain, "Sifting the Sports," *Galt Daily Reporter*, October 5, 1948, 12.
18. "Indians Remember Black in Pennant Celebration," *The Sporting News*, October 13, 1948, 4.
19. Mark Armour, "Ellis Kinder," SABR Biography Project.
20. Bruce Nash and Allan Zullo, *The Baseball Hall of Shame 2* (New York: Pocket Books, 1986), 115.
21. "Cleveland Goes Batty as Tribe Grabs Flag," *Youngstown Vindicator*, October 5, 1948, 1.
22. Laurie Brain, "Sifting the Sports," *Galt Daily Reporter*, October 5, 1948, 12.
23. "The Indians Come Through," *Youngstown Vindicator*, October 5, 1948, 12.
24. "Bearden Toast of Cleveland After Victory," *Oakland Tribune*, October 5, 1948, 28.

Chapter 5

1. "One-Way Ticket to Home for Walks in Dean's Days," *The Sporting News*, August 25, 1948, 2.
2. J.G. Taylor Spink, "Looping the Loops," *The Sporting News*, August 25, 1948, 2
3. "Threat Should Bring Yawns," *The Sporting News*, July 7, 1948, 2.
4. Dan Daniel, "A.L. Tightening Gag on Foul Gab on Field," *The Sporting News*, August 4, 1948, 1.
5. *Ibid.*, 2.
6. Fred Schuld, "Pat Seerey," SABR Biography Project.
7. "Yanks Borrow Rooter for Series with Indians," *The Sporting News*, September 1, 1948, 2.
8. Mark Stewart, "Pete Reiser," SABR Biography Project.
9. Pat Lynch, "Clubs Televising Cutting Own Throats—Shaughnessy," *The Sporting News*, November 24, 1948, 8.
10. "Spread of Video Networks Offers Problems for Minors," *The Sporting News*, November 24, 1948, 8.

Chapter 6

1. Laurie Brain, "Sifting the Sports," *Galt Daily Reporter*, October 5, 1948, 12.

2. "Dave Barry Quotes," Brainyquote.com.

3. Leo H. Petersen, "World Series Opener Pits Sain, Feller on Mound," *Tuscaloosa News*, October 6, 1948, 10.

4. Jack Hand, "Series Combatants Together at Braves Field," *Calgary Herald*, October 6, 1948, 11.

5. "Cleveland Favored at 13–5 Odds to Capture Top Baseball Crown," *Reading Eagle*, October 6, 1948, 14.

6. Whitney Martin, "High Mound Will Aid Feller," *Calgary Herald*, October 6, 1948, 14.

7. "Hotel Rooms Scarce in Cleveland," *Saskatoon Star-Phoenix*, October 6, 1948, 12.

8. "Friday Real Series Day; Crazy Cleveland Waits," *Youngstown Vindicator*, October 7, 1948, 1.

9. *Ibid.*, 20.

10. Leo H. Petersen, "World Series Opener Pits Sain, Feller on Mound," *Tuscaloosa News*, October 6, 1948, 10.

11. Al Abrams, "Sidelight on Sports," *Pittsburgh Post-Gazette*, October 5, 1948, 14.

12. Jack Hand, "Chilling Rain Expected for Initial Clash," *Sarasota Herald-Tribune*, October 6, 1948, 8.

13. Rogers Hornsby, "Hornsby Picks Indians in Five," *Pittsburgh Press*, October 6, 1948, 26.

14. "World Series Notes," *Reading Eagle*, October 6, 1948, 14.

Chapter 7

1. Leo H. Petersen, "World Series Opener Pits Sain, Feller on Mound," *Tuscaloosa News*, October 6, 1948, 10.

2. *Ibid.*

3. *Ibid.*

4. *Ibid.*

5. Jack Hand, "Feller to Toss for Indians; Sain for Braves in Opener," *Prescott Evening Courier*, October 5, 1948, 5.

6. "Indians Favored in Series on Power Hitting Strength," *Calgary Herald*, October 6, 1948, 20.

Chapter 8

1. Mutual Broadcasting System's radio broadcast of Game One of the 1948 World Series, October 6, 1948.

2. Jack Hand, "Braves Win 1–0 Opener on Two Lone Singles," *Sarasota Herald-Tribune*, October 7, 1948, 7.

3. "Series Begins Under Rain Threat," *Saskatoon Star-Phoenix*, October 7, 1948, 16.

4. Bill Nowlin (editor), *Spahn, Sain and Teddy Ballgame: Boston's (Almost) Perfect Baseball Summer of 1948* (Burlington, MA: Rounder Books, 2008), 329.

5. "Feller, Sain Set to Duel in Opener," *Calgary Herald*, October 6, 1948, 22.

6. Leo H. Petersen, "World Series Opener Pits Sain, Feller on Mound," *Tuscaloosa News*, October 6, 1948, 10.

7. "World Series Notes," *Reading Eagle*, October 6, 1948, 14.

8. David Cataneo, *Peanuts and Crackerjack* (Nashville: Rutledge Hill Press, 1991), 245–6.

9. "Indians Heavily Favored," *Calgary Herald*, October 6, 1948, 22.

10. Hugh Fullerton, Jr., "Cleveland Strategy Backfires in Opener," *Calgary Herald*, October 7, 1948, 24.

11. Mutual Broadcasting System's radio broadcast of Game One of the 1948 World Series, October 6, 1948.

12. *Ibid.*

13. *Ibid.*

14. Gayle Talbot, "Sain Wins First Game, 1–0," *Saskatoon Star-Phoenix*, October 7, 1948, 22.

15. Paul Dickson, *Bill Veeck: Baseball's Greatest Maverick* (New York: Walker, 2012), 158.

16. "Warren Spahn," SABR Oral History Collection, May 8, 2001.

17. Jack Hand, "Pickoff Decision is Target in Initial Battle," *Youngstown Vindicator*, October 7, 1948, 40.

18. *Ibid.*

19. *Ibid.*

20. *Ibid.*

21. *Ibid.*

22. Mutual Broadcasting System's radio broadcast of Game Two of the 1948 World Series, October 7, 1948.

23. "Umpire Stewart Under Fire After Photos Published," *Calgary Herald*, October 8, 1948, 25.

24. Jack Hand, "Disputed Base Play Marks 1948 World Series Opener," *Calgary Herald*, October 7, 1948, 24.

25. Bob Feller and Bill Gilbert, *Now Pitching, Bob Feller: A Baseball Memoir* (New York: Sports Publishing, 1990), 165–166.

26. *Ibid.*
27. Jack Hand, "Disputed Base Play Marks 1948 World Series Opener," *Calgary Herald*, October 7, 1948, 24.
28. *Ibid.*
29. Bill King, "Sain Silent in Victory," *Calgary Herald*, October 7, 1948, 24.
30. "Billy Awed by Pitching," *Saskatoon Star-Phoenix*, October 7, 1948, 16.
31. "Braves Fool Mack," *Reading Eagle*, October 7, 1948, 38.
32. Leo H. Peterson, "Spahn Opposes Indians After Braves Cop Opener," *Tuscaloosa News*, October 6, 1948, 12.
33. *Ibid.*
34. "Feller Doesn't Think Too Much of Boston Braves," *Sarasota Herald-Tribune*, October 7, 1948, 7.
35. Rogers Hornsby, "Feller's Bases on Balls Beat Him, Says Hornsby," *Oakland Tribune*, October 7, 1948, 27.
36. "Two Breaks Needed to Get Rickert into World Series," *Reading Eagle*, October 7, 1948, 38.
37. Jim Calorgero, "Weatherman and Indian Rooters Both Wrong About Opening Game," *New London Evening Day*, October 7, 1948, 20.
38. Bob Feller and Bill Gilbert, *Now Pitching, Bob Feller: A Baseball Memoir* (New York: Sports Publishing, 1990), 162.
39. Jim Calorgero, "Weatherman and Indian Rooters Both Wrong About Opening Game," *New London Evening Day*, October 7, 1948, 20.
40. Patrick L. Kennedy and David Keefe, "Remembering the Wigwam (Part Two)," *BU Today*, April 13, 2012.
41. "Court Adjourned!" *Boston Globe*, October 6, 1948, 26.

Chapter 9

1. "Billy Awed by Pitching," *Saskatoon Star-Phoenix*, October 7, 1948, 16.
2. *Ibid.*
3. "Underdog Braves Take World Series Lead," *Saskatoon Star-Phoenix*, October 7, 1948, 16.
4. "Satch's Chances Slim of Starting Game for Cleveland," *Calgary Herald*, October 7, 1948, 24.
5. *Ibid.*
6. Grantland Rice, "Veteran Newsman Rates Series Opener Best Pitched Since '05," *Calgary Herald*, October 7, 1948, 24.

Chapter 10

1. "Bob Lemon Quotes," Brainyquote.com.
2. Bill Nowlin (editor), *Spahn, Sain and Teddy Ballgame: Boston's (Almost) Perfect Baseball Summer of 1948* (Burlington, MA: Rounder Books, 2008), 145.
3. *Ibid.*
4. Jim Kaplan, "Warren Spahn," SABR Biography Project.
5. Jon Barnes, "Bob Lemon," SABR Biography Project.
6. *Ibid.*
7. Mutual Broadcasting System's radio broadcast of Game Two of the 1948 World Series, October 7, 1948.
8. Oscar Fraley, "Major Star First Year," *Greensburg Daily Tribune*, October 6, 1948, 21.
9. Mutual Broadcasting System's radio broadcast of Game Two of the 1948 World Series, October 7, 1948.
10. *Ibid.*
11. Sheldon Appleton, "Frank McCormick," SABR Biography Project.
12. Mutual Broadcasting System's radio broadcast of Game Two of the 1948 World Series, October 7, 1948.
13. "Lemon Pitches Great Ball to Win Second Game 4–1," *Saskatoon Star-Phoenix*, October 7, 1948, 1.
14. Hugh Fullerton, "That's One, Now 3 More," *Saskatoon Star-Phoenix*, October 8, 1948, 14.
15. "That's One, Now 3 More," *Saskatoon Star-Phoenix*, October 7, 1948, 14.
16. Jack Hand, "Boudreau Sets Pace as Tribe Tops Spahn, 4–1," *Sarasota Herald-Tribune*, October 8, 1948, 7.
17. "Cleat-torn Boston Infield Blamed for Series 'Boots,'" *Youngstown Vindicator*, October 8, 1948, 34.
18. "Series Jottings," *Calgary Herald*, October 7, 1948, 24.
19. Grantland Rice, "Series Short on Thrills So Far," *Saskatoon Star-Phoenix*, October 8, 1948, 14.
20. Joe Reichler, "Boudreau's Pickoff Play Most Talked-About Series Feature Thus Far," *Williamson Daily News*, October 8, 1948, 13.
21. "Cleveland Votes For 34 Shares," *Saskatoon Star-Phoenix*, October 7, 1948, 16.
22. "Lemon and Boudreau Star in Win Over Boston Club," *Saskatoon Star-Phoenix*, October 8, 1948, 14.

Chapter 11

1. "That's One, Now 3 More," *Saskatoon Star-Phoenix*, October 7, 1948, 14.
2. "Bearden Stars as Cleveland Rocks Braves," *Altus Times-Democrat*, October 8, 1948, 1.
3. "Satch Paige Has Praise for Catchers," *Calgary Herald*, October 8, 1948, 21.
4. Grantland Rice, "Braves' Vernon Bickford Today Caries Much of Series Burden," *Calgary Herald*, October 8, 1948, 21.
5. *Ibid.*

Chapter 12

1. Les Masterson, "Vern Bickford," SABR Biography Project.
2. Whitney Martin, "Indians Gain 2-1 Edge in Series on 2-0 Win," *Meriden Record*, October 9, 1948, 1.
3. Leo H. Petersen, "Cloudy Skies Greet Third Series Game," *Greensburg Daily Tribune*, October 8, 1948, 1.
4. Mutual Broadcasting System's radio broadcast of Game Three of the 1948 World Series, October 8, 1948.
5. "Vern Received Mid-Season Raise," *The Sporting News*, August 25, 1948, 3.
6. Mutual Broadcasting System's radio broadcast of Game Three of the 1948 World Series, October 8, 1948.
7. Rogers Hornsby, "Old-Time Baseball Features Series," *Pittsburgh Press*, October 9, 1948, 6.
8. Mutual Broadcasting System's radio broadcast of Game Three of the 1948 World Series, October 8, 1948.
9. Fritz Howell, "Tribe Takes Win in Stride," *Calgary Herald*, October 9, 1948, 24.
10. Mutual Broadcasting System's radio broadcast of Game Three of the 1948 World Series, October 8, 1948.
11. "Bearden Pitches Indians to 2nd Win Over Boston," *Calgary Herald*, October 8, 1948, 1.
12. Jack Hand, "Bearden Stars, Cleveland Leads Series," *Sarasota Herald-Tribune*, October 10, 1948, 7.
13. Rogers Hornsby, "Old-Time Baseball Features Series," *Pittsburgh Press*, October 9, 1948, 6.
14. Whitney Martin, "Indians Win 2-0 Over Braves; 80,000 Jam Cleveland Stadium," *Youngstown Vindicator*, October 8, 1948, 1.
15. Al Abrams, "Sidelights on Sports," *Pittsburgh Post-Gazette*, October 9, 1948, 10.
16. Gayle Talbot, "Gromek and Feller Could Spell End of World Series," *Calgary Herald*, October 9, 1948, 24.
17. *Ibid.*
18. Al Abrams, "Sidelights on Sports," *Pittsburgh Post-Gazette*, October 9, 1948, 10.
19. *Ibid.*
20. Rogers Hornsby, "Old-Time Baseball Features Series," *Pittsburgh Press*, October 9, 1948, 6.
21. "World Series," *Ellensburg Daily Record*, October 8, 1948, 4.
22. "World Series Notes," *Ellensburg Daily Record*, October 9, 1948, 3.
23. Hugh Fullerton, "Smart Relief Hurling Too Late Taking Over," *Calgary Herald*, October 9, 1948, 21.

Chapter 13

1. "Boudreau: Key is Fourth Game," *Saskatoon Star-Phoenix*, October 9, 1948, 16.
2. "Cleveland Hats are Off to Gene Bearden," *Saskatoon Star-Phoenix*, October 9, 1948, 18.
3. "Boudreau: Key is Fourth Game," *Saskatoon Star-Phoenix*, October 9, 1948, 16.
4. "Cleveland Hats are Off to Gene Bearden," *Saskatoon Star-Phoenix*, October 9, 1948, 18.
5. Jack Hand, "Gromek and Feller Could Spell End of World Series," *Calgary Herald*, October 9, 1948, 21.
6. *Ibid.*
7. Grantland Rice, "Johnny Sain Braves' Last Hope in Series Devoid of Thrills," *Calgary Herald*, October 9, 1948, 21.
8. Hugh Fullerton, "Smart Relief Hurling Too Late Taking Over," *Calgary Herald*, October 9, 1948, 21.
9. Grantland Rice, "Johnny Sain Braves' Last Hope in Series Devoid of Thrills," *Calgary Herald*, October 9, 1948, 21.

Chapter 14

1. Warren Corbett, "Steve Gromek," SABR Biography Project.

2. *Ibid.*
3. Mutual Broadcasting System's radio broadcast of Game Four of the 1948 World Series, October 9, 1948.
4. *Ibid.*
5. *Ibid.*
6. *Ibid.*
7. *Ibid.*
8. *Ibid.*
9. "Gromek Halts Braves 2–1 for Third Indian Win," *Lewiston Morning Tribune*, October 10, 1948, 8.
10. "This Speaker Says Boudreau is Tops for Shortstops," *Tuscaloosa News*, October 10, 1948, 9.
11. *Ibid.*
12. "Boudreau Was Too Tagged, Braves Claim," *Lewiston Morning Tribune*, October 10, 1948, 8.
13. Richard Sandomir, "Cleveland Indians in 1948: A Story of Integration," *New York Times*, October 23, 2016 (online version).
14. *Ibid.*
15. Warren Corbett, "Steve Gromek," SABR Biography Project.
16. "Ex-Indian Sewell Says Tribe's Tops," *Tuscaloosa News*, October 10, 1948, 9.
17. Red Smith, "Cleveland Club Has Babysitter Service at Park," *Boston Globe*, October 10, 1948, 1.

Chapter 15

1. "Gromek Terms Indian Win 'Great Thrill,'" *Lewiston Morning Tribune*, October 10, 1948, 8.
2. *Ibid.*
3. Hy Hurwitz, "Potter Surprise Choice Against Feller Today," *Boston Globe*, October 10, 1948, 1.

Chapter 16

1. Mutual Broadcasting System's radio broadcast of Game Five of the 1948 World Series, October 10, 1948.
2. *Ibid.*
3. *Ibid.*
4. Mutual Broadcasting System's radio broadcast of Game Five of the 1948 World Series, October 10, 1948.
5. Eddie T. Jones, "Robert Feller Fails in Big Chance to Capture World Series Victory," *Toledo Blade*, October 11, 1948, 22.
6. "Satchel Paige," u-s-history.com.
7. Mutual Broadcasting System's radio broadcast of Game Five of the 1948 World Series, October 10, 1948.
8. *Ibid.*
9. "Feller Roughed Up; Loses 11–5," *Calgary Herald*, October 11, 1948, 16.
10. Mutual Broadcasting System's radio broadcast of Game Six of the 1948 World Series, October 11, 1948.
11. Hugh Fullerton, "Spahn Gives Braves Hope,' *Saskatoon Star-Phoenix*, October 11, 1948, 24.
12. *Ibid.*
13. Mutual Broadcasting System's radio broadcast of Game Six of the 1948 World Series, October 11, 1948.
14. Hugh Fullerton, "Spahn Gives Braves Hope,' *Saskatoon Star-Phoenix*, October 11, 1948, 24.
15. Harold Kaese, "Braves Save Own, League Prestige; Hope to Equal Bucs' 1925 Stunt," *Boston Globe*, October 11, 1948, 6.

Chapter 17

1. "Rapid Robert Loses Sting," *Pittsburgh Press*, October 11, 1948, 23.
2. "Veeck May Buy Chicago Sox," *Pittsburgh Press*, October 11, 1948, 23.
3. Vince Johnson, "Spahn Sends Series Back to Boston," *Calgary Herald*, October 11, 1948, 16.
4. Al Abrams, "Sidelight on Sports," *Pittsburgh Post-Gazette*, October 11, 1948, 20.
5. Chester L. Smith, "The Village Smithy," *Pittsburgh Press*, October 11, 1948, 23.

Chapter 18

1. Gayle Talbot, "4–3 Win Gives Series to Cleveland," *Saskatoon Star Phoenix*, October 12, 1948, 14.
2. Mutual Broadcasting System's radio broadcast of Game Six of the 1948 World Series, October 11, 1948.
3. *Ibid.*
4. *Ibid.*
5. *Ibid.*
6. Gayle Talbot, "4–3 Win Gives

Series to Cleveland," *Saskatoon Star Phoenix*, October 12, 1948, 14.

7. Ibid.

8. Mutual Broadcasting System's radio broadcast of Game Six of the 1948 World Series, October 11, 1948

9. Gayle Talbot, "4–3 Win Gives Series to Cleveland," *Saskatoon Star Phoenix*, October 12, 1948, 14.

10. "'We'll Get Them Next Year' Say Series Losers," *Calgary Herald*, October 12, 1948, 23.

11. Roger Birtwell, "Dad Bearden Sees a Dream Come True," *The Sporting News*, October 20, 1948, 7.

12. "Bearden Victories? In the Hat!" *The Sporting News*, October 20, 1948, 7.

13. Stan Baumgartner, "Indians Prove Superiority in Taking 'Hurlers' Series,'" *The Sporting News*, October 20, 1948, 8.

14. Paul Dickson, *Bill Veeck: Baseball's Greatest Maverick* (New York: Walker, 2012), 160.

15. "Indians Get Big Welcome in Hometown," *Youngstown Vindicator*, October 12, 1948, 1.

16. Ibid., 10.

17. Dickson, *Bill Veeck*, 161.

18. Grantland Rice, "Cleveland Ran True to Advance Form in Winning World Series," *Calgary Herald*, October 12, 1948, 23.

19. Ibid.

20. "Gov. Warren and Lou Boudreau Head List of 'Most Virile Men,'" *Boston Globe*, October 12, 1948, 1.

21. Mary Cremmen, "Dom DiMaggio Takes Wellesley Girl as Bride," *Boston Globe*, October 11, 1948, 1.

Chapter 19

1. Azquotes.com.

2. "Lefty Gomez Quotes," Baseball-Almanac.com.

Chapter 20

1. Sidney Davis, "Red Barrett," SABR Biography Project.

2. Paul Dickson, *The Hidden Language of Baseball: How Signs and Sign-Stealing Have Influenced the Course of Our National Pastime* (New York: Walker, 2003), 66.

3. Bill Nowlin (editor), *Spahn, Sain and Teddy Ballgame: Boston's (Almost) Perfect Baseball Summer of 1948* (Burlington, MA: Rounder Books, 2008), 92.

4. John McMurray, "Phil Masi," SABR Biography Project.

5. Sidney Davis, "Marv Rickert," SABR Biography Project.

6. Warren Corbett, "Steve Gromek," SABR Biography Project.

Chapter 21

1. Lester Smith, "Braves Set Sail on Sea of Red Ink," *The Sporting News*, March 25, 1953, 1.

2. Bill Nowlin (editor), *Spahn, Sain and Teddy Ballgame: Boston's (Almost) Perfect Baseball Summer of 1948* (Burlington, MA: Rounder Books, 2008), 2.

3. David M. Jordan, *Closing 'Em Down: Final Games at Thirteen Classic Ballparks* (Jefferson, NC: McFarland, 2010), 32.

4. Dan Daniel, "Braves' Shift to Milwaukee Voted by NL," *The Sporting News*, March 25, 1953, 3.

5. Lester Smith, "Braves Set Sail on Sea of Red Ink," *The Sporting News*, March 25, 1953, 1.

6. Ibid.

7. Patrick L. Kennedy and David Keefe, "Remembering the Wigwam (Part Two)," *BU Today*, April 13, 2012.

8. Scott McLaughlin, "Boston Braves supporters lament another missed opportunity for a Red Sox-Braves World Series," WEEI website (Audacy.com), October 26, 2021.

9. "Boston Sets New Mark for Crowds," *The Sporting News*, August 26, 1915, 3.

Chapter 22

1. Les Masterson, "Vern Bickford," SABR Biography Project.

2. Bob Dolgan, "'Thin Man' to the rescue," *Cleveland Plain Dealer*, August 16, 1998, 10-C.

3. Joseph Wancho, "Joe Gordon," SABR Biography Project.

4. Ed McAuley, "Indians a Vanished Tribe, Without '48 Zip," *The Sporting News*, October 5, 1949, 12.

5. Warren Corbett, "Steve Gromek," SABR Biography Project.
6. Rick Balazs, "Jim Hegan," SABR Biography Project.
7. *Ibid.*
8. *Ibid.*
9. Saul Wisnia, "Tommy Holmes," SABR Biography Project.
10. *Ibid.*
11. Jon Barnes, "Bob Lemon," SABR Biography Project.
12. *Ibid.*
13. John McMurray, "Phil Masi," SABR Biography Project.
14. Sidney Davis, "Nels Potter," SABR Biography Project.
15. John McMurray, "Connie Ryan," SABR Biography Project.
16. Jan Finkel, "Johnny Sain," SABR Biography Project.
17. Jon Daly, "Billy Southworth," SABR Biography Project.
18. *Ibid.*
19. Jim Kaplan, "Warren Spahn," SABR Biography Project.
20. Alexander Edelman, "Eddie Stanky," SABR Biography Project.
21. "Bill Summers," Wikipedia.
22. "Veeck as in Wreck," Goodreads.com.
23. Saul Wisnia, "Bill Voiselle," SABR Biography Project.
24. *Ibid.*
25. *Ibid.*

Chapter 23

1. Anthony Castrovince, "Whereabouts of Tribe's '48 Title Pennant Remains a Mystery," MLB.com, October 22, 2016.
2. Warren Corbett, "Bill Veeck," SABR Biography Project.
3. Anthony Castrovince, "Whereabouts of Tribe's '48 Title Pennant Remains a Mystery," MLB.com, October 22, 2016.
4. *Ibid.*

Bibliography

Books

Allen, Lee. *The National League Story*. Rev. ed. New York: Hill & Wang, 1965.
Bradlee, Jr., Ben, *The Kid: The Immortal Life of Ted Williams*. New York: Little, Brown, 2013.
Cataneo, David. *Peanuts and Crackerjack*, Nashville: Rutledge Hill, 1991.
Dark, Alvin, and John Underwood. *When in Doubt, Fire the Manager*. New York: E.P. Dutton, 1980.
Dickson, Paul. *Baseball's Greatest Quotations*. New York: HarperCollins, 1991.
_____. *Bill Veeck: Baseball's Greatest Maverick*. New York: Walker, 2012.
_____. *The Hidden Language of Baseball: How Signs and Sign-Stealing Have Influenced the Course of Our National Pastime*. New York: Walker, 2003.
Einstein, Charles, ed. *The Baseball Reader*. New York: Bonanza, 1989.
Epplin, Luke. *Our Team: The Epic Story of Four Men and the World Series That Changed Baseball*. New York: Flatiron, 2021.
Eskenazi, Gerald. *Bill Veeck: A Baseball Legend*. New York: McGraw-Hill, 1988.
Feller, Bob. *Bob Feller's Strikeout Story*. New York: Grosset and Dunlap, 1947.
Feller, Bob, with Bill Gilbert. *Now Pitching, Bob Feller: A Baseball Memoir*. New York: Sports Publishing, 1990.
Hirshberg, Al. *The Braves: The Pick and the Shovel*. New York: Waverly House, 1948.
Jordan, David M. *Closing 'Em Down: Final Games at Thirteen Classic Ballparks*. Jefferson, NC: McFarland: 2010.
Kiersh, Edward. *Where Have You Gone, Vince DiMaggio?* New York: Bantam Books, 1983.
Longert, Scott H., *Bad Boys, Bad Times: The Cleveland Indians and Baseball in the Prewar Years, 1937–1941*. Athens: Ohio University Press, 2019.
Moore, Joseph Thomas. *Pride Against Prejudice: The Biography of Larry Doby*. New York: Greenwood, 1988.
Nash, Bruce, and Allan Zullo. *The Baseball Hall of Shame 2*. New York: Pocket Books, 1986.
Nowlin, Bill, ed. *Spahn, Sain and Teddy Ballgame: Boston's (Almost) Perfect Baseball Summer of 1948*. Burlington, MA: Rounder, 2008.
Reichler, Joseph L., ed. *The World Series: A 75th Anniversary*. New York: Simon & Schuster, 1978.
Rosenburg, John M. *They Gave Us Baseball*. Harrisburg, PA: Stackpole, 1989.
Schneider, Russell. *The Boys of Summer of '48*. Urbana, IL: Sports Publishing, 1998.
_____. *Tales from the Tribe Dugout*. Champaign, IL: Sports Publishing, 2002.
Shatzkin, Mike, ed. *The Ballplayers*. New York: William Morrow, 1990.
Ward, Geoffrey C., and Ken Burns. *Baseball: An Illustrated History*. New York: Alfred A. Knopf, 2010.
Zoss, Joel, and John S, Bowman. *The American League*. New York: Bison, 1986.
_____. *The National League*. London: Bison, 1986.

Bibliography

Newspapers

Altus Times-Democrat
Baltimore Afro-American
Boston Globe
Boston Herald
Boston Post
BU Today
Calgary Herald
Chicago Daily News
Cleveland Plain Dealer
Cleveland Press
Cleveland Times
Cornell Daily Sun
Detroit Free Press
Ellensburg Daily Record
Eugene Register-Guard
Galt Daily Reporter
Gettysburg Times
Greensburg Daily Tribune
Lewiston Daily Tribune
Meriden Record
Milwaukee Journal
Milwaukee Sentinel
New London Evening Day
New York Herald Tribune
New York Mirror
New York Times
New York World-Telegram
Oakland Tribune
Pittsburgh Post-Gazette
Pittsburgh Press
Prescott Evening Courier
Reading Eagle
St. Petersburg Times
Sarasota Herald-Tribune
Saskatoon Star-Phoenix
The Sporting News
Toledo Blade
Tuscaloosa News
Wall Street Journal
Williamson Daily News

Online Resources

Audacy.com
Baseball-almanac.com
Baseball-reference.com
Cleveland.com
ESPN.com
MLB.com
Retrosheet.org
SABR.org
Thedeadballera.com
ThisGreatGame.com
U-S-History.com
VintageDetroit.com
Youtube.com

Oral History Collections

Morehead State University, Steve Hamilton Oral History Collection
    Johnny Sain
National Baseball Hall of Fame and Museum
    Lou Boudreau
    Bob Feller
    Bob Lemon
    Joe Paparella
SABR Oral History Collection
    Warren Spahn
Louis B. Nunn Center for Oral History, University of Kentucky Libraries
    Larry Doby
    Bill Veeck

Podcast

Robinson, Eddie. "A World Series Win," *The Golden Years of Baseball*. Apple Podcasts, December 31, 2020.

Index

Aaron, Hank 199, 225
Abbott, Bud 85
Abrams, Al 133, 134, 170
"Across the Field" (song) 145
Adelis, Pete 66
USS *Alabama* (ship) 29, 191
Allyson, June 205
Altrock, Nick 116
Antonelli, Johnny 16
Armour, Mark 194
Ashburn, Richie 204
"Auld Land Syne" (song) 62

Bagby, Jim 22
Banyard, Steve 123–124
Barber, Red 82
Barlick, Al 196
Barney, Rex 67
Barry, Dave 70
Barry, Jack 18
Benny, Jack 84
Benzaquin, Paul 198
Berardino, Johnny 193
Berg, Moe 161
Bero, Johnny 43
Berra, Yogi 39, 45, 218, 227
Berry, Charlie 15
Berry, Neil 44
Big State League (minor league) 204
Biondi, Reno 183
Birtwell, Roger 181, 190, 196
Black, Don 32–33, 56, 134–135, 206
Blades, Ray 67
Boone, Aaron 206
Boone, Bret 206
Boone, Daniel 206
Boone, Ray 164, 206
Borden, Joe 5
Boston Braves Historical Association 191, 200–201
Bradlee, Ben, Jr. 48

Brady, Bob 201
Brain, Laurie 56, 57, 70
Braves' Baseball in Your living Room (TV program) 205
Brissie, Lou 38
Broeg, Bob 216
Brown, Joe E. 176
Brown, Willard 25
Burdette, Lew 195
Burnett, Dick 217
Burns, Ed 87
Byrnes, James F. 83

California League (minor league) 224
Calorgero, Jim 99, 100
Campanella, Roy 18
Castrovince, Anothny 231
Cavalcade of Sports (radio program) 77
Chapman, Ray 22, 148
Chapman, Sam 38
Cheaper by the Dozen (book) 2
Christopher, Russ 43, 162, 207–208
Churchill, Ernie 85
Churchill, Winston 1
Ciano, Galeazzo 186
Clemens, Roger 16
Cobb, Ty 1, 10, 68, 129
Coleman, Joe 38
Collins, Rip 99
Como, Perry 2
Considine, Bob 36–38
Coolidge, Calvin 84
Coolidge, Grace 84
Cooney, Johnny 17
Cooper, Mort 93
Corbett, Gene 63
Corbett, Warren 35
Costas, Bob 211
Costello, Lou 85
Coy, Wayne 69
Crandall, Del 199–200, 217, 224

247

Cremmen, Mary 184
Crosby, Bing 2
Cunningham, Bill 224

Daley, Arthur 56, 192
Daniel, Dan 198
Day, Doris 2
Deal, Charlie 7
Dean, Dizzy 62
Dean, Hank 85
Delahanty, Ed 64
Dent, Bucky 190
Dickson, Paul 182
DiMaggio, Dominic 184
DiMaggio, Joe 29, 30, 39, 43, 61, 67–68
Dinneen, Joseph F., Jr. 198
Dobson, Joe 50
Doerr, Bobby
Doyle, Jim 46
Doyle, Dr. Roger T. 19
Duffy, Hugh 5, 198
Durocher, Leo 61, 209, 226
Dykes, Jimmy 212

Earley, Joe 26
Easter Parade (film) 2
Eaton, Francis 6
Edwards, Bruce 12
Epplin, Luke 29

Fain, Ferris 38
Feador, Jeremy 232
Fein, Nat 62
Feller, William 28
Fernandez, Nanny 68
Ferrell, Wes 68
Finkel, Jan 223
Finley, Charlie 209, 210, 219
Fithian, Elizabeth 148–149
Fitzgerald, Ray 207
Fitzgerald, Tom 196–197
Fonseca, Lew 192
Fowler, Dick 38
Fox, Nellie 228
Fraley, Oscar 111
Frick, Ford 17, 207, 227
Furillo, Carl 17, 18

Gable, Clark 183
Gaedel, Eddie 229
Gaffney, James E. 6, 9
Gandhi, Mahatma 1
Garcia, Mike 212, 213–214
Gehrig, Lou 64
General Hospital (TV program) 193
Gerlach, Larry R. 219
Gibbons, Frank 39

Godfrey, Arthur 2
The Golden Years of Baseball (podcast) 222
Goldstein, Spud 182
Gomez, Lefty 188
Good Morning, America (TV program) 218
Goodman, Benny 84
Gore, Artie 67
Gowdy, Curt 207
Gowdy, Hank 7
Greenberg, Hank 193, 206
Groth, Johnny 44
Guglielmo, Angelo 65–66
Gwynn, Tony 68

Hamlet (film) 2
Hand, Jack 75, 78–79, 94, 96, 116, 132–133, 137–138
Harder, Mel 55
Harder, Sandy 55
Harding, Warren 106
Harrah, Toby 186
Harridge, Will 63–64, 84, 95
Harris, Bubba 63
Harris, Mickey 61
Harrist, Earl 25
USS *Helena* (ship) 52
Henrich, Tommy 40
Hern, Gerald V. 5, 15
Hitchcock, Billy 15
Hogue, Bobby 235
Holbrook, Bob 195
Hope, Bob 100
Howell, Fritz 132
Hurst, Bruce 16
Hurth, Charley 65
Hurwitz, Hy 81, 151, 165
Hutchinson, Freddie 41
Hutton, Betty 84

I Remember Mama (film) 2
International Artists Committee 183

Jackson, Joe 21
Jackson, Reggie 190
James, Bill 7, 98
Johnson, Billy 39
Johnson, Vince 170
Johnson, Walter 93
Johnstone, Jay 217
Joost, Eddie 38

Kaese, Harold 12, 166, 225
Kauff, Benny 160
Kaufman, Ewing 216
Keeler, Wee Willie 68

Index

Kelley, Joseph B. 17
Kelly, King 5, 198
The Kid from Cleveland (movie) 193, 205
King, Bill 97
Kitty League (minor league) 66
Klein, Chuck 64
Kramer, Jack 44, 50
Kretlow, Lou 44
Kuhel, Joe 64
Kuhn, Bowie 207

Lafata, Joe 204
Landrum, Don 215
Lane, Frank 212
Larsen, Don 218, 220
Lee, Peggy 2
Levan, Jesse 228
Lewis, Franklin 55
Lewis, Whitey 70
Life (magazine) 37-38, 111
Logan, Johnny 195
Lollar, Sherm 217
Longfellow, Henry Wadsworth 198
Lopat, Eddie 39
Louis, Joe 85
Lowe, Bobby 64
Lundquist, Carl 17, 78, 95
Lyons, Al 235

Mails, Johnny 148
Majeski, Hank 38
Malesky, Bill 66
Maney, Joe 11
Manley, Effa 25, 182
Maranville, Rabbit 7, 198
Marchildon, Phil 64-65
Marshall, Cuddles 39
Martin, Billy 216, 222
Martin, Whitney 72, 123, 133
Masterson, Les 123
Mathews, Eddie 195
Mature, Victor 183
Mayo, Eddie 43
Mays, Carl 148
Mays, Willie 225
Mazur, Ronald 56
McCarthy, Tommy 5
McCosky, Barney 38
McDermott, Mickey 61
McDonough, James A. 73-74
McGowan, Bill 64
McNulty, Frank 200
McQuinn, George 39
Morrow, Art 38
Mountain State League (minor league) 126
Much Ado About Nothing (play) 183

Muckerman, Richard 63
Murnane, Tim 8-9
Murrell, Paul 63
Musial, Stan 68, 189
"My Hero" (song) 133

Nason, Jerry 134, 181
Nehf, Art 93
Nobles, Tom 65-66
"Notre Dame Victory March" (song) 145

Oakland Oaks 93
"The Old Gray Mare" (song) 219
O'Leary, J.C. 10
Olivier, Laurence 2
O'Malley, Walter 196
O'Neill, Steve 43
Onslow, Jack 228
Ott, Mel 61, 135
Outlaw, Jimmy 44

Parade (magazine) 200
Parker, Dan 63
Parnell, Mel 48, 50
Patrick, Van 82
Peck, Hal 164, 220
Pesky, Johnny 44, 53
Petersen, Leo H. 70
Power, Tyrone 39
Price, Jackie 24

Quinn, John 17

Raschi, Vic 39, 45
Red River (film) 2
Reiser, Pete 68, 218
Rennie, Rud 54
Reynolds, Allie 39, 61
Richards, Paul 217
Rickey, Branch 25
Rittner, Don 60
Rizzuto, Phil 39, 204
Robinson, Jackie 24, 25, 66, 147, 182, 209, 227, 228
Robinson, Wilbert 22
Rockwell, Norman 200
Roden, Ralph 17
Romeo, Blake J. 197
Rose, Pete 12
Rudolph, Dick 7
Ruel, Muddy 94
Ruether, Dutch 96
Rugo, Guido 11
Ruhl, Oscar K. 25
Russell, Jim 19
Russo, Bob 9

Index

Ryan, Ellis 206, 229
Ryan, Tommy 179–180

Sain, Doris 84
Sammy Kaye Orchestra (musical group) 111
Sandomir, Richard 147
Saturday Evening Post (magazine) 11, 200
Scarborough, Ray 44
Scheib, Carl 38
Schmidt, Butch 7
Scully, Vin 203
Selee, Frank 5
Sewell, Joe 148
Shakespeare, William 183
Shea, Spec 45
Shore, Dinah 2
Shoun, Clyde 235
Simmons, Herbert 9
Slapnicka, Cy 28
Smith, Chester L. 146, 151, 170
Smith, Elmer 22
Smith, Jack 183
Smith, Lester 198
Smith, Red 148–149
Snyder, Frank 10
Sockalexis, Louis 21
Southern Association (minor league) 65
Spahn, Gregory 76
Spence, Stan 60
Spink, J.G. Taylor 12, 31, 54–55, 182
Stalin, Josef 1
Stallings, George 6, 83
Steinbrenner, George 216, 217, 222
Stenberg, Raynhild 73, 197
Stephens, Vern 60
Stewart, Bud 64
Stewart, Jimmy 205
Stewart, Mark 68
Stewart, Paul 191
Stoneham, Horace 69
Stratton, Monty 205
The Stratton Story (film) 205
Sturgeon, Bobby 235
Suder, Pete 32
Sullivan, Ed 2
Sullivan, George 100
Suzuki, Ichiro 68

Talbot, Gayle 72
Tamblyn, Russ 193
Tebbetts, Birdie 42–43, 54
This Week in Baseball (TV program) 204
Thompson, Hank 25
Time (magazine) 28, 68, 172
Toast of the Town (TV program) 2
"Too Fat Polka" (song) 2
Toporcer, Specs 99
Tourtellette, Shane 192
The Treasure of the Sierra Madre (film) 2
Truman, Harry 182
Twombley, Wells 83
Tyler, Lefty 7

Valo, Emer 38
Vander Meer, Johnny 67
Vecsey, George 35
Veeck, Bill (Sr.) 23
Verban, Emil 67
Vernon, Mickey 216

Waddell, Rube 28, 29
Wagner, Honus 118, 146
Wakefield, Dick 46
Walker, Dixie 30
Wambsganss, Bill 22
Ward, Frank B. 166–167
Ward, John Montgomery 6
Warren, Earl 183
Weart, William G. 8
Weisman, Harold 26, 55
Wertz, Vic 65
Western Association (minor league) 204
Wexler, Sam 65
Whalen, Tom 199
White, Ernie 255
Whitman, Burt 87
Whitted, Possum 7
Wilks, Ted 61
Williams, Joe 192
Wilson, Robert G. 100
Wisnia, Saul 230
Wynn, Early 212, 216

Yastrzemski, Carl 219
Yawkey, Tom 53, 206

Zoldak, Sam 65, 119, 235